THE PHONOLOGICAL INTERPRETATION OF ANCIENT GREEK

This volume treats systematically the variation found in the successive stages of the development of all ancient Greek dialects. It combines a synchronic approach, in which generative rules expound phonological divergencies between the systems of different dialects, with a diachronic statement of unproductive and mostly pan-Hellenic shifts.

Professor Bubeník presents a phonetic description and structural phonemic analysis of the best-known variant - Classical Attic of the 5th century B.C. - and displays and contrasts the vocalic and consonantal inventories of all the other dialects classified according to their major groups. Derivational histories of individual dialects are examined in their juxtaposition, to ascertain which rules are shared by various dialects and which are dialect-specific. The pan-dialectal framework enables Bubeník to capture various relationships among genetically related dialects which are missed in atomistic and static treatments, and to show more convincingly the extent of their similarity and their systemic cohesion.

This volume makes a significant contribution to both classical scholarship and current theory of language change by offering new analyses of a variety of phonological and morphophonemic problems presented by a dead language and its dialects.

VÍT BUBENÍK is a member of the Department of Linguistics at Memorial University.

PHOENIX
Journal of the Classical Association of Canada
Revue de la Société canadienne des études classiques
Supplementary Volume xix
Tome supplémentaire xix

VÍT BUBENÍK

The Phonological Interpretation of Ancient Greek: A Pandialectal Analysis

UNIVERSITY OF TORONTO PRESS
Toronto Buffalo London

©University of Toronto Press 1983
Toronto Buffalo London
Reprinted in paperback 2014
ISBN 978-0-8020-5476-0 (cloth)
ISBN 978-1-4426-5165-4 (paper)

Bubeník, Vít, 1942-
The phonological interpretation of Ancient Greek

(Phoenix. Supplementary volume 19 =
Tome supplémentaire 19)
Includes indexes.
Bibliography: p. xiv. 242
ISBN 978-0-8020-5476-0 (bound) ISBN 978-1-4426-5165-4 (pbk.)

1. Greek language - Dialects - Phonology - History.
2. Greek language - Phonology. I. Title.
II. Series: Phoenix (Toronto, Ont.).
Supplementary volume 19

PA265.B82   481'.5   C82-095009-2

Publication of this book is made possible by grants from the Canadian Federation for the Humanities, using funds provided by the Social Sciences and Humanities Research Council of Canada, and from the Publications Fund of University of Toronto Press.

To the memory of my father

OLDŘICH BUBENÍK (1908-1973)

who was my first teacher of Ancient Greek

φύλλα τὰ μὲν τ'ἄνεμος χαμάδις χέει, ἄλλα δέ θ'ὕλη

τηλεθόωσα φύει, ἔαρος δ'ἐπιγίγνεται ὥρη

ΙΛΙΑΔΟΣ Ζ, 147-8

PREFACE

This book is based on my research in the area of Ancient Greek dialects and Mycenology going back to 1966. Its subject has been treated by many classical scholars for several generations. However, in recent years more up-to-date linguistic methods have been applied consistently in this area. It is no exaggeration to claim that Ancient Greek represents one of the most interesting and challenging fields among extinct Indoeuropean languages for both the diversity and the multiplicity of its dialects and its time depth. The fact that the subject of the variation in a language like Greek is far from being exhausted was one of the main impulses which directed my research. Furthermore I believe that an understanding of regional variation in the dead language has a great relevance for the study of the same phenomenon in its living descendant. Greek will undoubtedly continue to be one of the most rewarding areas of study of linguistic change.

    I must gratefully acknowledge the advice and assistance of Dr. A. Bartoněk in the initial stages of my work. He was my supervisor in the years when I was working on my doctoral dissertation 'Pádová syntax mykénského dialektu' (The Syntax of Case in Mycenaean Greek), which I submitted to the Faculty of Arts, University J.E. Purkyně in Brno, in 1969. I benefited enormously from his profound knowledge of Ancient Greek dialects and his linguistic insights. I wish to thank Dr. A. Erhart, who taught me general and historical linguistics. Next I must thank the Department of Classics and University J.E. Purkyně for allowing me to spend five months in Greece, where I could pursue my study of dialect inscriptions.

    After I had moved to Canada I had the opportunity to discuss various problems of Ancient and Modern Greek phonology and phonological theory in general with Professor W.S. Allen

(University of Cambridge), Dr. J. Hewson (Memorial University), Professor F.W. Householder (Indiana University), Dr. B. Newton (Simon Fraser University), Dr. I. Warburton (University of Reading) and Dr. L. Zgusta (University of Illinois). All these scholars made valuable comments and suggestions on earlier drafts of my work.

My colleagues at Memorial University Dr. S. Clarke, Mr. L. Smith and Mr. B. O'Dwyer proofread various parts of the manuscript and provided invaluable assistance in the matter of style. I am especially grateful to Dr. J. Hewson who read the whole manuscript and saved me from a number of unhappy statements. It is hardly necessary to say that none of these people is in any way responsible for any shortcomings or errors in my work; these remain solely my responsibility.

St. John's
August 31, 1976

I am also indebted to two anonymous readers of the University of Toronto Press for their candid suggestions on my presentation of certain problems in phonology and morphophonemics, and for sharpening my perception of some theoretical issues.

And finally, it is my pleasant duty to acknowledge the generous support of Memorial University of Newfoundland which helped me by two Vice-President's Research Grants to offset the typing and publishing costs connected with the production of this manuscript.

St. John's
August 31, 1981   Vít Bubeník

CONTENTS

Preface vii
Illustrations xiii

CHAPTER ONE: INTRODUCTION 3
1.1 Aims 3
1.2 General Approach 6
1.3 Methodology of Ancient Greek Dialectology 14
1.4 The Classification of Ancient Greek Dialects 22
1.5 The Decline of Ancient Greek Dialects 29

CHAPTER TWO: VOWELS 32
2.1 The Vowels of Attic and Other Greek Dialects 32
2.1.1 The Vowels of Classical Attic 32
2.1.2 The Vowels of the Greek Dialects About 350 B.C. 35
2.1.3 The Alphabet 39
2.2 The Diphthongs of Classical Attic 39
2.3 Monophthongization of Proto-Greek Diphthongs
*ei and *ou 45
2.4 Fronting and Raising of Proto-Greek
*ā in Attic-Ionic 49
2.5 Compensatory Lengthening 56
2.5.1 First Compensatory Lengthening 56
2.5.2 Second and Third Compensatory Lengthening 59
2.5.3 Raising of Long Mid Vowels in Dialects 63
2.6 Vowel Sequences in Dialects 63
2.6.1 Height Dissimilation 63
2.6.2 Height Assimilation 68
2.7 Contractions in Attic and Other Dialects 69
Notes 74

CHAPTER THREE: CONSONANTS
3.1 The Consonants of Attic and Other Dialects 77

3.1.1 The Consonants of Classical Attic 77
    3.1.1.1 Phonemic Variants 79
    3.1.1.2 Phonological System 82
    3.1.1.3 Geminates 84
    3.1.1.4 Aspirates 86
    3.1.1.5 Continuants and Sonorants 87
3.1.2 The Consonants of the Greek Dialects 87
3.1.3 Phonotactics of Classical Attic Consonants 89
    3.1.3.1 Dyadic Clusters 89
    3.1.3.2 Triadic Clusters 91
3.2 Phonology of Aspirates 96
3.2.1 Phonotactics of Aspirates 96
3.2.2 Phonetic Reconstruction of Clusters Φθ and Χθ 98
3.3 Grassmann's Law 101
3.4 Frication of Classical Aspirates 105
3.5 Dental and Velar Palatalization 110
3.6 Reflexes of Proto-Greek Labiovelars in Classical Dialects 116
3.7 Development of Proto-Greek Sonorant Clusters in Classical Dialects 120
Notes 127

CHAPTER FOUR: THE ACCENTUAL SYSTEM 133
4.1 The General Limiting Rule 133
4.2 Minor Rules and Enclisis of Accent 140
    4.2.1 Minor Rules 140
    4.2.2 Enclisis of Accent 142
4.3 Historical Origins of the Greek Accent Pattern 145
    4.3.1 Vedic and Greek 145
    4.3.2 Three Syllable Rule 152
    4.3.3 Analogical Accent Levelling 155
4.4 Circumflex in Final Syllables of Thematic Nouns 160
4.5 Function of Accent in Ancient Greek Dialects 169
4.6 Typology of Accent in Ancient Greek Dialects 172
4.7 Situation in Modern Greek Dialects 177
Notes 182

CHAPTER FIVE: INTERPLAY BETWEEN SOUND CHANGE AND ANALOGY 188
5.1 Personal Endings of Thematic and Athematic Verbs 188
5.2 Athematic Inflection of Contract Verbs 193
5.3 Athematic Verbs 'be', 'go' and 'say' 201
5.4 Perfect with Aspirate 208
5.5 Perfect Participle 211
Notes 218

Contents xi

SELECT BIBLIOGRAPHY 222

INDEX OF NAMES 227

INDEX OF GREEK WORDS AND WORD FORMS 229

ILLUSTRATIONS

1-1. The Regions of Ancient Greece 2
1-2. Convergence and divergence in the history of Greek dialects 31
2-1. Vocalic phonemes of Classical Attic (5th B.C.) 33
2-2. Distinctive features of the vocalic phonemes of Classical Attic 34
2-3. Vocalic phonemes of Laconian (about 350 B.C.) 35
2-4. Distinctive features of the vocalic phonemes of Laconian (about 350 B.C.) 35
2-5. Vocalic phonemes of Elean (about 350 B.C.) 36
2-6. Vocalic phonemes of dialects with the 4-grade vocalic system 37
2-7. Vocalic phonemes of Boeotian (about 350 B.C.) 38
2-8. Vocalic phonemes of post-Classical Attic-Ionic (about 350 B.C.) 38
2-9. Distinctive features of the vocalic phonemes of post-Classical Attic-Ionic (about 350 B.C.) 38
2-10. Short and long diphthongs in accented syllables 43
2-11. Monophthongization of the diphthong *ei* 46
2-12. Vocalic phonemes of Arcado-Cypriot, Aeolic and Doric dialects (after the 1st compensatory lengthening) 63
2-13. Vocalic phonemes of Attic-Ionic, North-West and Saronic dialects (after the 1st compensatory lengthening and raising of mid vowels) 63
2-14. Attic rules of vocalic contraction 70
3-1. Distinctive features of consonantal phonemes of Classical Attic 83
3-2. Consonantal phonemes of Classical Attic 87
3-3. Consonantal phonemes of pre-Classical Attic-Ionic and Classical Arcadian 88

xiv Illustrations

3-4. Consonantal phonemes of Boeotian and
        and Central Cretan 88
3-5. Consonantal phonemes of Ionic and Lesbian 89
3-6. Dyadic clusters (I) Obstruent + Obstruent 89
3-7. Dyadic clusters (II) Stop + Sonorant 90
3-8. Dyadic clusters (III) Sonorant + Stop
     (IV) $\begin{Bmatrix} \text{Sonorant} \\ \text{Sibilant} \end{Bmatrix} + \begin{Bmatrix} \text{Sonorant} \\ \text{Fricative} \end{Bmatrix}$ 90
3-9. Triadic clusters of Ancient Greek 92
3-10. Triadic clusters (V)
$\begin{Bmatrix} \text{Sonorant} \\ \text{Sibilant} \\ \text{Velar Stop} \end{Bmatrix}$ + Peripheral Stop + Coronal Obstruent 93
3-11. Triadic clusters (VII)
$\begin{Bmatrix} \text{Sonorant} \\ \text{Sibilant} \\ \text{Velar Stop} \end{Bmatrix}$ + Stop + Sonorant 94
3-12. Triadic clusters (VIII)
$\begin{Bmatrix} k \\ n,r \\ s \end{Bmatrix}$ + Sibilant + Stop 95
3-13. Obstruents of Hellenistic Greek 108
3-14. Obstruents of Greek of the Transitional
        Period (300 - 600 A.D.) 109
3-15. Dialect geography of reflexes of Proto-Greek
      clusters *ss, *ts, *t(h)j, *k(h)j, *tw, *dj
        and *gj 117
4-1. Accent typology of Balto-Slavic languages
        and Ancient Greek dialects 177
5-1. Dialect geography of thematic, athematic
        and contract verbs 200
5-2. Distribution of morphemic variants of
        Present and Perfect Participle
        in Vedic 217

The Phonological Interpretation of Ancient Greek

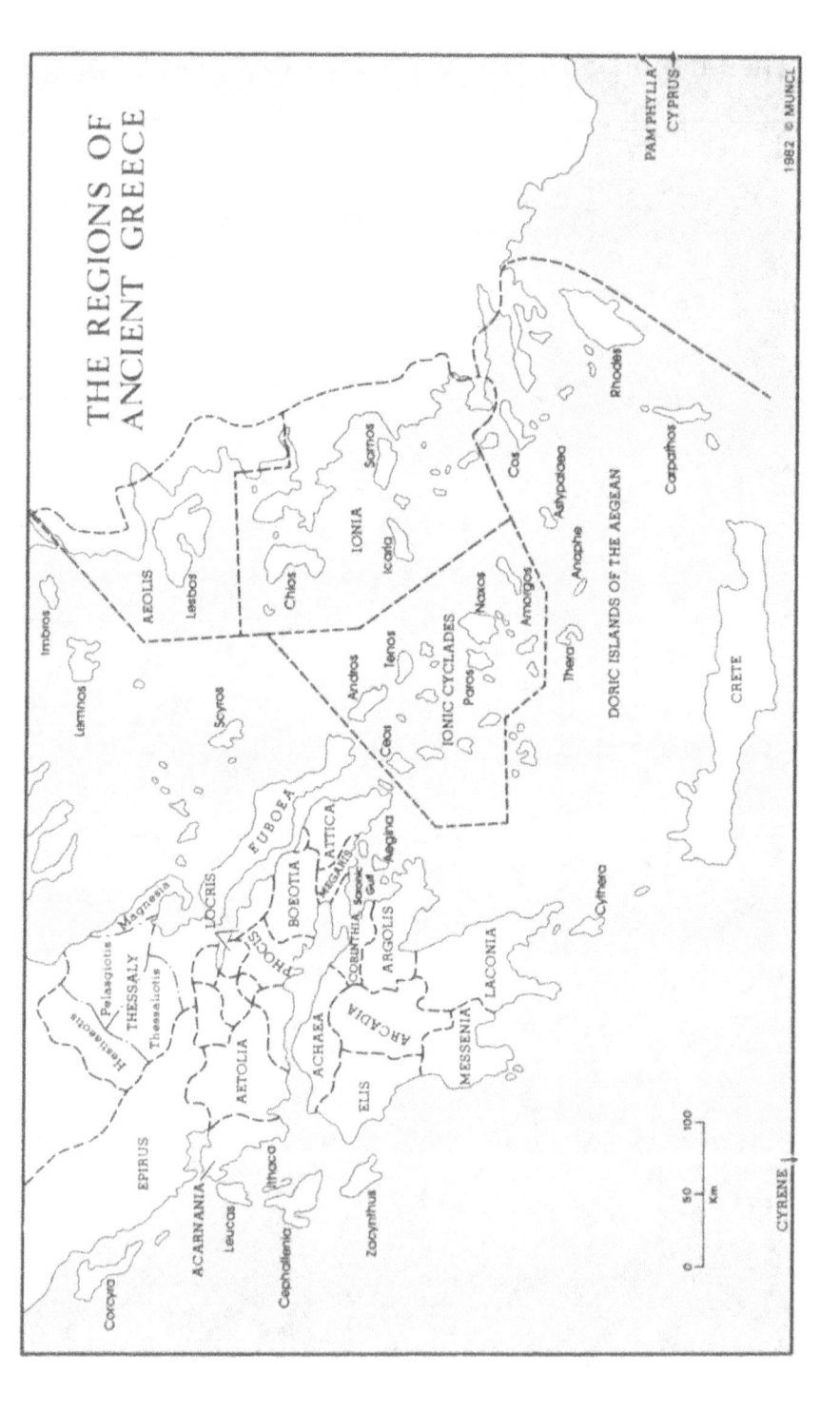

1

Introduction

1.1 AIMS

The aim of the present monograph is a systematic presentation of the most likely historical processes that are responsible for the variation found in successive stages of the development of the major dialectal groups of Ancient Greek. I will be interested in accounting for the changes that have affected the sound structure of Ancient Greek dialects over the period of approximately one thousand years in all areas where Greek was spoken. Generally speaking I will attempt to explain the variation in Ancient Greek as
(a) a function of the *time* dimension
    Mycenaean (1400 - 1100)
    post-Mycenaean (1100 - 700)
    Classical (700 - 350)
    Hellenistic (350 - 150)
    Graeco-Roman (150 B.C. - 300 A.D.)
(b) a function of the *space* dimension.
The geographical area where the Ancient Greek dialects were spoken (the southern part of the Balkan peninsula, the adjacent islands and a part of the land mass of Asia Minor) may be surveyed on map 1-1. The dialects of overseas settlements (Corcyra, Italy, Sicily, Hellespont, Euxine, etc.) will be excluded from my discussion (or used only as evidence for the dialect of a particular metropolis).

  The documentary evidence is rich but uneven and with considerable gaps. The primary documents are represented by the corpus of the Greek alphabetic inscriptions (from the end of the 8th c. down to the Christian Era) and the corpus of Linear B tablets (from the 14th to the 12th c.). Our primary documents can in no way be compared as to reliability and extent with materials which are at the disposal of

students of living dialects. The limitations under which the
dialectology of a dead language labours are well-known. First
of all, where the students of living dialects are dealing with
the phonetic reality elicited from speakers of particular
dialects, historical dialectology can only interpret written
documents, a technique which is attended with various
difficulties. The spelling itself is merely a graphic representation of the phonetic reality. This becomes especially
obvious when it comes to such important matters as accent or
external sandhi, where the written documents are really 'dumb'.
For instance, given our knowledge of the Attic accent system
and our rudimentary knowledge of the Doric accent system we
may wonder about the placing of the accent in the Hellenistic
Greek spoken in the Peloponnese or elsewhere in the old Doric
areas:

  Attic   αἱ γυναῖκες ἔλαβον 'the women took'
  Doric   αἱ γυναίκες ἐλάβον
  Hellenistic αἱ γυναίκες ἐλάβοσαν

We may hypothesize that there were speakers of Hellenistic
Greek who would stress γυναῖκες in the Doric way by placing
the acute on the penult. Such a hypothesis is obviously hard
to verify unless we find a phonetic description of the case by
an ancient grammarian or, what is more difficult, unless we
discover a parallel in Modern Greek dialects, which will
necessarily remain of doubtful value.

 In the second place, linguists have to keep in mind that
writing systems are conservative and that graphemic change
lags behind phonetic change. This is a commonplace in all
languages and again it is quite easily demonstrable in
living languages. However, in our case it is sometimes
quite difficult to know whether a particular inscription
shows predominantly historical spellings or phonetic
spellings, a distinction which of course has considerable con-
sequences for the relative chronology of sound change.
Particularly the disappearance of some dialectal phenomenon
from the inscriptions of a certain community during several
generations need not imply the fact that this phenomenon
disappeared also from the *colloquial usage* of the dialect.
What is sometimes a quite likely explanation is that the
phenomenon disappeared from the *literary usage* of the dialect,
i.e., the scribes (as in the later inscriptions from the time
of the Attic Koine) realized that this phenomenon was simply
a kind of 'provincialism' which was to be avoided for various
reasons. Unfortunately, we are not always in a position to
prefer one of the above solutions.

 As Nagy-Householder (1972:36) put it: 'in fact, we may
posit as a general principle that the constraints and licences
of the various Greek orthographic systems are the primary key

5 Introduction

to evaluating the nuances of the underlying phonological systems.' Quite often, however, the value of this primary principle is substantially lessened by various caprices of ancient scribes.

If we find late spellings ἐκγδοθῆ or ἐκγ βασιλέως (instead of etymological ἐκδοθῆ, ἐκ βασιλέως), we certainly can make a case for phonetic spelling, which attempts to capture a phonetic reality [egdot$^{h}\bar{e}$]. The voiced [g] is here a result of the natural voicing of a voiceless stop before a voiced one. However, what are we to think about spellings like ἐκγ πόλεως where voicing is out of question?

In spite of these difficulties the genuine task of historical dialectology should be a reconstruction of the most likely sequence of historical linguistic events which entail an internal dialectal differentiation of the language (and of course even internal differentiation of the main dialectal groups and individual dialects) at any stage of its history. In accordance with this basic tenet my principal aim should be to 'explain' the interdialectal variation at several historical stages before the Classical Era, and likewise the usage of the Classical and post-Classical Era itself.

In the case of a living language, the prerequisite of any phonological interpretation is a reliable phonetic description. In the case of a dead language, the phonetic 'description' (the reliability of which falls far short of the reliability of the phonetic description of any living language) should rather be called phonetic 'reconstruction'.

Phonetic reconstruction of Ancient Greek was a preoccupation of several generations of classical philogists culminating in Sturtevant (1940) and Grammont (1948). W.S. Allen, *Vox Graeca* (1968, 1974) supersedes all the previous accounts by being a thorough synchronic treatment which brings into discussion many valuable parallels from dead and modern languages. The dialect analyzed is fifth-century Attic, but there are also diachronic considerations regarding earlier and later stages and references to other dialects. The book contains also a revised description of the Greek tonal accent and stress.

Nowadays it is no exaggeration to claim that we have a sufficiently exact idea of how Classical Attic was pronounced, even if there are still some details which are disputable. The principal techniques employed in phonetic reconstruction were also refined. They are based on the interpretation of the following types of data, according to Allen (1974:vii):
1) statements by contemporary grammarians and other writers
2) word-play, contemporary etymologies, and onomatopoeia
3) representations in other ancient languages
4) subsequent developments

6 Phonological Interpretation of Ancient Greek

5) spelling conventions and variants
6) the internal structure of the language itself.

The points 3) and 4) represent external evidence (in space and time); the rest can be called internal evidence. The interpretation of representations in other ancient languages is attended with particular difficulties, and it is hard to know sometimes whether we are dealing with phonetic transcriptions or with simple transliterations.

1.2 GENERAL APPROACH

Dialects arise because some sound changes fail to diffuse over a whole speech community; the ultimate causes of this phenomenon are of course extralinguistic. Thus e.g., Ionic fronting process ā → ǣ failed to diffuse through Attic territory and we can talk about an incomplete sound change: Attic χώρα 'land' versus Ionic χώρη. In this way arise differences in patterns of alternation e.g., the Proto-Greek intervocalic consonantal cluster *sm was subject to the regressive assimilation of sibilant *sm → mm only in the Aeolic dialectal group. In all other dialects fricative weakening s → h (with subsequent loss of voiceless breathing and compensatory lengthening) took place: Attic εἰμί 'I am' versus Lesbian ἔμμι. The ultimate causes of this 'choice' of two different directions (= diachronic split) have to do with spatial and temporal separation of speakers of Proto-Ionic and Proto-Aeolic.

A description of interdialectal variations among Ancient Greek dialects in terms of the sequence of actual events is formalizable, if each change is labeled a 'rule'. The sequential character of historical sound-changes will then be represented by the formal descriptive device of linear rule ordering. From the point of view of historical linguistics, the concept of a rule is important not because it 'explains' various alternations, but because a particular change has not taken place in all dialects (= a rule did not apply in all dialects, in other terminology). In this sense then we can account for various alternations observable in individual dialectal groups or dialects. Stricto sensu, rules do not have any explanatory power, since they are simply descriptive devices, (they permit a certain economy and elegancy of statement; they are easy to survey, etc.); sequences of rules simply give a mechanism for description, not for a historical explanation. So, in the following, by establishing the rules which account for dialectal variations I will mean the specification of the geographical distribution of sound-changes.

Linguists usually try to explain the astonishing variety of phonetic and phonological differences in related dialects

7 Introduction

(or genetically related languages) by reducing them, as much
as is possible and reasonable. The formal device of this
reductionism is a *protoform* (in diachronic linguistics) or
underlying form (in synchronic linguistics). In the last two
decades, a considerable effort has been exerted on the
solution of the problem of multiplicity of surface forms.
Thus orthodox generativists will claim that all dialects of
a single language have identical underlying representations.
According to many linguists this view represents a reasonable
hypothesis, since it can explain interdialectal communication.
To be sure, the fact of the mutual comprehension alone is not
considered by many others as a sufficient argument to allow
the linguist to set up identical underlying representations.
The reasons are obvious: where does mutual comprehension
start and where does it end? There are mutually incomprehen-
sible dialects and, on the other hand, mutually comprehensible
languages.

We may start with the examination of some data from several
dialects at the time of about 350 B.C.:

	'carrying' (Part Fem)	'of the horse' (Gen Sg)	'two horses' (Dual)
Attic	φέρουσα /pʰerūsa/	ἵππου /hippū/	ἵππω /hippō/
Corinthian	φέρουσα /pʰerōsa/	ἵππου /hippō/	ἵππω /hippǭ/
Laconian	φέρωha /pʰerōha/	ἵππω /hippō/	ἵππω /hippō/
Theran	φέρωσα /pʰerōsa/	ἵππου /hippǭ/	ἵππω /hippǭ/
Lesbian	φέροισα /pʰeroisa/	ἵππω /ippō/	ἵππω /ippō/
Central Cretan	φέρονσα /pʰeronsa/	ἵππω /hippō/	ἵππω /hippō/
West Argolic	φέρονσα /pʰeronsa/	ἵππου /hippǭ/	ἵππω /hippǭ/

What kind of explanation can we offer for all those
different forms of feminine participle 'carrying'? We may
recapitulate the traditional explanation offered by historical
phonetics preferring to work 'downstream' from the proto-form
established on the basis of (external) comparative evidence
(e.g., Cretan φερονσα, Lesbian φέροισα, Sanskrit *bharatī* and
Avestan *barantī* suffice to establish both Proto-Indoeuropean
*bherontjə and Proto-Greek *pʰerontja). Then we have to

assume that later on /t/ before a palatal glide was palatalized and affricated, yielding something like $p^heront's'ja$ [$p^heronča$]. Subsequently the affricate was fricated and depalatalized resulting in historically documented $p^heronsa$. Later on, according to Lejeune (1972:129), the nasal lost its closure and yielded a voiced fricative, which was unstable and changed into a palatal glide. In Lesbian /j/ formed a diphthong with the preceding vowel; in other dialects, the voiced fricative lost its articulation completely and prolonged with its glottal vibrations the preceding vowel. Thus according to Lejeune we are dealing with a diachronic split:

$$p^heronsa \longrightarrow p^heroFsa \begin{matrix} \longrightarrow p^herojsa \\ \searrow p^her\bar{o}sa \end{matrix}$$

Or we may prefer to work 'upstream' from the data of individual dialects back to the proto-form. Attic, Corinthian and Laconian forms are apparently easy to explain. What is responsible for the differences may be labelled the *raising* of long mid vowel $\bar{\varrho} \to \bar{o} \to \bar{u}$ (as in Early Modern English /stōn/ 'stone' goes back to the Middle English /stǭn/ and /mūn/ 'moon' to /mōn/). If we assume that $p^heronsá$ underlies these three forms, we have to postulate a phonological process, by which the nasal was lost before a sibilant (this process is responsible for the difference between other dialects and the dialects spoken in Crete and Argolis, where -*ns*- is preserved). Even this form would not be 'deep' enough since it would not explain alternations like $p^heront + os$ (Gen Sg Masc) or the Lesbian form $p^heroisa$. Taking into account these forms we would arrive at $*p^herontja$ as the form which 'underlies' all the forms in dialects. Without going into any further details, comparative reconstruction of Proto-Greek on the basis of individual dialects could be formalized by linearly ordered 'rules' as below:

	-ontja				
Affrication	-ont^{s}ja				
t $\longrightarrow \emptyset$	-onsja				
Depalatalization	-onsa	<u>Central Cretan, West Argolic</u>	*Metathesis of glide*	-oinsa	
n $\longrightarrow \emptyset$ (+ Lengthening)	-ōsa	<u>Theran</u>		-oisa	<u>Lesbian</u>
Raising	-ọ̄sa	<u>Corinthian</u>			
Raising	-ūsa	<u>Attic</u>			

9   Introduction

It goes without saying that a derivational sequence of this kind does not represent anything like a synchronic process of individual dialects, which explains why these dialects are mutually comprehensible. This sequence is *diachronic* not synchronic. In other words, by this scheme I do not mean that speakers of Cretan were deriving their form $p^heronsa$ from underlying *$p^herontja$ by applying rules of *affrication*, *t-deletion* and *depalatalization*; that speakers of Attic were doing the same and in addition were applying further rules of *n-deletion* and two *raisings* to generate their $p^her\bar{u}sa$. This kind of 'synchronic' analysis would only repeat the historical events, which actually took place in these dialects over a period of centuries (and many of these changes were shared by various dialects). All I intend to do with similarly specified derivational histories is to formalize my descriptions of the sound-changes taking place in time. By such a presentation I hope to achieve a greater degree of explicitness and more systematic presentation of such sound-changes than are to be found in various works on historical phonetics of Ancient Greek.

This is not to say that synchronic processes in various dialects (especially in those subject to rapid change) did not repeat parts of this diachronic derivational scheme. Thus in Attic the raising process $\bar{\rho} \rightarrow \bar{u}$ appears to have been a synchronic rule in the 4th c., i.e., speakers of Attic could notice at a certain time that their fathers said /pherọsa/ (they contrasted /pherọsa/ and /t^{h}ūmos/ θυμός) but their own pronunciation was /pherūsa/ (with a contrast /pherūsa/ and /t^{h}ūmos/). Consequently, for one generation we may suppose *pherọsa* as an underlying form of *$p^her\bar{u}sa$*. Or in Central Cretan the loss of a nasal before a sibilant was certainly at one time a synchronic rule. In this dialect the final cluster *-ns* was preserved before a vowel but *-n-* was lost if the following word began with a consonant, e.g. τονς ἐλευθερους   tons + V
but τος καδεσταvς   tons + C ⟶ tos + C
Consequently, we are justified in postulating a synchronic rule of nasal-deletion for Central Cretan in the 5-4th c.

Quite often it is extremely difficult to keep apart descriptions of diachronic changes and synchronic processes. This is true a fortiori for dead dialects, where we have to specify the synchronic cut. Analyzing Greek dialects synchronically around 400 B.C. we may attempt to represent the relationship between historical sound-changes and synchronic processes in the following diagram where the dotted lines represent diachronic events, which took place during roughly a thousand years and are irrelevant synchronically:

10 Phonological Interpretation of Ancient Greek

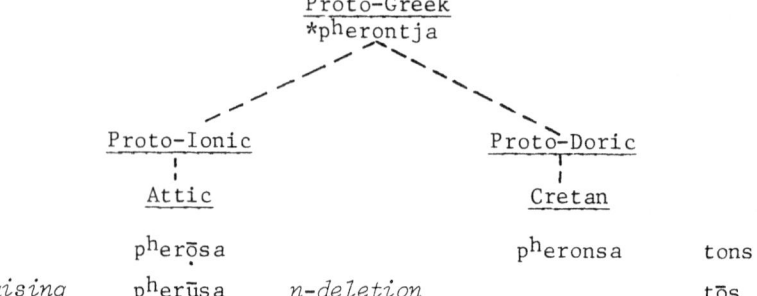

	Attic		Cretan	
	pʰerōsa		pʰeronsa	tons
Raising	pʰerūsa	n-deletion		tōs

It is hard to imagine that the subconscious knowledge of the speakers of individual Greek dialects included something like the whole schema on page 8. Even if morphophonemic analysis of Ancient Greek qua language needs underlying representations like *pʰerontja, it still does not mean that speakers of individual dialects of Ancient Greek generated their forms in such or a similar way. This schema is only our description of diachronic changes not a generative model for speakers. We may add that even the communication between two regional variants (e.g., between Attic and Cretan) does not mean that the speakers establish a common set of underlying representations. As is observable daily in connection with any living language, it simply means that both sides build certain dialectal correspondences in their grammars (sometimes called diaphonemes). Some linguists prefer a common diasystem for all the dialects but the point remains that the psychologically real substance for speakers are those sets of correspondences. An Athenian visitor to the Central Crete or the island of Lesbos in the 4th c. B.C. could simply become 'aware' that /ō/ and /ū/ in his dialect correspond to a single /ō/ in the speech of Cretans or Lesbians.

On the other hand, it is easy to show the structural parallelism between morphophonemic and pandialectal analysis and to demonstrate that these two methods are essentially complementary. To take a simple example from Attic, we may formalize the morphophonemic alternation of the type $ag + \bar{\rho}$ 'I lead' ~ $\bar{e}g + on$ (Imperfect) by deriving the Imperfect from underlying $\bar{e} + agon$ by the Augmentation and Low Vowel Rule and the alternation $pʰain\bar{o}$ 'I reveal' ~ $\acute{e}pʰ\bar{e}na$ (Aorist) from underlying $\acute{e}pʰansa$ by the Resonant Aorist Rule (according to Sommerstein (1973:25, 51, 62)):

	e + agon		épʰānsa
Augmentation	āgon	Resonant Aorist Rule	épʰāna
Low Vowel Rule	ḕgon		épʰēna

11   Introduction

This synchronic sequence will appear as identical with the diachronic sequence which is establishable by means of pan-dialectal analysis: Doric *stālā*, Aeolic *stallā*, Attic *stēlē* (< Proto-Greek *stalnā); Doric *éph̄ana* 'I revealed', Attic *éph̨ēna* (< Proto-Greek *éphansa):

	stalnā	éphansa	
Lengthening	stālā	éph̄ana	Doric
Fronting	stǣlǣ	éph̄æna	
Raising	stēlē	éph̨ēna	Attic

It is precisely here where linguists disagree - some accept all the units given by the morphophonemic analysis as synchronic entities, some try to give to these units different temporal interpretations. Whereas the derivational history of Attic *stēlē* is only a sequence of diachronic events, that of *éph̨ēna* qualifies for both: a sequence of historical changes and - given the morphophonemic alternation *phainǭ* ~ *éph̨ēna* - the synchronic process. Obviously, the forms *éph̄ana* and *āgon* which are crucial in the morphophonemic analysis of Attic, are more 'abstract' than the surface phonemes of pandialectal analysis which works with real Doric forms *éph̄ana* and *ēgon*.

Linguists describing a language either synchronically or diachronically tacitly assume that the multiplicity of forms is reducible to a common underlying form or proto-form. However, in both descriptions the identity hypothesis may be counterbalanced by a 'diversity' hypothesis. We may simply assume that the dialectal variation is an inherent property of both a present day language and its ancestral proto-language. For instance, it might be hard to specify sequences of sound-changes separating the following forms from a single proto-form:

Attic	τέτταρες	'four'	Boeotian	πέτταρες
Ionic, Arcadian	τέσσερες		Lesbian	πέσσυρες
West Greek	τέτορες		Homeric	πίσυρες

This would be tantamount to deriving all four vowels /e, o, a, u,/ from a single underlying vowel *V:

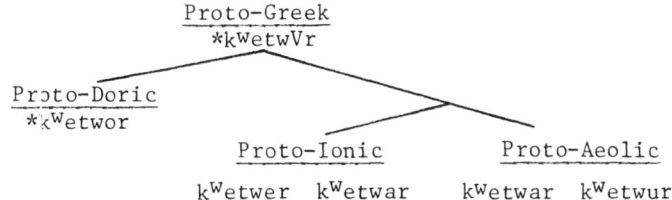

Thus in historical retrospective we may view Greek way back in the 2nd Millenium B.C. as a dialectally undifferentiated language (= identity hypothesis) or as a cluster of dialects, ancestors of classical dialects, even if nobody can say anything more definite about them (= diversity hypothesis).

At this place we have to admit that our starting point of all derivations, i.e., our reconstructions of Proto-Greek, are in a sense apriori hypotheses whose status appears to be justified only by the internal regularities found in the Greek dialects. They introduce a unifying principle in the diversity and multiplicity of the dialect forms which in their totality make the Greek language.

In the case of a dead language the internal reconstruction of the phonological systems of its individual dialects is quite a demanding undertaking. Whilst the diachronic description establishes the most likely sequence of historical sound-changes, which are responsible for the present stage of individual dialects, we should also explain synchronically the distribution of contrasts in individual dialects, i.e., the relationship of simultaneous elements in the system, not the substitution of one by another in time. Thus we may observe that in the 4th c. speakers of Attic had the same long high back vowel /ū/ in both the participle φέρουσα and the Gen Sg ἵππου; speakers of Corinthian had the same half-close back /ọ̄/, and speakers of Laconian long mid back /ō/ in both words. The speakers of Attic or Corinthian could contrast Gen Sg ἵππου and Dual ἵππω (/ū/ versus /ō/ or /ọ̄/ versus /ọ̄/), whereas the speakers of Laconian could not. On the other hand, contrasts were distributed in a totally different way in Lesbian φέροισα and ἵππω (diphthong /oi/ and monophthong /ō/), Central Cretan φερονσα and ἱππω (sequence /on/ and long mid back /ō/) and West Argolic (sequence /on/ and half-close /ọ̄/). Gen Sg and Dual were homophonous in Lesbian and Central Cretan but not in West Argolic:

Attic		Corinthian, Theran, West Argolic	
hippū	hippō	hippọ̄	hippọ̄
Gen Sg	Dual	Gen Sg	Dual

Messenian, Laconian, Lesbian, Central Cretan

hippō

Gen Sg   Dual

The present monograph will deal not only with the phonetic description and phonemic analysis but also with the *internal reconstruction* of individual dialects. At this point it is worth mentioning that the internal reconstruction of individual dialects would sometimes be impossible without the previously established initial stage (= Proto-Greek), which

13   Introduction

in its turn was established by means of *comparative reconstruction*. It means that Greek protoforms can be established by means of evidence from other Indo-European languages. There is nothing illicit in such a method, since the relationship between the internal and comparative (= external) reconstruction is reciprocal. It would make no sense to claim that comparative reconstruction, or vice versa, that all internal reconstruction must be completed before the other reconstruction can begin. This can be demonstrated quite easily from the data of IE languages e.g., the form of the Present Participle Feminine 'carrying':

Sanskrit	bháratī	Common Indo-Iranian	?	
Avestan	bárəntī			
Doric	phéronsa			Proto-Indo-
Ionic	phérōsa	Common Greek	?	European ??
Aeolic	phéroisa			
Old Church Slavic	berǫ̃šti	Common Balto-Slavic	?	
Lithuanian	-anti			

The internal reconstruction of Proto-Greek has been demonstrated on the preceding pages. The same result would be arrived at externally by comparing Indo-Iranian *bharantī* and (reconstructed) Balto-Slavic *bérontī* with Greek data from individual dialects. Both Indo-Iranian and Balto-Slavic show that there was originally a consonant cluster *-nt-* (which shows up only in the Masculine counterpart in Greek *phérontos*). Since the Feminine Participle in Indo-Iranian belongs to *ī-stems* and in Balto-Slavic to *jo-stems*, this would lead to a reconstruction of the Proto-Greek *ja-stem* *pʰérontja*. Thus the solution of the problem is seen to be as follows:

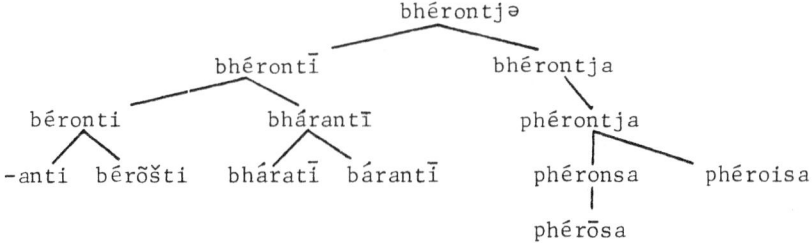

Summing up, we have seen that the internal reconstruction (= morphophonemics) of a single dialect handles sound units in connection with grammatical meaning (φέρουσα ~ φέροντος) and that on the basis of this alternation we may establish an underlying representation |pʰérontja|; pandialectal analysis

14 Phonological Interpretation of Ancient Greek

handles sound units in connection with one lexeme in different
dialects (Ionic φέρουσα, Doric φέρονσα and Aeolic φέροισα) and
leads to Proto-Greek *phérontja; and finally, the external
reconstruction (= comparative method) handles sound units in
connection with one lexeme in different genetically related
languages and yields *phérontja (or its PIE ancestor
*bhérontja).

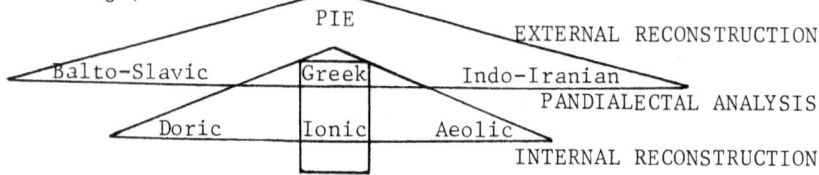

As commented by Anttila (1972:278) all these methods are
essentially complementary in that they use the same mechanism
and 'give ultimate units from which there is one mapping
relation to the lower units ... from which one started.' A
corollary of this situation is the complementarity of syn-
chrony and diachrony. Pandialectal analysis is basically a
descriptive synchronic work on dialects of a single language.
Nevertheless, we may draw on the results of comparative
method to confirm our inferences (for instance, a diaphoneme
|kʷ| is establishable on the basis of interdialectal corres-
pondences between Ionic (τίς 'who', τηλόθεν 'from afar') and
Aeolic (Thessalian κίς, Lesbian πήλοθεν). This may be con-
firmed externally by comparative evidence of Latin *quis* or
Hittite *kuiš*. Thus an abstract diaphoneme of synchronic pandialectal analysis turns out to be identical with a concrete
protophoneme of historical comparative method.

  1.3 METHODOLOGY OF ANCIENT GREEK DIALECTOLOGY

Some methodologically significant works in the area of
Ancient Greek dialectology and linguistics have appeared in
the seventies. Before reviewing these I would like to mention
some older compilations which will remain valuable sources of
data and information for any future investigator on the field
of Ancient Greek dialects.

  Three detailed handbooks dealing with Ancient Greek dia-
lects appeared early in the 20th c.:
A. Thumb, *Handbuch der griechischen Dialekte* (Heidelberg 1909)
C.D. Buck, *Introduction to the Study of Greek Dialects*
(Boston 1910)
F. Bechtel, *Griechische Dialekte* (Berlin 1921-24)

  All these three works (especially the last one) have more or
less the character of loose compilations which methodologically
do not proceed beyond collecting and classifying of data. This
is unfortunately true even about the later editions of Thumb's

work:
A. Thumb - E. Kieckers, *Handbuch der griechischen Dialekte I* (Heidelberg 1932), dealing with West Greek dialects.
A. Thumb - A. Scherer, *Handbuch der griechischen Dialekte II* (Heidelberg 1959), dealing with Aeolic, Arcado-Cypriot, Attic-Ionic and Mycenaean.
An inclusion of the Mycenaean dialect and the analysis of its phonology based on the latest achievements in Mycenology is the most significant contribution of A. Scherer.

C.D. Buck's *The Greek Dialects* (1955) surpasses methodologically all other previous works which present separate treatment of the several dialects. He considered data from all dialects simultaneously from a more or less synchronic viewpoint and elaborated a new and quite exact classification of Ancient Greek dialects. In his systematic exposition (under the heads: Vowels, Consonants, External Combination, Inflection, Word-Formation, Syntax) he discussed a large number of dialectal phenomena. On pp. 141-180, there are summaries of the characteristics of the several groups and dialects and there is also a valuable chart of the distribution of many important pecularities common to several dialects. Buck's approach consists basically in the drawing of isoglosses and heteroglosses, which link and separate various dialects, and in the specification of the geographical distribution of individual linguistic phenomena.

The next step to take was to quantify differences and conformities and express them algebraically. This has been done by R. Coleman in his *The Dialect Geography of Ancient Greece* (1963), who selected 51 dialectal phenomena from Thumb and Buck and attempted a detailed classification of 24 dialects with the help of *correlation coefficients*. These were established by the following method: Where dialect A exhibits x items and dialects B and C respectively $x - b$, $x - c$ items comparable to A, then if p of these $x - b$ and q of these $x - c$ are identical with A, the correlation coefficient of A and B is given by the formula $\frac{p}{x - b}$ and of A and C by the formula $\frac{q}{x - c}$. The most significant of these figures were then used in a geographic table *Greek Dialectal Affiliations*, where the arrows point to dialects of highest correlation, and 'reciprocality' is denoted by a double-headed arrow (e.g., Attic and Ionic are 'reciprocal' dialects with correlation coefficient 0.80; Aeolic dialects have following coefficients: Lesbian - Thessalian 0.56, Thessalian - Boeotian 0.58, but Lesbian - Boeotian only 0.35; the lowest correlation coefficient exists between Cypriot and Corinthian 0.13). Unfortunately Coleman did not provide a detailed account of occurrences of the 51 selected phenomena in his 24 selected dialects, consequently his figures are hard to check; nevertheless his attempt is to be considered as an interesting pioneer attempt at a classification of Ancient Greek dialects with the help of statistical methods.

Statistical methods introduced into Greek dialectology by R. Coleman were further developed by A. Bartoněk in his typological analysis of the West Greek dialects entitled *Classification of the West Greek Dialects at the Time about 350 B.C.* (1972). In contrast to Coleman, who elaborated coefficients of conformities between individual dialects, Bartoněk established *coefficients of the differences*. The reason for this was that the author considered the number of isoglosses between the individual West Greek dialects as too high, whereas it was possible to specify the most distinct intra-Doric heteroglosses. The author also felt that a dialectal classification should start by stressing the distinguishing not the common factors. The number of heteroglosses between any pair of 18 West Greek dialects can be ascertained on Table B (pp. 130-3), which presents 44 selected dialectal phenomena. Table C 1 (Bartoněk 1972:138-9) indicates the number of relevant differences between the individual dialects. Table C 2 (1972:140-1), instead of *mere sums* of the single differences, gives the *differentiation coefficients* (obtained by dividing the number of *ascertained relevant differences* by the number of *items with distinctive relevance*. E.g., the coefficient of the relation between Phocian and Corinthian is represented by the quotient 11:42 = 0.26; this figure expresses in per cent the number of differences ascertained in proportion to the total number of all comparable cases, and finally, Table C 3 (1972:142), arranged in conformity with the geographic situation, presents a graphic survey of the closest interrelations within the West Greek dialectal world.

Diametrically opposed to these pandialectal studies is Lupaș's analysis of the best known variant of Ancient Greek. L. Lupas in her *Phonologie du grec attique* (1972) elaborated a phonological description of Classical Attic within a rigid structuralist (basically Trubetskoyan) framework on a strictly synchronic basis. The originality of her undertaking consists in the fact that she attempted a phonological description of the extinct language by methods applied in taxonomic descriptions of living languages (minimal pairs, phonotactics). A significant contribution of hers toward our deeper understanding of Attic phonology lies in her description of vocalic and consonantal allophones (pp. 57-103). Then she discusses the inventory of Attic phonemes and the phonological system. The features used for the description of the Attic phonological system are those of R. Jakobson and M. Halle (1956) –

diffuse, grave, flat and compact for vowels, compact, grave and tense for consonants. Phonological independence of the consonants /p,t,k,b,d,g,p^h,t^h,k^h,l,r,m,n,s/ is beyond doubt but there remain a number of borderline cases - geminates /pp,tt,kk,ss/ and geminated aspirates /pp^h,tt^h,kk^h/ - and she decided to include all these (and also geminated sonorants) among the consonantal phonemes of Attic. This might seem a well-founded assumption since there are minimal pairs for all geminates with the exception of /pp/ and the geminated aspirates /pp^h,tt^h,kk^h/. However, it is here that the limitations of the author's structuralist framework become most patent. Instead of being satisfied with handling the gemination by means of the prosodic feature short - long, she introduces also the feature tense - lax (only as a subcategory of the length) to cope with surface oppositions /p/ : /p^h/ and /pp/ : /pp^h/, etc.

	tense	lax
short	p	p^h
long	pp	pp^h

A paradox of this solution is obvious - the author must warn us that she does not consider geminated aspirates as more lax than non-geminated voiceless stops. The notation [-tense] for /pp^h/ is supposed to indicate only that geminated aspirates are less tense than geminated voiceless stops. This makes the feature tense - lax only a relative category, which can be easily disposed of from the description of Ancient Greek. Notice that all examples of geminated aspirates are borderline cases which can be ignored in the phonological analysis (mostly expressive words like ἀπφῦς 'papa', τίτθη 'nurse', τυτθός 'little', καγχάζω 'laugh aloud' and names like Βάκχος).

Lupaş's work remains purely static - naturally, she did not test her features on synchronic processes (or diachronic changes) of Attic. And, of course, she did not attempt to formalize any of her descriptions by means of her predominantly acoustic features.

The greatest achievements of structuralism have to do with the concept of sound change and relative chronology. Here must be mentioned works by Ruipérez (1956), Allen (1958), Bartoněk (1966) and Szemerényi (1968). Ruipérez was the first to introduce Martinet's principles in the area of Ancient Greek -- he attempted to describe and explain the development of the vocalic systems in Attic and Boeotian using the concepts of the dynamics of pressure (and counterpressure) in the phonemic system. Bartoněk, following

Ruipérez, reconstructed long-vowel systems of all known dialects at several pre-classical stages through the Classical Era down to the beginnings of the Hellenistic Koine ca. 350 B.C. Allen attempted the reconstruction of the prehistory of Greek dental and velar palatalization (further valuable refinements were provided recently in 1973b). Szemérenyi has elaborated at length on the relative chronology of alleged Attic reopening $ǣ$ to $ā$ and fronting $ū$ to $ǖ$. A common denominator of all these (and other) studies is a more or less rigid structuralist effort to describe and explain changing phonological subsystems of a language in terms of qualitative leaps (= systematic changes), paying due attention to the graduality of sound change.

Probably the most detailed exposé of the historical phonetics of Ancient Greek dialects is Lejeune's discursive and data-oriented presentation in a framework of traditional historical linguistics. His *Phonétique historique du mycénien et du grec ancien* (1972) is based closely on the editions of 1946 and 1955. The main changes involved the incorporation of Mycenaean data which entailed some changes in relative and absolute chronology. Lejeune's basic procedure is to posit proto-forms (obtained by external and/or internal reconstruction) and to specify the sequence of sound changes which are responsible for the variation in the language, which shows up as dialectal differences. (It may be observed that there is a similarity of method between historical phonetics and generative phonology, especially in the area of pandialectal study. And just as there are profound questions to be raised as to the historical reality of protoforms, there are equally important questions concerning the psychological reality of the underlying forms used by generativists). Lejeune puts a considerable effort into specifying the relative chronology of historical sound changes. (This procedure corresponds to rule ordering in generative phonology). The following passages (1972:130 and 22), regarding the development of the cluster -ns- (*ntj/i) may serve as an example:

> Les altérations diverses d'un groupe -νσ- secondaire sont de date rélativement récente. En ionien-attique, elles sont postérieures à la fermeture de $ā$ en η : $ᾰ$ allongé en $ā$ se conserve dans φᾶσι, πᾶσι, πᾶσα, etc. Dans le dorien de Théra et de Cyrène, les altérations, qui diffèrent pour les deux parlers (*-ονσα > ωσα à Théra, * - ονσα > οισα à Cyrène), sont posterieures à la date de leur séparation: 630 environ.
>
> le fait que Cyrène ait été fondée vers 630 par les Doriens

de Théra, et le fait qu'au IVe s. on observe le type παυσα
à Cyrène, le type πᾶσα à Théra, impliquent qu'au VIIe s.
on devait encore avoir le type πανσα à Théra.

Finally a few words regarding the generative presentation
of Ancient Greek. P. Kiparsky (1967a and 1973) is a pioneer
in using the technique of generative phonology in accentology.
A. Sommerstein, *The Sound Pattern of Ancient Greek* (1973),
elaborated an account of the most important rules governing
the pronunciation of sentences in the best known variant of
Ancient Greek - Classical Attic as spoken between about 480
and 320 B.C. The authors of these works strongly emphasize
that they are offering more adequate accounts than traditional
taxonomic descriptions and they put a considerable effort
into formalizing and ordering their generative rules.
Undeniably, the rules possess greater descriptive capacity,
which is inherent in their symbolism, and we apparently
achieve a deeper insight into workings of the language if we
can make our rules work. However, even if we manage to express ourselves more economically and abstractly it still
does not mean that we are achieving a real explanation of the
phenomena.

As shown above, the mechanism of the generativists' method
and that of historical linguists is identical - the rules/
sound changes of both operate on the underlying representations/protoforms which are reconstructable by means of
internal reconstruction/comparative method. If we examine
many of the sequences of rules in *The Sound Pattern of Ancient
Greek* it will appear that they simply recapitulate well-known
diachronic sequences of sound changes. On p. 28 Sommerstein
assumes that in Attic the underlying representations of the
present forms like ἐλπίζω 'hope' and φυλάττω 'guard' were
essentially the same as in older forms of the language
(*elpidjō* and *phulakjō* - reconstructable on the basis of
alternations like ἐλπίδ + ος and φύλακ + ος). Then he
requires the rules to convert the clusters gy, dy into zd,
and ky, ty, k^hy, t^hy into tt. These rules are: *Affrication*
(send all such clusters to dental stop + fricative),
Affricate Resolution (send /ts/ to [tt]), *Metathesis*
(metathesize /dz/ to [zd]):

	pʰulakyō	melitya	elpidyō
Affrication	pʰulatsō	melitsa	elpidzō
Affricate Resolution	pʰulattō	melitta	-
Metathesis	-	-	elpizdō

Now let us compare Lejeune's account (1972:79 and 113) in
terms of historical phonetics:

le groupe *ty a tendu vers une prononciation *ts; *ky est d'abord passé à *ty, puis a tendu à son tour vers *ts. Les groupes de forms *ts sont ensuite passés, selon les dialectes, soit à ss ... soit à tt. L'évolution des sonores a été parallèle ...

ce groupe sonore *dz a subi interversion (à laquelle échappe le groupe sourd *ts).

If we formalize Lejeune's account of diachronic sound changes separating proto-Greek forms and Attic forms, it will appear that not only the underlying representations of Attic are the same as in older forms of the language, but even the sequence of 'rules governing the pronunciation of sentences' only recapitulates a familiar diachronic sequence:

Sommerstein				Lejeune		
				dy	ty	dy
dy	ty	dy		ty		
ts	ts	dz		ts	ts	dz
tt	tt	-		tt	tt	-
-	-	zd		-	-	zd

This comparison may highlight one fact which is easily forgotten, namely, that the form of synchronic phonological rules was originally derived from descriptions of sound-changes. This is possible because historical changes leave behind alternations which allow for the elaboration of the synchronic order of rules (these thus have to reflect the historical sequence of sound-changes to a certain degree). In our case, whereas Lejeune presents a likely sequence of historical events, Sommerstein makes claim that this sequence reflects what went on in the brain of the speakers of Classical Attic when they uttered sentences. We have to keep in mind that this is only an attractive hypothesis, whose psychological reality is still being discussed; on the other hand, the historical statement represents a fact which is unaccessible to most speakers of language. Therefore I believe that the problem of how much the historical sequences are reflected in the synchronic order of application of phonological rules and what exactly is the nature of their interdependency deserves the careful attention of linguists. I will have the opportunity to examine some of the opinions concerning this matter at several places in the book.

However, the main interest of my study lies in presenting the coherent historical exposé. A challenging task in the research into the interrelations and history of the Ancient Greek dialectal world may be formulated thus: a systematic processual treatment of the historically real sequences of events which are responsible for the astonishing variety of all those forms found in about twenty Classical dialects. This task has been attempted in the present study.

My method will be basically that used by comparative linguistics for the reconstruction of proto-languages. As shown above this method may equally be applied to the dialects of a single language and may thus be called pandialectal analysis. On the basis of an examination of the cognate forms in various dialects I will postulate a common set of proto-forms (it will sometimes prove impossible to have a single proto-form) and try to reconstruct the most likely sequences of historical sound changes. These reconstructed sequences (= derivational histories) of individual dialects will be examined in their juxtaposition to ascertain which 'rules' are shared by various dialects and which are in individual dialects. This procedure may obviously be used to capture various relationships among genetically related dialects; relationships which are missed in structuralist typological studies. In this way we may show more convincingly the extent of similarity and the systematic cohesion of these dialects. Thus the internal differentiation of the Attic-Ionic group of dialects will be presented in this way:

	Attic	West Ionic (Euboic)		Central and East Ionic
		prākjō		
Palatalization	______	prāk'jō		______
Affrication	______	prāt's'jō		______
Depalatalization	______	prātsō		______
Progressive Assimilation	prāttō	prāttō	*Regressive Assimilation*	prāssō
Fronting	-	prǣttō		prǣssō
Raising	-	prę̄ttǭ		prę̄ssǭ

Even if some of the sequences elaborated in this book may be only pseudohistorical or open to 'reordering' they can be taken as convenient formulae which ultimately serve the purpose of elaborating the framework for the study of dialectal variation in Ancient Greek on an historical basis.

In working on derivational histories of individual dialects, one should not lose sight of the structural phonemic patterning of the most important dialectal groups. The statement that Elean low front *ǣ* derives from Proto-Greek *ē* through a lowering process has a certain explanatory value - but it is equally insightful and complementary to have the difference between Elean and other 'strict' Doric dialects (Laconian, Central Cretan, Cyrenaean) presented in terms of the total vowel pattern as a contrast between a quadrangular long-vowel system and a triangular system. It is after all on the psychologically real levels of phonetics and structural phonology, not on the intermediate steps of derivational histories, which are only our reconstructions, where we tell the difference between individual dialects.

These considerations entailed the necessity of a synchronic presentation of the best known of all Classical dialects - Attic (as spoken in the 5th c.) - in order to be able to contrast the phonemic inventories of other dialects. Classical Attic is presented in the framework of structural phonology. Phonological contrasts are established by means of minimal pairs and various problems connected with the specification of the vocalic and consonantal system are discussed.

1.4 THE CLASSIFICATION OF ANCIENT GREEK DIALECTS

The Greek language at the time of the earliest alphabetical records was already considerably diversified into a number of quite distinct dialects. Inscriptions written in epichoric alphabets give evidence of the existence of differing forms of speech right down to Hellenistic times. Only some of these became literary languages; by far the larger number of dialects, which never came to play any role in literature, are known only through the inscriptions of various Greek communities.

That the ancient Greeks enjoyed their differences in speech is well-known from the comedies of the Old and Middle Period where the authors parodied speakers of Doric dialects and Boeotian. Aristophanes could distinguish a speaker of the 'mild' Doric Megarian from a speaker of the 'strict' Doric Laconian. Plato (Cratylus 434 C) reports that Eretrian (West Ionic dialect spoken in Euboea) has σκληρότηρ 'hardness' for σκληρότης. In terms of phonetics, Plato noticed that in the pronunciation of the Eretrians the final sibilant was not accompanied by a turbulent airstream since its phonetic value was only an approximant [ɹ] - a phenomenon traditionally called 'rhotacism'. In the 4th c. it was observed that the 'correct' pronunciation of words like ξύλον 'wood' was with the front [ü], and the non-Attic [u] became a joke.

Unfortunately, apart from similar observations and scattered ethno-linguistic comments found mostly in Herodotus, Thucydides and Plato, we do not possess any systematic exposé coming from the Classical Period, when the provincial dialects were still in use. It is only in the 1st c. B.C., long after provincial dialects had been replaced by the Hellenistic Koine, that a more systematic passage regarding the existence of Ionic, Aeolic and Doric elements was written by Strabo in his Geography (VIII 1,2 p. 333). Strabo's tripartite grouping of Ancient Greek dialects based on geographical and thno-linguistic criteria is basically continued by modern scholars. To be sure, Strabo is only talking about four dialects - Ionic, Attic, Doric and Aeolic (to these the Hellenistic koine was sometimes added by the ancient grammarians) and he joined them into two pairs. The first pair, Attic-Ionic, is based on the 'identity' of the Old Attic and Ionic (the colonists who founded the Ionic cities on the Asiatic shore came from Attica according to Strabo). The second pair, Doric-Aeolic, is justifiable only by the ethnic and linguistic intermingling of the Doric and Aeolic dialects following the Dorian invasion. Strabo writes that the Aeolians after the arrival of the Dorians survived in the Peloponnese only as the inhabitants of Arcadia and Elis, and that Aeolic was spoken by the Greek inlanders everywhere north of the Isthmus (with the exception of Athens, Megara and Parnassian Doris). This statement shows that Strabo's Aeolic included everything which was not classifiable as Ionic, Attic or Doric.

Let us review some incontrivertible present day views on the classification of Ancient Greek dialects and present some linguistic evidence for it in terms of isoglosses and heteroglosses.

Regarding the Dorians of Ancient Greece there was a well-founded tradition that they came originally from the Northwest and throughout the historical period they formed well-defined groups geographically and linguistically. The tradition regarding their homeland in the North West is linguistically fully supported by the close relationship of the Doric dialects and North West Greek dialects (Aetolian, Locrian and Phocian). In modern scholarship, the Doric dialects are classified as a major sub-group of West Greek dialects, since in classical times these dialects were spoken mainly to the West of a line cutting the centre of the northern mainland from north to south, and were also spoken in Megara and the whole Peloponnese. In prehistoric times Doric dialects were brought to the islands of Crete, Melos, Thera, Rhodes, and Cos and to the adjacent coast of Caria.

Some general West Greek characteristics are as follows:
(a) West Greek dialects are so-called ti-dialects, while East Greek dialects (Ionic, Aeolic, Arcado-Cypriot) fricated /t/ before /i/ and may be labelled si-dialects:
  (3rd Pl Pres) <u>West Greek</u> φεροντι versus <u>Ionic</u>   φέρουσι
         and <u>Pamphylian</u> εξαγοδι   <u>Arcadian</u> φερονσι
                 [eksagōndi]   <u>Lesbian</u> φέροισι
  (3rd Sg Pres) <u>West Greek</u> τιθητι versus <u>East Greek</u> τίθησι
          and <u>Boeotian</u>   διδωτι   δίδωσι

(b) 1st Pl Pres ending φέρο-μες versus East Greek.φέρο-μεν

(c) Marker -ks- (instead of East Greek -s-) in the Future and Aorist of verbal stems in -ζω (the same phenomenon is also found in Arcado-Cypriot, Boeotian and Thessalian), e.g., Cretan δικακσει (= δικάσει). (All equivalent forms given in brackets will be from the Attic dialect).
(d) So-called 'Doric future' in -σεω (elsewhere -σω) e.g., Cretan πραξιομεν (= πράξομεν) with height dissimilation $eo \longrightarrow io$
(e) Pronominal forms like Dat Sg ἐμιν (= ἐμοί), τιν (= σοί)
  Gen Sg ἐμεο (= ἐμοῦ), τεο (= σοῦ)
  West Greek dialects are traditionally subdivided into:
  i) 'strict' Doric dialects (Laconian, Messenian, Cretan and Cyrenaean)
  ii) 'middle' Doric dialects (West Argolic and East Aegean Doric)
  iii) 'mild' Doric dialects (dialects spoken in the Saronic gulf: Megarian, Corinthian and East Argolic, and North West dialects).

'Strict' Doric dialects do not distinguish between Proto-Greek /ē,ō/ and the secondary /ē,ō/ arising through the compensatory lengthenings and isovocalic contractions. Their vocalic system preserves the Proto-Greek system of long vowels /ī,ē,ā,ū,ō/ with three levels of aperture.

On the other hand, 'middle' and 'mild' Doric dialects changed the Proto-Greek 3-level system into a 4-level one /ī, ē, ẹ̄, ā, ū, ọ̄, ō/. The close mid vowels /ẹ̄/ and /ọ̄/ resulted here from compensatory lengthenings and isovocalic contractions.

The remaining 'non-West' Greek dialects belong to three groups: Ionic, Arcado-Cypriot and Aeolic.

The Ionic group (or Attic-Ionic) is made up of Attic and Ionic dialects spoken on the island of Euboea, the Cycladic islands and on the coast of Asia Minor. The linguistic unity of these areas is fully supported by ancient tradition and archaeological evidence. That the insular Ionians were akin to the inhabitants of Attica was a well-known fact in the Greek history, this being the result of the Ionian colonization of the Aegean islands. This Ionian colonization reached the Asiatic shore sometime in the Dark Age (11 - 9th c.). What is uncertain is the original extent of the Ionic territory on the European mainland. According to Strabo, Ionians lived even in the Peloponnese, and it could be that at least the entire shore of the Saronic gulf was once Ionic, before the local dialects were replaced by Doric dialects.

Some notable Attic-Ionic characteristics are:
(a) Fronting and raising of Proto-Greek $*\bar{a} \longrightarrow \bar{æ} \longrightarrow \bar{ę}$
(b) 3rd Pl Aorist of athematic verbs, and Aorist Passive

endings in -σαν (elsewhere in -ν):
  ἔθεσαν, ἐλύθησαν elsewhere ἔθεν, ἐλύθην
(c) 3rd Sg Impf ἦν 'he was', elsewhere ἦς (<*ēs + t)
(d) Movable -n in verbal forms in -σι(ν) and -ε(ν) in the environment before both vowels and consonants
(e) Pronominal forms: Nom Pl in -εις elsewhere in -ες
  Attic ἡμεῖς 'we' versus Lesbian ἄμμες, Doric ἅμες
       ὑμεῖς 'you'   ὔμμες   ὕμες
              Acc Pl in -έας (or -ᾶς) elsewhere in -ε
  Attic ἡμᾶς 'us' versus Lesbian ἄμμε, Doric ἅμε
       ὑμᾶς 'you'   ὔμμε   ὕμε

Arcadian (spoken in central Peloponnese) and Cypriot are two 'peripheral' dialects that have in common a number of peculiarities which are unknown (or only sporadically documented) elsewhere. In view of their geographic disparity this is astonishing, especially when we recall that our written documents come from the 5th and 4th c. Presently it is believed that these two dialects represent remnants of the originally homogenous dialect(s) of Mycenaean Greece. According to some scholars even the dialect spoken in Pamphylia (southern coast of Asia Minor) belongs to this group; others classify it as belonging to the Aeolic group. Pamphylian is poorly recorded and the only major inscription does not suffice to decide the matter.

In Arcado-Cypriot (but there is some evidence even from Pamphylian and Lesbian) short mid vowels in certain positions are raised /e,o/ ⟶ /i,u/:

i) /e/ before a dental nasal (even elsewhere but the evidence is scanty)
   Arcadian ἰν 'in' (= ἐν), ἰνδικος 'right' (= ἔνδικος)
            μινονσαι 'remaining' (= μένουσαι)
   Cypriot ἰναλινω 'write upon'
ii) final /o/, and /o/ before a labial nasal
   Arcadian ὀπυ [hopu] 'under' (= ὑπό [hupo])
            ἐγαμαντυ 'got married' (= ἐγήμαντο)
            ὑμοιος 'similar' (= ὁμοῖος)
   Cypriot γενοιτυ 'happen' (= γένοιτο)

Other most notable characteristics of Arcado-Cypriot are dative constructions of prepositions ἀπυ and ἐξ (elsewhere ἀπό and ἐξ + Genitive) and some special lexical items like κας 'and' (elsewhere καί), πος 'near by' (elsewhere πρός), etc.

In modern scholarship the Aeolic group includes the dialect of the island of Lesbos, and Thessalia and Boeotia on the European mainland. There are some fundamental isoglosses linking these three dialects:

(a) Proto-Greek labiovelars *k^w and *g^w became labials /p/ and /b/ in all environments (elsewhere only before non-high back vowels and consonants).
(b) Aeolic dialects have the marker -*ont*- in the Perfect Participle, where other dialects have the original marker -*ŏt*- e.g., Lesbian κατεληλύθοντος 'descend' (= κατεληλυθότος).
(c) /o/ instead of /a/ before or after liquids e.g., Lesbian στρότος 'army' (= στρατός), Thessalian βροχυς 'short' (= βραχύς).

On the other hand, there are considerable diversities between Boeotian-Thessalian and Lesbian explainable partially by their geographical distance and the influence of neighbouring dialects - West Greek influence on Boeotian and Thessalian greater in the case of the West Thessalian area (= Thessaliotis) and Ionic influence on Lesbian. Perhaps the most important diversity regards the Proto-Greek clusters of the type $\begin{Bmatrix} \text{Liquid} \\ \text{Nasal} \end{Bmatrix}$ + Sibilant, Sibilant + $\begin{Bmatrix} \text{Nasal} \\ \text{Liquid} \end{Bmatrix}$ and *ln. These are reflected as geminates in Thessalian and Lesbian but non-geminates in Boeotian, e.g., Proto-Greek *g^we/oln- Lesbian βόλλομαι 'wish', βόλλα 'counsel', Thessalian βελλομαι but Boeotian βειλομαι, βωλα (cf. West Greek δειλομαι, βωλα); Proto-Greek *esmi 'I am', Lesbian, Thessalian ἔμμι but Boeotian ἐμι.

Only Boeotian among Aeolic dialects has a geminate /tt/ for Proto-Greek clusters *ts, *t(h)j and *k(h)j. Lesbian and Thessalian (with some exceptions) show /ss/, e.g. Proto-Greek *kārukjō,   Beotian καρυττω 'proclaim'
*met^hjos   μεττος 'middle'
but Lesbian καρύσσω
             μέσσος

CLASSIFICATION OF CLASSICAL GREEK DIALECTS (5th c. B.C.)

I. WEST DIALECTS

'mild' Doric
    1 North-West group (Aetolian, Locrian, Phocian)
    2 Saronic group (Corinthian, Megarian, East Argolic)

'middle' Doric
    3 West Argolic
    4 East Aegean group (Doric dialects spoken on the islands Thera, Rhodes, Cos)

'strict' Doric
    5 Cretan group (Central Cretan, East Cretan) and Cyrenaean
    6 Laconian-Messenian group (Laconian,

Messenian)
Achaean subgroup (spoken in North
Peloponnesian Achaea)
7 Elean (isolated dialect of a transitional
type between the North West group and
Peloponnesian Doric)

II. ATTIC-IONIC DIALECTS

1 Attic
2 West Ionic (Euboean)
3 Central Ionic (Cycladic)
4 East Ionic (Ionic of Asia Minor)

III. ARCADO-CYPRIOT

1 Arcadian
2 Cypriot
3 Pamphylian (classified as Aeolic by some scholars)

IV. AEOLIC DIALECTS

1 Lesbian
2 Thessalian group (with several regional varieties spoken in Pelasgiotis, Thessaliotis, Hestiaeotis, and Magnesia)
3 Boeotian

Quite problematic is the reconstruction of dialect prehistory and the origins of the main historical divisions; undoubtedly this will continue as the most disputed facet of Greek dialectology. The old theory of the invasion of Greece by three separate waves of Greek-speaking people sometime during the 2nd Millenium is insufficient, since this theory simply transfers the problem without attempting a solution. The three main dialectal groupings of Ancient Greece are simply identified with the three independent invasions and the historical diversity of Greek dialects reflects a further internal differentiation of these groups after their arrival in Greece. As summed up by Chadwick (1969:81), the three-wave theory implies that the formation of the Greek language took place *outside* Greece and this seems to be unnecessary. There is some archaeological evidence that the first Greek speakers could be identical with the carriers of the Middle Helladic culture and that they might have entered some parts of Greece before the end of the 3rd Millenium i.e., the genesis of the Greek language can be set *inside* Greece (or the southern Balkan area).

The only incontestable fact of the dialectal differentiation of the Greek world in the Late Helladic (or Mycenaean) period is the absence of West Greek characteristics

in the language of the tablets written in Linear Script B.
This is not surprising, given the isolation of the West
Greek tribes in the mountainous North-West. One of the first
coherent reconstructions of dialect prehistory, elaborated
by Risch (1955), presents a basic dialectal difference
between the *ti-* and *si-* dialects in the Late Helladic period:
the *ti-* dialect group comprised the Mycenaean ancestors of
both Classical Doric and Aeolic dialects (= *North Greek* area),
and the *si-* dialect group comprised the language of LB texts,
which was labelled as proto-Ionic-Arcado-Cypriot (= *South Greek*).

Chadwick's reconstruction (1963:8) of dialect prehistory
differs from the earlier theory of Risch in the substitution
of 'Achaean' for Aeolic, thus allowing Aeolic and Arcado-
Cypriot to form subgroups of Achaean:

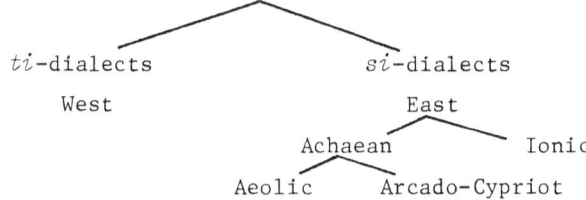

ti-dialects   *si*-dialects
West   East
       Achaean   Ionic
   Aeolic   Arcado-Cypriot

The language (or dialect) of Linear B texts, so-called
Mycenaean, is surprisingly undifferentiated, whether the
texts come from Crete or the Peloponnese. Various hypotheses
have been elaborated to explain this fact. Some scholars see
Mycenaean as a *supradialectal formation* arising out of a mixture of Proto-Arcado-Cypriot, Proto-Ionic and Proto-Aeolic
elements. This kind of Koine-formation supposedly ended its
existence with the fall of the culture which it served, as
the mixed interdialectal speech of the population living
directly in the Mycenaean centers (Mycenae, Pylos, Thebes on
the mainland: Knossos, Phaistos, Tylissos, etc. in Crete).
Other scholars think of Mycenaean as an *extinct dialectal
branch* of the late Helladic stem of Greek dialects.

According to Bartoněk (1972:19) Mycenaean was originally
spoken in the Peloponnese and is most *closely related to*
(but not fully identical with) the postulated Late Helladic
ancestor(s) of the *Arcado-Cypriot group;* Mycenaean also seems
to be *closely linked up* with the postulated ancestor of the
Aeolic group.

Thus the hypothetical differentiation of Greek dialects
spoken in the Late Helladic period (= the last centuries of
the 2nd Millenium) is more or less a back-projection of the
four principal dialectal groups of the classical times. The
criterion is basically a *geographical* one:

Proto-Doric \} autonomous dialectal units
Proto-Aeolic

Proto Ionic \} two closely linked dialectal groups
Proto-Arcado-Cypriot

Thus we may propose the following scheme:

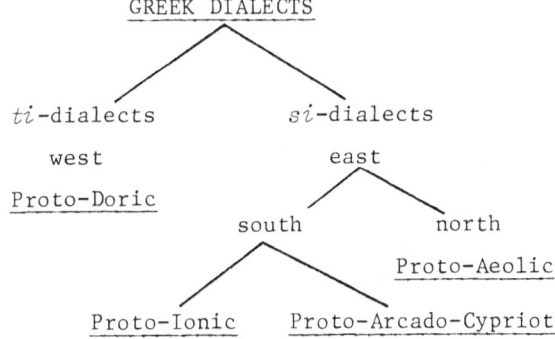

1.5 THE DECLINE OF CLASSICAL DIALECTS

The spread of Attic-based Koine (starting in the 4th c. B.C.) caused the apparent gradual disappearance of the provincial dialects. The reasons for the ultimate supremacy of Attic are to be sought in the political, social and cultural conditions back in the 5th c. At this time Athens became the political and intellectual centre of Greece, and the Attic dialect became the recognized 'standard' language of literary prose. This can be observed first of all in the territory of the related Ionic dialects, which were the first to yield to the pressure of Attic and lose their identity as distinct dialects. Some signs of this may be seen in Ionic inscriptions from various islands already by the 5th c., and from the beginning of the 4th c. in the inscriptions from Ionic cities in Asia Minor. It was this kind of Attic-based Koine, well established in territory originally Ionic and in several respects modified and enriched by Ionic elements (the most characteristic feature of this influence being the substitution of Ionic σσ for the ττ of 'pure' Attic e.g., θάλασσα), that the Macedonians spread through the whole of the Eastern Mediterranean and made an official language of their empire by the end of the 4th c.

The detailed history of the gradual eclipse of other dialectal groups will be a subject of another study of mine (in preparation). We can safely assume that local dialects continued to be spoken in the countryside long after they had been overlaid by Attic Koine and had lost their prestige among the urban upper class. The practical consequence of this situation was that dialects ceased to be used in inscriptions. This is unfortunate for us since the failure of this primary source prevents us from having adequate evidence regarding the length of survival of individual dialects, as a means of oral communication, especially in originally non-Ionic territories.

According to Debrunner (1954:34-69), Doric dialects proved to be most tenacious of all, especially in the Peloponnese and East Aegean regions (island of Rhodes). During the 3rd and 2nd c. B.C. the local Doric dialects of the Peloponnese were replaced in official inscriptions by the Doric Koine of the Achaean League. This dialectal formation was essentially Doric retaining distinctive West Greek dialectal characteristics, but with a trend to eliminate local peculiarities and with a strong admixture of forms from Attic Koine. After the dissolution of the Achaean League by the Romans (in 146 B.C.), the Doric Koine, in its turn, was replaced in official inscriptions by common Hellenistic Koine. In Rhodes, which was never humiliated by the Romans, there are still in the 1st c. A.D. many inscriptions in the more or less consistent local variant of late East Aegean Doric. There is even some evidence in contemporary writers that Doric dialects continued to be spoken in the 1st and 2nd c. A.D. Thus Suetonius (Tib. 56) indicates that in the 1st c. A.D. 'Dorice Rhodii loquuntur'. Dio Chrysostom, about 100 A.D., met an old woman in the Peloponnese who was 'δωρίζουσα τῇ φωνῇ'. According to Pausanias (4.27.11), Messenians were still using their Doric dialect in the 2nd c. A.D.

While by the end of the 2nd c. B.C. all inscriptions from the Ionic islands and Asia Minor are in Hellenistic Koine, the Aeolic dialect was used in the inscriptions of the island of Lesbos until the 1st c. B.C. Thessalian and Boeotian did not last so long. An interesting phenomenon was the 'revival' of Lesbian dialect in the 2nd c. A.D., when there appeared some inscriptions in a sort of 'corrupted' Lesbian. Scholars do not agree if this was only an artificial revival, a piece of antiquarianism, which had nothing to do with the dialect which had long ceased to be spoken, or a real revival to literary use of a dialect which perhaps had survived throughout the interval of several centuries as a local patois. Considering the situation in other peripheral areas (such as the Doric Peloponnese or Rhodes), the second possibility is certainly very likely, especially if we recall that Aeolic accentuation was quite different from Attic. The same is true of Doric dialects (see below Chapter Four, p. 153 ff.), as partly documented by late inscriptions from the remote regions of

31   Introduction

the Peloponnese and Crete. Doric dialects (or rather local variants of the Hellenistic Koine coloured by Doric dialect features) persisted for several centuries into the Christian Era.

As is well-known, Modern Greek dialects go back ultimately to the Hellenistic Koine, with the one notable exception of Tsakonian, which derives not from the Hellenistic Koine but from some type of late Peloponnesian Doric (as mentioned above, this was contaminated by Attic Koine in the 2nd - 1st c. B.C.). Modern Tsakonian is completely isolated from Modern Peloponnesian dialects and is spoken in several villages only, located on the seaward slopes of Mount Parnon in the east Peloponnese.

The phenomena of *convergence* and *divergence* in the history of Greek dialects can be diagrammed as in Figure 1-2.

Figure 1-2.   Convergence and divergence in the history of Greek dialects.

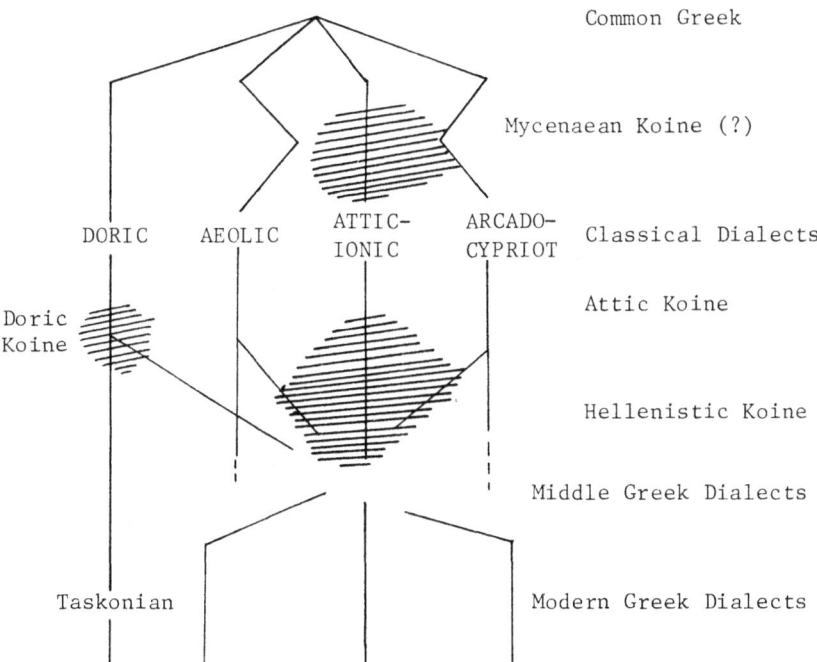

2

Vowels

2.1 THE VOWELS OF ATTIC AND OTHER GREEK DIALECTS

2.1.1 *The Vowels of Classical Attic*

The phonological system of Classical Attic vowels can be established on the basis of the following commutation tests:

(a) front - back
(b) low - non-low and high - non-high
(c) round - non-round
(d) half-close - half-open
(e) short - long

Examples are mainly taken from Lupaş (1972:126-31):

(a) e - o λέχος 'bed' - λόχος 'ambush'

ẹ̄ - ọ̄ λυπεῖν 'be pained' (Inf) - λυποῦν (Part Neuter)

ẹ̄ - ọ̄ ἄλλην 'other' (Acc Sg Fem)-ἄλλων (Gen Pl)

i - u πίστις 'faith' - πύστις 'inquiring'

ī - ū μηνίω 'be wroth against' - μηνύω 'reveal'

ẹ̄ - ā νίκης 'victory' (Gen Sg) - νίκας (Acc Pl)

(b) a - e φύλακας 'guards' (Acc Pl) - φύλακες (Nom Pl)

i - e λύθητι 'loose' - λύθητε (2nd Pl Imp
(2nd Sg Imp Aor Pass)- Aor Pass)

ī - ẹ̄ νίκη 'victory' - νείκη 'quarrels' (Pl)

u - o τύκος 'mason's hammer' - τόκος 'childbirth'

ū - ọ̄ νῦν 'now' - νοῦν 'mind' (Acc Sg)

(c) o - a λυσόμενος (Part Fut - λυσάμενος (Part Aor
Middle) Middle)

33 Vowels

ō - ā νῑκῶν 'conquer' (Part) - νῑκᾶν (Inf)
(d) ē - ē̜ φιλεῖτε 'love' (2nd Pl Ind) - φιλῆτε (2nd Pl Subj)
ō - ō̜ χρυσοῦμεν 'gild' (1st Pl Ind) - χρυσῶμεν (1st Pl Subj)
(e) a - ā λυπηρά 'painful' (Pl Neuter) - λυπηρᾱ́ (Sg Fem)
e - ē λύετε (2nd Pl Ind) - λύητε (2nd Pl Subj)
e - ē̜ ἔχομεν 'have' (1st Pl Pres) - εἴχομεν (1st Pl Impf)
i - ī ἱκετεύομεν 'supplicate' (1st Pl Pres) - ῑ̔κετεύομεν (1st Pl Impf)
o - ō̜ κακός 'bad' (Adj) - κακῶς (Adv)
o - ō λόγος 'word' (Nom Sg) - λόγους (Acc Pl)
u - ū ὑβρίζομεν 'be insolent' (1st Pl Pres) - ὑβρίζομεν (1st Pl Impf)

For the purpose of interdialectal comparison Classical Attic vowels will be presented by means of the traditional pseudoarticulatory diagram in Figure 2-1.

Figure 2-1. Vocalic phonemes of Classical Attic (5th B.C.)

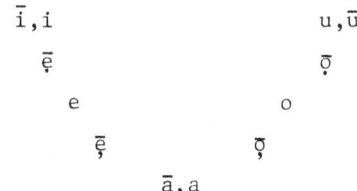

Key-words:

/ī/	νῑ́κη	'victory'	/ū/	θῡμός	'spirit, mind'
/i/	πίστις	'faith'	/u/	λυπηρός	'painful'
/ē/	εἰμί	'I am'	/ō̜/	φεύγουσα	'fleeing' (Fem)
/e/	λέχος	'bed'	/o/	λόχος	'ambush'
/ē̜/	φημί	'I say'	/ō/	χώρᾱ	'country'
/a/	ἄλλος	'other'			
/ā/	πράττω	'I make'			

An alternative way of presenting Attic phonemes is a classificatory matrix. Five features are necessary to specify all Attic phonemes: a prosodic feature of length (± long), two articulatory features specifying the highest position of the tongue in a vertical dimension (± high, ±

low), a horizontal dimension (± front) and an articulatory feature of lip shape (± round).

Figure 2-2. Distinctive features of the vocalic phonemes of Classical Attic.

	i	ī	e	ē	ẹ̄	a	ā	u	ū	o	ọ̄	ǭ
Long	−	+	−	+	+	−	+	−	+	−	+	+
Low	−	−	−	−	+	+	+	−	−	−	−	+
High	+	+	−	−	−	−	−	+	+	−	−	−
Front	+	+	+	+	+	−	−	−	−	−	−	−
Round	−	−	−	−	−	−	−	+	+	+	+	+

A problem arises in deciding how to classify the short mid vowels /e/ and /o/ of Classical Attic. Lupaș classifies them as compact (= low):

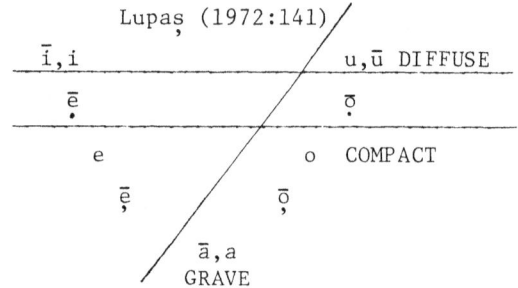

My main reason for classifying the short mid vowels as non-low stems from other dialects (Arcado-Cypriot, Lesbian and 'strict' Doric dialects) which have 3-grade vocalic systems as opposed to the 4-grade systems of Attic and other dialects. In these dialects neither the long nor the short mid vowels exhibit the low - non-low opposition. This results in a non-low specification for *e/o* and there is no reason for assuming a difference in 4-grade systems.

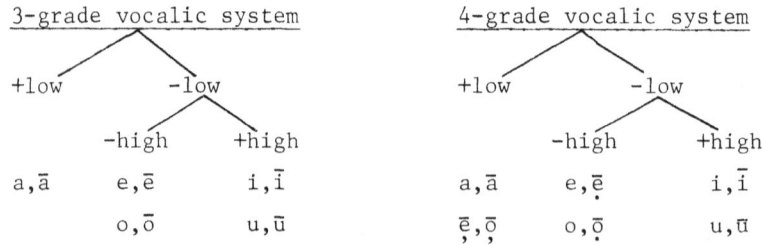

In other words, dialects with 4-grade vocalic system (like Attic) contrasted long mid vowels as low and non-low (or half-open and half-close) but dialects with 3-grade vocalic system (like Laconian) did not know this contrast.

2.1.2 *The Vowels of the Greek Dialects about 350 B.C.*

Ancient Greek dialects spoken in the 4th c. B.C. can be classified into two major groups (with several subgroups) according to their vocalic systems: those possessing a 3-grade vocalic system and those possessing a 4-grade vocalic system. All dialects have the palatal glide /j/ and the velar glide /w/, which form diphthongs with several vowels.
(i) The first group of dialects with the 3-grade vocalic system is represented by 'peripheral' dialects:
  a) The Arcado-Cypriot group
  b) Lesbian (Aeolic group)
  c) The 'strict' Doric dialects (Laconian, Messenian, Central Cretan and Cyrenaean)

In historical retrospective it can be said that these dialects preserved the Proto-Greek vocalic system of five short and long vowels.

Figure 2-3. Vocalic phonemes of Laconian (about 350 B.C.)

$$\bar{\imath},i \qquad\qquad\qquad \bar{u},u$$
$$\bar{e},e \qquad o,\bar{o}$$
$$\bar{a},a$$

The key words for Laconian are the same as those of Classical Attic with these differences:

ημι   /ēmi/   'I am'
φαμι /phāmi/ 'I say'   φευγωσα /pheugōsa/ 'fleeing' (Fem)

Note: ημι and φευγωσα are spelled in the Ionic alphabet.

Figure 2-4. Distinctive features of the vocalic phonemes of Laconian (about 350 B.C.)

	i	ī	e	ē	a	ā	u	ū	o	ō
Long	−	+	−	+	−	+	−	+	−	+
Low	−	−	−	−	+	+	−	−	−	−
High	+	+	−	−	−	−	+	+	−	−
Front	+	+	+	+	−	−	−	−	−	−
Round	−	−	−	−	−	−	+	+	+	+

The dialect spoken in Elis (West Peloponnese) differs from all other 'peripheral' dialects by its front low æ. Thus in Elean there are three low vowels (ǣ, *a*, *ā*) - only two elsewhere, and five front vowels (*ī*, *i*, *ē*, *e*, *ǣ*) - only four elsewhere.

Figure 2-5. Vocalic phonemes of Elean (about 350 B.C.).

```
    ī,i                          u,ū
       ē,e                  o,ō
                a
              ǣ    ā
```

The source of Elean ǣ was the Proto-Greek *ē̄ which was lowered in this dialect. A new secondary ē̩ resulted from the first compensatory lengthening (or contraction $e + e$) sometime in the 10th c. This hypothesis is based on the observation that since the earliest Elean inscriptions (first half of the 6th c.) the primary Proto-Greek *ē̄ is spelled with the letter A, which at the same time was also used for the Proto-Greek ā. Since it is unlikely that Proto-Greek ē̄ changed into ā in this dialect, it is believed that the Elean reflex of Proto-Greek *ē̄ is a front low vowel ē̄ or rather ǣ. On the other hand, the new secondary ē̩, which originated through the first compensatory lengthening or contraction, is spelled with the letter E. For the difference in spelling, contrast Elean Ϝρατρα /wrǣtrā/ 'verbal agreement' from Proto-Greek *wrētrā (preserved in Attic ῥήτρα /rē̩trā/ with εμεν /ēmen/ 'to be' from Proto-Greek *esmen (⟶ ehmen ⟶ ēmen).

Some of the Attic contrasts (4-grade vocalic system) did not exist or were distributed differently in the 'peripheral' dialects (Arcado-Cypriot, Lesbian and 'strict' Doric dialects, which show 3-grade vocalic system).

In Attic-Ionic the opposition front low /ē̩/ - back low /ā/ differentiates the Gen Sg and Acc Pl of stems in -ā. The forms found in various other dialects are differentiated additionally in some other segment or are homophonous:

	Gen Sg		Acc Pl	
Attic-Ionic	νίκης	/nīkē̩s/	νίκας	/nīkas/
Cretan, Argolic	νικας	/nīkās/	νικανς	/nīkans/
Lesbian, Elean	νικας	/nīkās/	νικαις	/nīkais/
Theran, Cyrenaean	νικας	/nīkās/	νικας	/nīkās/

In Attic this opposition also differentiates Singular and Dual in the Nominative. However, even in Attic this opposition was limited; it did not appear in stems in -eā -iā -rā. Furthermore dual forms are rare in dialects (they are not documented in Ionic and Cretan inscriptions). The Boeotian example illustrates the analogical extension of the Masculine -ō into the Feminine (incidentally, Boeotian had the opposition /ē̩/ - /ā/):

37 Vowels

	Singular	Dual
Attic	δραχμή 'drachm'	δραχμά (δύο)
Boeotian	δραχμα	δραχμαω (δυο)

In Attic-Ionic the opposition half-close /ọ̄/ - half open /ǭ/ is used to differentiate the 3rd Pl Indicative and Subjunctive of thematic verbs. In other dialect groups we find the opposition short /o/ - long /ō/ (as in Attic-Ionic in the 1st and 2nd Pl):

	3rd Pl Ind.		3rd Pl Subj.	
Attic-Ionic	φέρουσι	/pʰerọ̄si/	φέρωσι	/pʰerǭsi/
Doric	φεροντι	/pʰeronti/	φερωντι	/pʰerōnti/
Lesbian	φέροισι	/pʰeroisi/	φέρωισι	/pʰerōisi/
Arcadian	φερονσι	/pʰeronsi/	φέρωνσι	/pʰerōnsi/

In Attic-Ionic this opposition is also used to differentiate the Indicative and Subjunctive of contract verbs in -e (with the exception of the 1st Sg) and -o (with the exception of singular forms). This was impossible in peripheral dialects, where the Indicative and Subjunctive of contract verbs in -o were homonymous:

	Indicative		Subjunctive	
Attic-Ionic	χρυσοῦμεν	/kʰrūsọ̄men/	χρυσῶμεν	/kʰrūsǭmen/
'strict' Doric	χρυσομες	/kʰrūsōmes/	χρυσομες	/kʰrūsōmes/
(in the Ionic alphabet)	χρυσωμες		χρυσωμες	

(ii) The second group of dialects, characterized by a 4-grade vocalic system, is represented by the 'mild' and 'middle' Doric dialects, Euboean and Pamphylian.

  a) <u>North-West dialects</u> (Aetolian, Locrian, Phocian)
  b) <u>Megarian</u> and <u>Argolic</u> (both East and West)
  c) <u>East Aegean Doric</u>
  d) <u>Euboean</u> (Ionic dialect of the island of Euboea)
  e) <u>Pamphylian</u>

Figure 2-6. Vocalic phonemes of dialects with the 4-grade vocalic system.

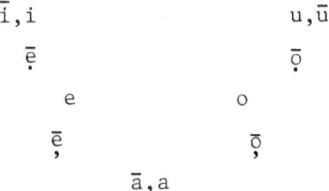

38 Phonological Interpretation of Ancient Greek

The dialect spoken in Boeotia differed from the above system in that it did not have the contrast between a half-close and half-open back vowel:

Figure 2-7. Vocalic phonemes of Boeotian (about 350 B.C.)

    ī,i   u,ū

     ē̇

        e   o,ō

     ē̦

          ā,a

The Classical Attic vocalic system was changed through the fronting of high back vowels $\breve{u} \longrightarrow \breve{ü}$ and raising of a half-close back $\bar{\varrho} \longrightarrow \bar{u}$ about 400 B.C. The same changes took place in the insular Ionic dialects (with the exception of Euboean).

Figure 2-8. Vocalic phonemes of post-Classical Attic-Ionic (about 350 B.C.).

    ī,i   ü,ü   ū

     ē̇

        e   o

     ē̦   ō

        ā,a

Following is a set of words showing differences between Classical Attic (see p. 33) and post-Classical Attic-Ionic:

    θυμός   /tʰümós/   'spirit, mind'

    λυπηρός   /lüpērós/   'painful'

    φεύγουσα   /pʰeúgūsa/   'fleeing' (Fem)

Figure 2-9. Distinctive features of the vocalic phonemes of post-Classical Attic-Ionic (about 350 B.C.)

	i	ī	e	ē̇	ē̦	a	ā	ü	ǘ	ū	o	ō
Long	−	+	−	+	+	−	+	+	−	+	−	+
Low	−	−	−	−	+	+	+	−	−	−	−	−
High	+	+	−	−	−	−	−	+	+	+	−	−
Front	+	+	+	+	+	−	−	+	+	−	−	−
Round	−	−	−	−	−	−	−	+	+	+	+	+

2.1.3 The Alphabet

In terms of the pre-Euclidean, epichoric, alphabet and the post-Euclidean (after 403/2 B.C.) Ionic alphabet, phonetic values of the Classical and Post-Classical Attic were represented as below:

Pre-Euclidean Alphabet	Ionic Alphabet	Phonemic Values (5th c.)	(4th c.)
I	I	i,ī	i,ī
E,EI	EI	ẹ̄	ẹ̄
E	E	e	e
E	H	ẹ̄	ẹ̄
A	A	a,ā	a,ā
Y	Y	u,ū	ü,ǖ
O	O	o	o
O	Ω	ǭ	ǭ
O,OY	OY	ọ̄	ū

e.g. 5th c. spellings   4th c. spellings

    ΑΛΛΟΝ /allon/   ΑΛΛΟΝ /allon/
    ΑΛΛΟΝ /allǭn/   ΑΛΛΩΝ /allōn/
    ΑΛΛΟΣ /allǭs/   ἈΛΛΟΥΣ /allūs/
    ΟΥΤΕ /ǭte/   ΟΥΤΕ /ūte/

2.2 THE DIPHTHONGS OF CLASSICAL ATTIC

In the following discussion the main emphasis will be on the surface contrasts of Classical Attic. We are aware of the fact that it is controversial to claim that language can have short and long diphthongs.[1]

Classical Attic had nine diphthongs,[1] five short and four long. [ei] can be regarded as a combinatory variant of /ē/ before a vowel while long diphthongs [āu] and [ōu] result only from the contraction $o + au$.

Short			Long	
[ei]	ui	eu	ēi	ēu
oi			ōi	[ōu]
ai		au	āi	[āu]

Short and long diphthongs generally occur in all environments with the following restrictions:

a) short diphthongs do not occur before high vowels
b) diphthongs [ei] and /ui/ do not occur before consonants
c) long diphthongs [āu], [ōu] and /ēu/ occur only before consonants

Phonotactics of Attic Diphthongs

Short	ei	oi	ai	ui	eu	au
before non-high vowel	+	+	+	+	+	+
before consonant	−	+	+	−	+	+
finally	+	+	+	+	+	+

Long	ēi	ōi	āi		ēu	āu	ōu
before vowel	+	+	+		−	−	−
before consonant	+	+	+		+	+	+
finally	+	+	+		−	−	−

Note that long diphthongs before vowels are much more restricted:[2]

/āi/ occurs before mid back vowels (with the exception of /ọ̄/)
/ēi/ occurs before mid vowels (with the exception of /ē/)
/ōi/ occurs before non-high vowels (with the exception of /ẹ̄/

Given these restrictions only the following minimal pairs are possible for short diphthongs (only diphthongs with the identical first or second component will be contrasted):

a) /au/ − /eu/
- V : αὔω 'light a fire' − εὔω 'singe' (Homeric)
- C : αὐλή 'court' − εὐλή 'worm'
- # : αὖ 'again' − εὖ 'well'

b) /au/ − /ai/
- V : παύω 'stop' − παίω 'beat'
- C : αὐτῶν 'self' (Gen Pl) − αἰτῶν 'asking a favor' (Part)
- # : αὖ 'again' − αἰ 'if' (Homeric)

c) /ai/ − /ui/
- V : μαῖα 'midwife' − μυῖα 'fly'
- # : ?

d) /ai/ − /oi/
- V : ?
- C : καινός 'new' − κοινός 'common'
- # : κακαί 'bad' (Fem Pl) − κακοί (Masc Pl)

e) /ai/ − /ei/
- V : λαῖαι 'stones' − λεῖαι 'smooth' (Fem Pl)
- # : ?

f) /ei/ − /oi/
- V : εἵην 'send' (Opt Aor) − οἵην 'such' (Acc Sg)
  <u>Ionic</u>

41   Vowels

    - # : πόλει 'city' (Dat)   - πόλοι 'pivots'

g) /ei/ - /ui/
    - V : θεῖον 'divine' (Neuter) - θυῖον 'resin'
    - # :   ?

h) /ei/ - /eu/
    - V :   ?
    - # : βασιλεῖ 'king' (Dat)   - βασιλεῦ (Voc)

i) /oi/ - /ui/ ?

Long diphthongs in Classical Attic present various difficulties in phonological interpretation. So far as their origin is concerned, they were inherited from PIE in some cases (in word-final position; before a consonant they were shortened by so-called Osthoff's Law), while in other cases they resulted from Greek contractions.

Given the restrictions on the occurrence of short and long diphthongs only the following minimal pairs contrasting short and long diphthongs of identical quality are possible:

			- V	- C	- #
a)	/ei/ :	/ēi/	+	−	+
b)	/oi/ :	/ōi/	+	+	+
c)	/ai/ :	/āi/	+	+	+
d)	/eu/ :	/ēu/	−	+	−

a) /ei/ : /ēi/
    - V : εἶα   'on, up'   - ᾖα   'I went'
    - # : (τῷ) πάθει 'accident' - (τῇ) πάθῃ 'misfortune' (Dat)
        (Dat)
    - C : This contrast did not exist. Examples like εἶμεν 'that we may be' (Optative of εἶναι) versus ᾖμεν 'we went' (Imperfect of ἰέναι) or εἶτε 'that you may be' versus ᾖτε 'you went' are to be phonemisized as /ĕmen/ - /ēimen/, not /eimen/ - /ēimen/.

b) /oi/ : /ōi/
    - V : οἴου   'think' (Imp)- ᾤου   'you thought' (Impf)
    - # : (οἱ) λόγοι 'words' (Nom)- (τῷ) λόγῳ 'the word' (Dat)
    - C : οἴχου   'go' (Imp)   - ᾤχου   'you went' (Impf)

Lesbian

φέροισι 'they carry' (Ind) - φέρωισι (Subj)

c) /ai/ : /āi/
    - V : ῥαίων 'smashing' (Part)- ῥᾴων   'easier'

- # : (αἱ) οἰκίαι 'houses'   - (τῇ) οἰκίᾳ 'house' (Dat)
           (Nom)
- C :   ?

d) /eu/ : /ēu/
- C : εὔξασθε 'pray' (Imp) - ηὔξασθε 'you prayed' (Impf)
  εὔνων   'well-disposed'- ηὔνων   'I sent to sleep'
  (Gen Pl of εὔνους)   (Impf of εὐνάω)

e) [āu] cannot be considered a phoneme of Attic. It results only from the contraction of ο + αυ ⟶ āu (Ionic [ōu])

Attic ταὐτό(ν) [tāuto(n)] 'the same'
Ionic τωὐτό [tōuto]

In the case of the preposition πρό 'before' progressive assimilation is operative even in Attic, since otherwise the preposition would be obliterated. See the hapax πρωὐδᾶν [prōudān] 'to declare first' (Aristophanes).

	Ionic
	to + auto
Progressive Assimilation	toouto
Contraction	tōuto

	Attic		
	to + auto		pro + audān
Regressive Assimilation	taauto	*Progressive Assimilation*	prooudān
Contraction	tāuto	*Contraction*	prōudān

In the case of diphthongs in accented syllables the phonetic opposition short versus long can be interpreted phonologically in two ways:
a) short versus long (as in the case of monophthongs) or
b) a diphthong accented on the first segment (= high pitch located on the first mora) versus a diphthong accented on the second segment (= high pitch located on the second mora).

In the antepenultimate syllable only the first analysis of diphthongs is possible εὔξασθε 'pray' (Imp) vs. ηὔξασθε 'you prayed' (Aorist), i.e. short /éu/ vs. long diphthong /ēú/ with the high pitch located on the second mora. The high pitch cannot be located on the first mora, since this would breach the general rule of Greek (see 4.1, p. 133 ff).

Both analyses are possible in the case of penultimate and final accented syllables. Thus the opposition εὗρε 'find' (Imp of Aorist) vs. ηὗρε 'he found' (Aorist), or εὔχου 'pray'

43 Vowels

(Imp) vs. ηὔχου 'you prayed' (Impf) can be interpreted as a short /eu/ vs. long diphthong /ēu/. Since, however, the high pitch can occur on either the first or the second mora, we can interpret this opposition as between a diphthong accented on the first segment /éu/ versus a diphthong accented on the second segment /eú/ and disregard the length of the first segment. In other words, this analysis shows that Attic in its spoken form did not exhibit the contrast short vs. long diphthong. (Imperative εὗρε and the 3rd Sg ηὗρε could be homophonous /héure/ without any risk of inhibiting the communication). Notice, however, that in the Middle Voice Imperative εὑροῦ and the 2nd Sg Indicative ηὕρου were not homophonous.

Similarly in the case of final accented syllables the opposition ἀργυροῖ 'silvern' (Pl Nom) vs. ἀργυρῷ 'to the silvern' (Dat Sg) can be interpreted as a short /oi/ vs. long diphthong /ōi/. On the other hand, the opposition ποταμοί 'rivers' (Pl Nom) vs. ποταμῷ (Dat Sg) may be interpreted as a diphthong accented on the second segment /oí/ vs. diphthong accented on the first segment /ói/.

Figure 2-10. Short and long diphthongs in accented syllables.

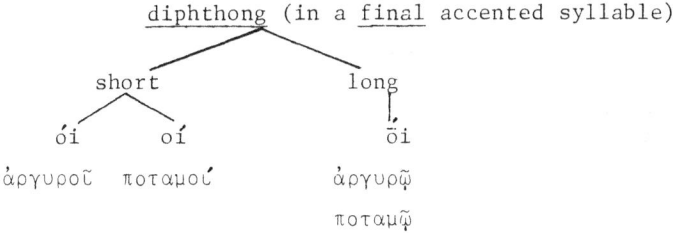

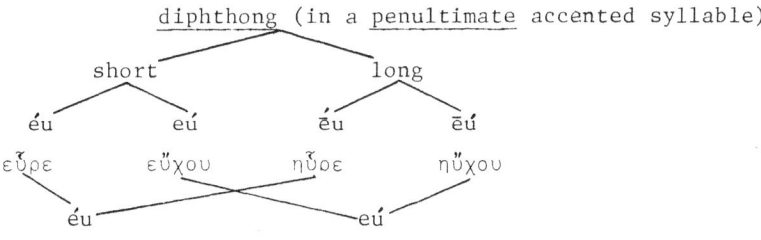

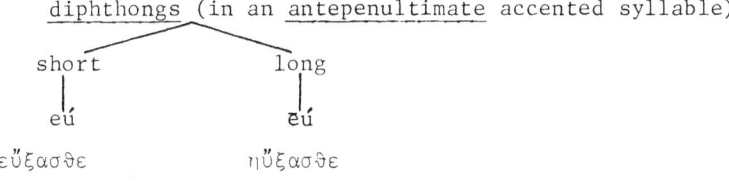

According to Allen (1974:80) long diphthongs in the environment before a vowel are to be evaluated not as diphthongs but simply as sequences of long vowel + palatal or velar glide, thus /āi/ = /ā/ + /j/. Consequently, the above minimal pairs would not be nominal pairs:

ῥᾴων/rāiōn/ vs. ῥαίων/raiōn/ would not be analyzed as /āi/ versus /ai/ but as /rājǭn/ vs. /raiǭn/.

This seems only to be a notational variant of the preceding solution. It implies a different syllabification in that the first word is to be segmented with the high front segment in the second syllable: $r\bar{a} - j\bar{\varrho}n$ as compared with the second with the high front element in the first syllable: $rai - \bar{\varrho}n$. In the case of external sandhi (when a final long diphthong is followed by an initial vowel) we may assume the loss of the morpheme boundary, e.g. τῷ ὄρνιθι/tō + jórnithi/ 'to the bird'. Allen cites spelling habits as evidence for this kind of analysis, e.g. Ionic τη Αφροδιτηι 'to Aphrodite' where the prevocalic palatal glide /j/ is omitted, since it was automatic in the environment after a front vowel. In the environment after a back vowel, as in our case, we may hypothesize that the palatal glide was optional - there could be speakers who would realize the above phrase as $t\bar{o} + ornit^{h}i$ with hiatus. In other words, long diphthongs in prevocalic position cannot be considered as full fledged phonemes, since they prove to be unstable, their second component can be lost or separated by syllabic boundary:

	/tōi + órnit^{h}i/	/tōi + patrí/
	[tǭjórnit^{h}i]	[tǭjpatrí]
or	[tǭórnit^{h}i]	[tǭpatrí]

Their phonemic status could be saved in terms of more abstract phonology, where morphological considerations bear on phonological phenomena. Thus the representation /rāi-ǭn/ versus /rai-ǭn/ would be supported by evidence that speakers of Attic were aware of the morphemic boundary in ῥᾴων (-ων is a suffix of other comparatives). Following this, it would seem that some speakers did have the contrast /āi/ versus /ai/, depending of course on their having palatal glide in the environment between back vowels. On the other hand, there were speakers without the palatal glide for whom all the above forms could be pronounced with hiatus:

[rāǭn]   versus   [raiǭn]

[tē + ap^{h}roditē]

We are on firmer ground in the environment before a

consonant or pause, where it is safer to assume that long
diphthongs have a phonemic status. However, even in cases
like /éuksasthe/ versus /éuksasthe/, /lógoi/ versus /lógōi/,
we may wonder about the stability of the opposition between
short and long diphthongs (manifested phonetically as the
opposition between 'normal' and 'delayed' glide). In fact,
we expect such a marked opposition to be unstable unless
supported by concomitant quality differences.[3] There are
independent reasons to think that this contrast was an
orthographic artifact. Colloquial Attic could certainly
tolerate homophony of the above forms - the homonymic clash
between the Aorist Imperative /éuksasthe/ [éuksasthe] and
Aorist Indicative /éuksasthe/ [éuksasthe] was certainly no
major problem in oral communication. There was, as a matter
of fact, no homonymic convergence of τῷ λόγῳ and οἱ λόγοι,
in the case when the Dat Sg and Nom Pl were used with an
article. Of equal importance, other dialects (e.g. <u>Arcadian</u>)
fail to show the opposition at all: τοι λογοι /toi logoi/ is
both Nom Pl and Dat Sg.

2.3 MONOPHTHONGIZATION OF PROTO-GREEK DIPHTHONGS
*ei and *ou

The dates proposed for the introduction of this process
vary from the 7th to the 5th c. according to different
scholars. Bartoněk (1966:77) is sure that monophthongization
of both these diphthongs occurred prior to 650 B.C. Schwyzer
(1938:233) dates this change as late as the 5th c. B.C. A
piece of direct evidence for the early date is that the
earliest known Attic inscription (ca. 725 B.C.) shows the
form τοτον = τοῦτον which might indicate that the monophthongization of the diphthong /ou/ into /ọ̄/ was under way as
early as the end of the 8th c. B.C. In terms of relative
chronology Bartoněk (1966:118) suggests that in Attica, Ionia
and the Cyclades the diphthongs /ei/ and /ou/ were monophthongized into /ẹ̄/ and /ọ̄/ either *prior* to the fronting process /ū/ ⟶ /ǖ/ or *simultaneously* with it.

In my view, the earlier estimate for the monophthongization
should be discarded in favour of the 5th c. for a number of
reasons. Reexamination of data in Meisterhans-Schwyzer
(1900:20,26,63) shows that documents belonging to the 5th c.
still make the distinction between

/ei/ spelled *EI*, and /ẹ̄/ spelled *E*
/ou/ *OY* /ọ̄/ *O*

The following confusions in spelling may prove that the monophthongization /ei/ ⟶ /ẹ̄/ and /ou/ ⟶ /ọ̄/ took place in preconsonantal position before the 5th c. B.C.

46   Phonological Interpretation of Ancient Greek

κε͂μαι (IG I² 1078 etc.)   vs.   εἰμί   (ibid. 1001, etc.)
τότον Gen Pl of οὗτος   βουλεῖ (ibid. 115,3)
       (IG 1² 247, etc.)

In the environment before the vowels, the inscriptions of the
5th and 4th c. hesitate between spellings *EI* and *E* e.g.
hιέρεια and hιέρεα, Πελειᾶται and Πελεᾶται etc. This seems to
indicate that the diphthong /ei/ was not monophthongized before
the vowels /a,e,o/ in the 5th and 4th c. It is hard to tell
when the diphthong /ou/ in the environment before vowel was
monophthongized since Attic inscriptions do not show alternative spellings *OY* and *O* (as in the case of *EI* and *E*).[4]

Further evidence for the delayed monophthongization of /ei/
before vowels, according to Allen (1974:79), can be derived
from the fact that the long close mid front vowel /ē/ was slower
to develop to a close /ī/ in a prevocalic than a preconsonantal
(or prepausal) position. This delay is taken to be the result
of the delayed monophthongization of a prevocalic /ei/ in
earlier times.

Thus in terms of relative-absolute chronology of sound-
change we can tabulate these developments as in Figure 2-11.

Figure 2-11. Monophthongization of the diphthong *ei* [after
              Allen (1974:74)].

	pre-5th c.	5-4th c.	4-3rd c. B.C.	1st-2nd A.D.	2-3rd A.D.
preconsonantal /ei/	ẹ̄		ī		
prevocalic /ei/	ei	ẹ̄		ī	
/ẹ̄/				ẹ̄	ī
/ai/					ẹ̄

[Reproduced by kind permission of the Cambridge University Press]

The monophthongal development *ai* ⟶ *ẹ̄* in Boeotian preceded
the same development in Hellenistic Koine by several centuries.
At the end of the 4th c. we already find spellings like
Ταναγρηω [tanagrēō] 'of Tanagra' (Attic Ταναγραίου [tanagraiū]),
Θειβηω [tʰẹ̄bẹ̄ō] 'Theban' (Attic Θηβαίου [tʰẹ̄baiū]).
As the latter example shows, even the raising *ẹ̄* ⟶ *ẹ̄* took
place much earlier in Boeotian.

Furthermore, we can venture a hypothesis that by the early
4th c. the long diphthong /ēi/, which was optionally realized
as a short diphthong [ei], underwent in its turn the monophthongization process that earlier affected the short diphthong

/ei/. This hypothesis is supported by the tendency in the
4th c. to replace *HI* /ēi/ by *EI* /ei/, e.g. ἀποκλήω~ἀποκλείω
'shut out', κλής ~ κλείς 'key', κλῆθρον ~ κλεῖθρον 'bolt',
λητουργῶ ~ λειτουργῶ 'perform public duties'. According to
Lupaș (1972:35) there is no evidence for these spelling alternations before the 5th c. The above facts support the
following relative chronology:

$$\bar{e}i \longrightarrow ei \longrightarrow \bar{e} \longrightarrow \bar{i}$$
$$ei \longrightarrow \bar{e}_{\cdot} \longrightarrow \bar{i}$$

Adding the absolute dimension, we posit the relationships
below:

	pre-5th	5th-4th	4th-3rd	2nd-1st
	$\bar{e}i \longrightarrow$	$ei \longrightarrow$	$\bar{e} \longrightarrow$	$\bar{i}$
preconson-antal	$ei \longrightarrow \bar{e}$	$\longrightarrow$	$\bar{i} \longrightarrow$	
prevocalic	$ei \longrightarrow$	$\bar{e}_{\cdot} \longrightarrow$		$\bar{i}$

Notice that /ē̩/ (from *ēi) was raised to /ī/ in Roman times
(2nd - 1st B.C.). Its development was later than the raising
of /ē̩/ (from *ei), which dates from the 4th - 3rd B.C.

It is hopeless to attempt to specify the relative chronology
of monophthongization by establishing a causal nexus between
this change and the fronting of $\bar{u}$ ($\longrightarrow \bar{ü}$) and the raising of
half-close back $\bar{o}_{\cdot}$ ($\longrightarrow \bar{u}$). Thus if we accept the old view
that the fronting of $\bar{u}$ ($\longrightarrow \bar{ü}$) took place quite early - in
the 7th c. according to Schwyzer (1938:233) and monoph-
thongization followed in the 6 - 5th c. - we would have a
plausible case for a drag-chain explanation:

$$\bar{ü} \xleftarrow{1} \bar{u} \qquad \bar{u}$$
$$\qquad\qquad\qquad \uparrow 2$$
$$\qquad\qquad\qquad \bar{o}_{\cdot} \quad \bar{o}_{\cdot} \xleftarrow{3} ou$$

If on the other hand the monophthongization preceded the
fronting, it undoubtedly preceded also the raising. Bartoněk
(1966:127) suggested that the change $\bar{o}_{\cdot} \longrightarrow \bar{u}$ was fully accom-
plished as late as 400 B.C. In this case a push chain is
motivated:

$$\bar{ü} \xleftarrow{3} \bar{u} \qquad \bar{u}$$
$$\qquad\qquad\qquad \uparrow 2$$
$$\qquad\qquad\qquad \bar{o}_{\cdot} \quad \bar{o}_{\cdot} \xleftarrow{1} ou$$

The corresponding evolution of the front vowels can be used
to further illuminate the push/drag-chain question. Consider
the following data:

48 Phonological Interpretation of Ancient Greek

	λείπω	βουλή	βουλῆς	καιρός	θυμός
Classical Attic (5th B.C.)	lépō̬	bo̬lêi	bo̬lê̂s	kairós	tʰūmós
4th – 3rd B.C.	lípō	būlê̬	būlê̂s		tʰümós
2nd – 1st B.C.		būlî̬			
1st – 2nd A.D.			būlḗs	kērós	
2nd – 3rd A.D.			būlī́s	kērós	
⋮					
Modern Greek	lípo	(vulí)	vulís	k'erós	θimós

It is of interest that the raising of preconsonantal ē̬ → ī̬, which was under way during the 4th – 3rd c. in Attic, took place much earlier in neighbouring Boeotian. This is obvious from the observation that the spellings which vary between *EI* and *I* in the 5th c. later occur as invariant *I*, when the Boeotians adopted the Ionic alphabet around 350 B.C.:

Boeotian	εχι	/ekʰī́/	'have'	Attic	ἔχει	/ekʰḗ̬/
	επιδει	/epīdḗ̬/	'when, since'		ἐπειδή	/epē̬dḗ̬/
	κιμενας	/kīmenās/	'laid'		κείμενας	/kḗ̬menās/

The raising of half-close mid vowels took place everywhere during the Hellenistic and Graeco-Roman period. It is possible that this phenomenon represents a contribution of Boeotian to Hellenistic Koine in the sense that the change may have started here, later on appeared in Attic, and still later spread to insular Ionic. We know that the raising of /ō̬/ never operated in West Ionic (= Euboean) and there is some evidence for delayed raising of /ē̬/. This is established on the basis of words spelled with *EI* /ē̬/ in Ionic inscriptions which already exhibit *I* /ī/ in Attic. Consider also the Doric equivalents:

Laconian	χηλιοι	'thousand'	Cretan	βωλα	'counsel'
Ionic	χείλιοι		West Ionic	βουλή	/bo̬lē̬/
Attic	χίλιοι		Attic-Ionic	βουλή	/būlē̬/
Theran	μηλιχιος	'mild, gracious'			
Attic-Ionic	μειλίχιος				
Attic (inscriptions)	μιλίχιος				
Cretan	Fημα	'dress'			

Ionic   εἷμα, εἱμάτιον
Attic   ἱμάτιον

With its two raisings, Attic is the most progressive of these three groups.[5] Ionic dialects with one raising on the front axis (and one or two on the back axis) occupy the middle position between Attic and the conservative 'strict' Doric dialects, which did not raise mid vowels at all. In summary, the sequence of sound-changes from Proto-Greek can be reconstructed as below:

	kʰeslioi	bolsā	
Fricative Weakening	kʰehlioi	-	
Compensatory Lengthening	kʰēlioi	bōla	Doric
Fronting	-	bōlǣ	
Raising	kʰẹ̄lioi Ionic	bǭlẹ̄	West Ionic
Raising	kʰīlioi Attic	būlẹ̄	Ionic

2.4 FRONTING AND RAISING OF PROTO-GREEK *ā IN ATTIC-IONIC

Proto-Greek *ā remains unchanged in all dialects with the exception of Attic-Ionic where ā was fronted (ā → ǣ) and subsequently raised (ǣ → ẹ̄):

Attic-Ionic		other dialects
τιμή	'honor'	τιμᾱ́
φημί	'I say'	φᾱμί

However, even Attic differs from the rest of Ionic dialects in not having ē but ā after front vowels *e*, *i* and liquid *r* e.g.

Attic		Ionic
γενεά	'family'	γενεή
οἰκία	'house'	οἰκίη
χώρα	'county'	χώρη

Two theories have been elaborated to explain this distribution of reflexes in the Attic-Ionic group of dialects. The first posits a continuous line of development while the second proposes a retrogressive stage:

1) Attic retained the Proto-Greek ā after front vowels and *r* while Ionic fronted ā to ǣ in all environments.

   Proto-Greek *ā ⟶ Attic ǣ (but not after front vowels or /r/)
              *ā ⟶ Ionic ǣ

2) Attic-Ionic changed Proto-Greek ā into ǣ and then Attic changed ǣ back into ā after front vowels and *r*:

50 Phonological Interpretation of Ancient Greek

Proto-Greek *ā ⟶ Attic-Ionic ǣ
(later) Attic ǣ ⟶ ā / {front vowel, r} _

The problem is further complicated by the fact that some Attic words show ǡ after *r*, e.g. κόρη 'girl', δέρη 'neck'. In many of these cases *r* was originally followed by *w*; consequently, the rule could be formulated for them. Unfortunately, examples like εἰρήνη 'peace' or κρήνη 'source' (from Proto-Greek *eirānā, *krānā; cf. Doric ἰράνā, κράνā) cannot be explained in such a way. The retrogressive theory has tended to be dominant in the linguistic literature. Szemerényi for example (1968:139-157) gives the following account in terms of relative-absolute chronology of historical sound change:

Stage 1: About 1000 - 950 B.C. Proto-Greek ā was narrowed into ǣ in the Ionic group of dialects. Loss of intervocalic *w* took place about the same time. The loss was complete in East Ionic, but incomplete in West Ionic (= Attic and Euboic):

		*newā	*hāmerā	*korwā
ā ⟶ ǣ		newǣ	hǣmerǣ	korwǣ
w ⟶ ∅/V-V		neǣ		

Stage 2: About 800 B.C. a 'new' long velar ā was introduced into the system of long vowels. This ā arose by the second compensatory lengthening (see p. 59): *pantja ⟶ pansa ⟶ pāsa. This innovation coincided with the reopening of the ǣ to ā in the environment after front vowels and *r*:

		*newā	*hāmerā
ā ⟶ ǣ		newǣ	hǣmerǣ
w ⟶ ∅/ V-V		neǣ	-
ǣ ⟶ ā/{front vowel, r} _		neā	hǣmerā

Stage 3: About 750 B.C. the opening influence of the *r* ceased to operate but the opening influence of the front vowels continued. At the same time, post-consonantal *w* was lost in West Ionic. This would have created a new *r* before ǣ which would be expected to condition ǣ ⟶ ā. By this time, however, *r* no longer conditioned the backing of ǣ:

		*newā	*korwā
ā ⟶ ǣ		newǣ	korwǣ
w ⟶ ∅/ V-V		neǣ	-
w ⟶ ∅/ r -		-	korǣ
ǣ ⟶ ā/front vowel -		neā	-

Meanwhile the vocalic sequence ea (from Proto-Greek *esa→ eha → ea) was contracted into the long front low vowel ǣ which remained unchanged even after r; however, the ǣ segments from this source become ā after front vowels (while not changing after r):

	*genesa	*oresa	*endewesa
	.	.	.
	.	.	.
	genea	orea	endeea
contraction	genǣ	orǣ	endeǣ
ǣ → ā/front vowel -	-	-	endeā

In other words, Szemerényi argues that the retrogression of ǣ ⎯ ā of West Ionic was simplified in the following way:

(1) about 800 B.C.   ǣ ⎯⎯→ ā/ { front vowel, r } -

(2) about 750 B.C.   ǣ ⎯⎯→ ā/ front vowel -

This would seem to be the weak part of Szemerényi's refinement of the relative scheme of the Attic 'Rückverwandlung' - for what reason should the opening influence of the /r/ cease after such a short time span?

Lejeune's theory (1972:234-6) is basically the same. According to him the narrowing ('fermeture') of ā into ǣ took place before the time of the second compensatory lengthening (restricted to the secondary consonantal group -ns-, see p. 59, *pantja ⎯→ pansa ⎯→ pāsa). It also preceded the contraction of a + e → ā (e.g. τιμάετε → τιμᾶτε), since the resulting ā remained unchanged in both Attic and Ionic dialects. The Attic-Ionic ǣ continued to close in articulatory height until it merged with the Proto-Greek ē. However, ǣ and ē still had not merged in 6th c. Cycladic (in Ionic dialects spoken on the islands of Amorgos, Naxos and Ceos). The difference in local alphabets indicates this: the grapheme H denotes the new ǣ while the grapheme E denotes the Proto-Greek *ē. Before the fusion of the new ǣ and the Proto-Greek ē was complete, conditioned reopening of the ǣ took place twice in Attic.

Lejeune also presents relative chronology of sound-change. According to him, the first reopening took place in the environment after r but desisted at the time of the contraction of e + a due to the merger of the resulting ǣ with the Proto-Greek *ē e.g. the Acc Sg *πλήρεα ⎯⎯→ πλήρη. This reopening dates from before the loss of postconsonantal w as well as the assimilation of the type rs ⎯→ rr, namely Attic κόρη 'girl' (*korwā), κόρρη 'temple' (< *korsā).

The second reopening took place later. During the second reopening the ǣ reopened after front vowels, e.g. Attic γενεά

Ionic γενεή, Attic καρδιά 'heart', Ionic κραδίη. The second
reopening must have followed the loss of intervocalic w and
the contraction of $e + a$ since the resulting $\bar{æ}$ reopens back
to $\bar{a}$ in the Acc Sg *ἐνδεέα ⟶ ἐνδεᾶ. The table below
illustrates the relative sequence of historical sound-changes
according to Lejeune's theory:

<u>1st reopening</u>

		*plēresa		
	*hāmerā	*plērea	*korwa	*korsā
$\bar{a} \longrightarrow \bar{æ}$	hāmerǣ	-	korwǣ	korsǣ
$\bar{æ} \longrightarrow \bar{a}/r$ -	hāmera	-	-	-
$e + a \longrightarrow \bar{æ}$	-	plērǣ	-	-
$w \longrightarrow ∅/r$ -	-	-	korǣ	-
$s \longrightarrow r/r$ -	-	-	-	korrǣ

<u>2nd reopening</u>

			*endewesa
	*genea	*newā	endeea
$\bar{a} \longrightarrow \bar{æ}$	geneǣ	newǣ	-
$w \longrightarrow ∅/V - V$	-	neǣ	-
$e + a \longrightarrow \bar{æ}$	-	-	endeǣ
$\bar{æ} \longrightarrow \bar{a}/front\ vowel$ -	geneā	neā	endeā

Lejeune's presentation of the Attic 'Rückverwandlung'
involves two difficulties. The first one is essentially the
same as the one found in Szemerényi's account; i.e. for some
unspecified reasons the 'opening influence' of r historically
precedes the opening influence of front vowels. The second
one becomes obvious if we juxtapose the derivational history
of κόρη and νέᾱ:

	*korwā		*newā
$\bar{a} \longrightarrow \bar{æ}$	korwǣ		newǣ
$\bar{æ} \longrightarrow \bar{a}/r$ -	-	$w \longrightarrow ∅ / V - V$	neǣ
$w \longrightarrow ∅/r$ -	korǣ	$\bar{æ} \longrightarrow \bar{a}/front\ vowel$ -	neā

Lejeune's version of the regressive hypothesis is rather
farfetched. The reopening rule is allowed to apply twice —

once *before* the loss of postconsonantal w and again *after* the loss of intervocalic w. However, these two rules can be easily collapsed:

$$\bar{æ} \longrightarrow \bar{a} / \left\{ {\text{front vowel} \atop r} \right\} -$$

Of course still another rule would be necessary to derive forms like ἐνδεᾶ:

$$\bar{æ} \longrightarrow \bar{a} / \text{ front vowel } -$$

Again we are left to ponder why the opening influence of the r ceased to operate.

These difficulties are obviated in the older progressive theory according to which there was no reopening of the $\bar{æ}$ to $\bar{a}$. From this point of view Attic retained Proto-Greek $*\bar{a}$, unchanged after front vowels and r, while Ionic fronted $\bar{a} \longrightarrow \bar{æ}$ without constraints of environment. As noted by Schwyzer (1938:188) this theory is simpler and more straightforward. The retrogressive and progressive theory both contain a basic assumption that the loss of intervocalic w precedes the loss of postconsonantal w. In the progressive theory the restricted fronting (Attic) and unrestricted fronting (Ionic) of the Proto-Greek $*\bar{a}$ are ordered together between these two losses. This is clear from the following derivations:

	Attic	
	*korwā	*newā
$w \longrightarrow \emptyset / V - V$	-	neā
Fronting	korwǣ	-
$w \longrightarrow \emptyset / r -$	korǣ	-

	Ionic	
	*korwā	*newā
$w \longrightarrow \emptyset / V - V$	-	neā
Fronting	korwǣ	neǣ
$w \longrightarrow \emptyset / r -$	kōrǣ	-

According to this theory the previous words would be derived as follows:

	Attic			
	*hāmerā	*korwā	*geneā	*newā
$w \longrightarrow \emptyset / V - V$	-	-	-	neā

54 Phonological Interpretation of Ancient Greek

(restricted) Fronting	hǣmerā	korwǣ	–	–
w ⟶ ∅ / r –	–	korǣ	–	–
Raising	hḛmerā	korḛ	–	–

Ionic

w ⟶ ∅ / V – V	–	–	–	neā
Fronting	hǣmerǣ	korwǣ	geneǣ	neǣ
w ⟶ ∅ / r – + *Compensatory Lengthening*	–	kōrǣ	–	–
Raising	hḛmerḛ	kǭrḛ	geneḛ	neḛ

It can be seen in the derivational history of contracted forms like Attic πλήρη, ὑγιᾶ or ὑγιῆ (in Plato) and ἐνδεᾶ (Neuter or Acc Masc of the adjectives πλήρης 'full', ὑγιής 'healthy', ἐνδεής 'lacking') that the source of the hypothesis about reopening of ǣ back to ā was only regressive assimilation of *e* to *a* in sequences $\begin{Bmatrix} u \\ i \\ e \end{Bmatrix}$ ea ⟶ $\begin{Bmatrix} u \\ i \\ e \end{Bmatrix}$ aa.

The existence of a *regressive* assimilation is further supported by the existence of other forms requiring a *progressive* assimilation. Furthermore, forms like ὑγιῆ (∼ ὑγιᾶ) could not be explained by the reopening hypothesis alone and would stand as exceptions. Such forms can, however, be derived easily if progressive and regressive assimilation are both posited:

	pléresa	hugiésa	
Fricative Weakening	pléreha	hugiéha	
h ⟶ ∅ / – V	plérea	hugiéa	Ionic (uncontracted)
Progressive Assimilation	pléree	hugiée	
Contraction	plḛrḛ́	hugiḛ̂	Attic
	endewésa	hugiésa	
Fricative Weakening	endewéha	hugiéha	
h ⟶ ∅ / – V	endewéa	hugiéa	
w ⟶ ∅ / – V	endeéa	–	
Regressive Assimilation	endeá́a	hugiáa	
Contraction	endeâ	hugiâ	Attic-Ionic

55 Vowels

In these derivations a certain inconvenience appears in the representation *plḗree, hugiée* at the stage after progressive assimilation, since the output of isovocalic contraction is regularly a raised vowel in Attic-Ionic: $e + e \longrightarrow \bar{e}$.
Since the vowel resulting from the contraction is low, if one of the contracting vowels is low, a more appropriate notation before the contraction would be *plḗreæ, hugiéæ, endeǽa*. Independent support is afforded by Ionic where it is known that long vowels developed in parallel fashion.

	Ionic		Attic
	-eā		-ea
Fronting	-eǣ	*Progressive Assimilation*	-eæ
Raising	-eē̞	*Contraction*	-ē̞

Here we should note the derivation of some more complicated forms belonging to εὐκλεής 'famous':

Acc Sg εὐκλ(ε)έα   Acc Pl εὐκλ(ε)έας

       εὐκλεᾶ (Pindar)   εὐκλεῖας (Homeric)

       εὐκλεῖα(poetic)   εὐκλεεῖς

Uncontracted forms

	ewésa		ewésas	
Fricative Weakening	ewéha		ewéhas	
$h \longrightarrow \emptyset / V - V$	ewé a		ewé as	
$w \longrightarrow \emptyset / V - V$	e é a εὐκλεέα		e é as εὐκλεέας
Syncopation	é a εὐκλέα		é as εὐκλέας

Contracted forms

	⋮		⋮	
	e é a		e é as	
Contraction (e + e)	ḗ a εὐκλεῖα		ḗ as εὐκλεῖας	
	(reaccented)		(reaccented)	
	ésa	ewéses		ewésa
Fricative Weakening	éha	ewéhes		ewéha
$h \longrightarrow \emptyset/V - V$	é a	ewé es		ewé a
$w \longrightarrow \emptyset/V - V$	–	e é es		e é a
Progressive Assimilation	é ẹ̄	–	*Regressive Assimilation*	e á a

Contraction $\hat{\bar{e}}$ e $\hat{\bar{e}}$s *Contraction* e $\hat{\bar{a}}$
($\acute{e} + \underset{\rtimes}{e}$)   ($\acute{a} + a$)

ψευδῆ   εὐκλεεῖς   εὐκλεᾶ

Let us recapitulate the most essential part of the previous discussion. In different dialects it is common for some sound-changes to occur at different times. In the case of the Ionic group of dialects the loss of postconsonantal w and fronting of $\bar{a}$ ($\rightarrow \bar{æ}$) occurred earlier in (East) Ionic than in Attic. Thus if we want our rules to imitate the sequential character of historical sound-changes the derivational scheme should look as follows:

	Attic	Ionic
	*korwā	*korwā
Fronting	–	korwǣ
$w \rightarrow \emptyset / r$ - + *Compensatory Lengthening*	–	kǭrǣ
Fronting	korwǣ	–
$w \rightarrow \emptyset / r$ -	korǣ	–
Raising	korḗ	kǭrḗ

In Attic the loss of postconsonantal w *followed* the fronting process. In Ionic, however, the ordering is irrelevant since for either order the result will be the same. The following derivation illustrates the ordering of the loss of w and compensatory lengthening before fronting:

	Attic	Ionic
	*korwā	*korwā
$w \rightarrow \emptyset / r$ - + *Compensatory Lengthening*	–	kǭrā
Fronting	korwǣ	kǭrǣ
$w \rightarrow \emptyset / r$ -	korǣ	–
Raising	korḗ	kǭrḗ

2.5 COMPENSATORY LENGTHENING

2.5.1. First Compensatory Lengthening

In the majority of Greek dialects, with the exception of the Aeolic group (Thessalian and Lesbian), Proto-Greek consonant clusters of a sibilant followed by liquid, nasal or velar semivowel (*sr, *sl, *sm, *sn, *sw) were affected by the fricative weakening $s \rightarrow h$. By this change the Proto-Greek *s inherited from PIE lost its typical articulation of

57 Vowels

a dental sibilant and changed into a voiceless glottal fricative *h*. The voiceless glottal fricative *h* was subsequently lost and this loss was accompanied by the *first compensatory lengthening* of the preceding short vowel:

	V	s	Sonorant
Fricative Weakening	V	h	Sonorant
Compensatory Lengthening	V̄		Sonorant

Doric σελᾱνᾱ 'moon' and χηλιοι 'thousand' from Proto-Greek **selasnā* and **kheslioi* exemplify these processes:

	selasnā	kheslioi
Fricative Weakening	selahnā	khehlioi
Compensatory Lengthening	selānā	khēlioi

In the same dialects Proto-Greek consonantal clusters of a sibilant following liquid or nasal (*rs, *ls, *ms, *ns) were simplified by the loss of the sibilant. This loss was accompanied by the compensatory lengthening of the preceding short vowel. In this case, however, the environment for compensatory lengthening is extremely limited since it occurs only in the sigmatic Aorist (see p. 122).

In the same dialects the Proto-Greek consonant cluster was simplified by the loss of the nasal, accompanied by the compensatory lengthening of the preceding short vowel.

The derivation of Doric ἐφᾱνα 'I showed' and στᾱλᾱ 'stele' from the Proto-Greek **ephansa* and **stalnā* illustrate this:

	ephansa		stalnā
s - Loss + Lengthening	ephāna	*n - Loss + Lengthening*	stālā

The traditional label *first compensatory lengthening* lumps together under the same heading the compensation for three distinct types of loss:
a) the loss of a glottal fricative before sonorants:
   h ⟶ ∅/ - Sonorant
b) the loss of a sibilant after sonorants (limited to the sigmatic Aorist):
   s ⟶ ∅/ Sonorant - V
c) the loss of a dental nasal after lateral liquid:
   n ⟶ ∅/ 1 - V

Linguists usually place the first compensatory lengthening around 1000 B.C. since the product of this lengthening (long /ā/) was subject to the fronting /ā/ ⟶ /ǣ/, which in its turn is supposed to have taken place *later* in the Attic-Ionic group.

The suggested date for Attic-Ionic fronting varies from

58 Phonological Interpretation of Ancient Greek

ca 1000 - 700 B.C. The end of the 8th c. B.C. is the time
of the earliest Attic-Ionic inscriptions. At this time
raising of the low front vowel into a middle one /ǣ/⟶
/ē̜/ is already documented, and this depends, of course, on
the existence of ǣ (< ā). Schwyzer (1938:233) places the
boundary between the 8th and 7th c. Lejeune (1947:17) includes fronting in the set of changes taking place 'towards
the end of the 2nd and in the beginning of the 1st millenium.'
Risch (1955:65) suggests the 10th or the 9th c. Bartoněk
(1966:101) prefers circa 900 B.C., the terminus post being
10th c. and the terminus ante 800 B.C. In terms of relative
chronology, Lejeune and Bartoněk argue that fronting ceased
to be active before the second compensatory lengthening.
According to Lejeune (1972:235)

> la fermeture avait cessé de se produire avant l'époque
> des allongments compensatoires récents (*πανσανς > πᾶσας)
> et des contractions de ǎ avec ě (*τῑμάετε > τῑμᾶτε), ę̄
> (τῑμάειν > τῑμᾶν) ou ǭ (*τῑμάητε > τῑμᾶτε); les ā qui en
> résultent ont subsisté en ionien et en attique, ainsi que
> les ā des mots d'emprunt postérieurs (Dārayavahuš:
> Δᾱρεῖος).

Similarly Bartoněk (1966:101) places Attic-Ionic fronting
between the operation of the 1st and the 2nd compensatory
lengthening:

Absolute-relative   *pántja

chronology   .

                                 *éphansa   .
1000 B.C. *1st Compensatory*
           Lengthening   éphāna   .
 900 B.C. *Fronting*   éphǣna   pánsa
 800 B.C. *Raising*   éphē̜na   *2nd Compensatory*
                                          Lengthening   pâsa

   Notice, however, that these facts can be explained without
reference to the suggested relative chronology. It might be proposed that the fronting of ā → ǣ failed to apply in pâsa not
because 'la fermeture avait cessé de se produire avant
l'époque des allongements compensatoires' but simply because,
if it did, the resulting paradigm would show morphemic variation like: *πῆς, παντός instead of πᾶς, παντός. In other
words, even if fronting had applied here its result might have
been levelled by analogy with other members of the paradigm.
Consequently, I would tend to believe that the fronting did
not apply inside of the paradigm of πᾶς, παντός. To say that
the fronting rule ceased to operate before 'l'époque

59 Vowels

des contractions' /a/ + /e/ ⟶ /ā/ involves other difficulties - a result of the same contraction in Doric is /ē/ and Doric did not front the low vowel /ā/. Thus against Attic ἔφηνα, τῑμᾶτε there is Doric ἔφᾱνα, τῑμῆτε:

	Attic		Doric	
	épʰāna		éphāna	
Fronting	éphǣna	tīmáete	-	tīmáete
Raising	éphēna	-	-	-
Contraction		tīmâte		tīmḗte

2.5.2 Second and Third Compensatory Lengthening

Some linguists distinguish between a 2nd and a 3rd compensatory lengthening. Both of these lengthenings presumably took place after the Attic-Ionic fronting $\bar{a}$ ⟶ $\bar{æ}$. The second lengthening of the type (*pantja ⟶) pansa ⟶ pāsa became a source of a new Attic-Ionic /ā/, where the Proto-Greek *a had been fronted several generations ago. The 2nd lengthening follows a fairly general tendency in Greek to weaken a nasal before a sibilant. The environment of the 2nd lengthening includes:
a) the secondary medial cluster -ns- derived from Proto-Greek *-ntj/i- (through affrication and depalatalization)
b) the primary final *-ns (in the Acc Pl, *tons Attic τούς, Laconian τως).

The 2nd lengthening did not extend to certain 'peripheral' dialects: Thessalian, Arcadian, West Argolic, Central Cretan, where forms like πανσα and φερονσα are found. In Lesbian, Cyrenaean (and also apparently in Theran) the palatal glide metathesized with the cluster ns or with s depending on whether the loss of n preceded or followed metathesis, and the form of the 3rd Pl -onsi (< *-onti) underwent 'metathesis (b)' -onsi ⟶ -oinsi (defined on p. 189):

	Lesbian and Cyrenaean		
	pʰeronti	pʰerontja	pantja
Affrication	pʰerontˢi	pʰerontˢja	pantˢja
t ⟶ ∅	pʰeronsi	pʰeronsja	pansja
Metathesis of glide	pʰeroinsi	pʰeroinsa	painsa
n ⟶ ∅	pʰeroisi	pʰeroisa	paisa (also <u>Theran</u>)

'peripheral' dialects (<u>Thessalian</u>, <u>Arcadian</u>, <u>West Argolic</u>, <u>Central Cretan</u>)

⋮   ⋮   ⋮

	pʰeronsi	pʰeronsja	pansja
	(Arcadian)		
Depalatalization	-	pʰeronsa	pansa
n ⟶ ∅	-	-	-

'peripheral' dialects (<u>Theran</u>, <u>Laconian</u>, <u>Messenian</u>, <u>Elean</u>)

	⋮	⋮	⋮
	pʰeronsi	pʰeronsja	pansja
Depalatalization	-	pʰeronsa	pansa
n ⟶ ∅ + *2nd Lengthening*	pʰerōsi	pʰerōsa	pāsa

Remaining dialects

	⋮	⋮	⋮
	pʰeronsi	pʰeronsja	pansja
Depalatalization	-	pʰeronsa	pansa
n ⟶ ∅ + *2nd Lengthening*	pʰerōsi	pʰerōsa	pāsa
Raising	pʰerǭsi	pʰerǭsa	-

The 3rd lengthening is limited to the clusters $\begin{Bmatrix} \text{Nasal} \\ \text{Liquid} \end{Bmatrix}$ + Velar glide (*nw, *rw, *lw - notice that the cluster *sw meets the structural description of the 1st lengthening). The effect of this process is to compensate for the loss of w after sonorants by lengthening the preceding vowel. It was active in Ionic outside Attic and West Ionic (= Euboean), in Argive (= the dialect of Argos) but not in Argolic, Cretan, Cyrenaean and East Aegean Doric. According to Bartoněk (1966:69) this process represented only a minor isogloss comprising the central and south-eastern sector of the Aegean region. Elsewhere w is lost following sonorants without a corresponding effect on the preceding vowel:

	*korwā	*derwā	*ksenwos
<u>Arcadian</u>	κορϝα 'girl'	δερϝᾱ 'neck'	ξένος 'guest'
<u>Attic</u>	κόρη	δέρᾱ	ξεῖνος
<u>Lesbian</u> (literary)	κόρᾱ	δείρη	ξεῖνος
<u>Ionic</u>	κούρη		
<u>Cretan</u>, <u>Cyrenaean</u>	κωρᾱ		ξηνος

61 Vowels

Lesbian ξέννος as well as ἕννεκα 'on account of', found in the late inscriptions and grammatical accounts of the Graeco-Roman period, may be considered Aeolic hypercorrections. They are based on a misunderstanding of the sources of Aeolic -nn-: *sn, *ns or *nj but not *nw. The reconstruction of *nw in *ksenwos is affirmed by Mycenaean ke-se-nu-wo /ksenwos/. On the other hand, it is likely that there was no *nw in ἕνεκα since Mycenaean spells this word e-ne-ka.

	Lesbian	Attic	Ionic	Cretan Cyrenaean
	korwā	korwā	korwā	korwā
Fronting	-	korwǣ	korwǣ	-
w ⟶ ∅ / Sonorant -	korā	korǣ	korǣ	korā
+ *3rd Lengthening*	-	-	kōrǣ	kōrā
Raising	-	korē̦	kō̦rē̦	-
	ksenwos	ksenwos	ksenwos	ksenwos
w ⟶ ∅ / Sonorant -	ksenos	ksenos	ksenos	ksenos
+ *3rd Lengthening*	-	-	ksēnos	ksēnos
Raising	-	-	ksḛnos	-

Alternatively Ionic forms like /kōrē̦/ can be explained by metathesis of velar glide (with parallel to the palatal glide metathesis in Lesbian and Cyrenaean):

	Ionic	Lesbian Cyrenaean
	korwā	pansja
Metathesis of glide	kourā	painsa
	⋮	⋮
	kourē̦ (=/kō̦rē̦/)	paisa

This possibility cannot be ruled out a priori; notice, however, that the derivation would not be as direct in words with a front vowel in the root like *ksenwos ⟶ ksḛnos.

The relative chronology of the 2nd and 3rd compensatory lengthening has been worked out by Bartoněk (1966:64-70, 174-5). The 3rd lengthening is shown to follow the 2nd lengthening by three generations between 800 and 700 B.C.:

62 Phonological Interpretation of Ancient Greek

Absolute-relative
chronology

		pʰeronti	
B.C.	epʰansa	pʰeronsi	korwā
1000 *1st Lengthening*	epʰāna	–	–
900 *Fronting*	epʰǣna	–	korwǣ
800 *Raising – 2nd Lengthening*	epʰḙ̄na	pʰerōsi	–
Raising	–	pʰerǭsi	korwḙ̄
700 *3rd Lengthening*	–	–	kōrḙ̄
Raising	–	–	kǭrḙ̄

Again it might be argued that there was in fact no third lengthening but that the lengthening of *pʰeronsi* and *korwǣ* took place at the same time. In fact all that is certain is that both followed the fronting $\bar{a} \rightarrow \bar{æ}$:

	epʰansa	pʰeronsi	korwā
1000 *1st Lengthening*	epʰāna	–	–
900 *Fronting*	epʰǣna	–	korwǣ
800 *Raising – 2nd Lengthening*	epʰḙ̄na	pʰerōsi	kōrḙ̄
Raising	–	pʰerǭsi	kǭrḙ̄

Finally, the picture for Ionic (excluding Attic) would be unchanged if the 3rd lengthening accompanied the 1st lengthening (prior to the fronting of $\bar{a} \rightarrow \bar{æ}$):

	epʰansa	korwā
1000 *1st Lengthening*	epʰāna	kōrā
900 *Fronting*	epʰǣna	kōrǣ
800 *Raising*	epʰḙ̄na	kǭrḙ̄

For these reasons it seems that there is not sufficient justification for a separate lengthening process in the environment before a *sonorant + velar glide*. It is probable that the putative 3rd lengthening was in fact the 2nd lengthening in some of the Doric dialects and the 1st lengthening elsewhere (e.g. in Ionic).

The whole theory of relative chronology is related to the European structuralist concept of the causality of sound change. The raising of $\bar{a} (\rightarrow \bar{e})$ following (or coinciding with) the raising of $\bar{æ} (\rightarrow \bar{e})$ is an instance of a push-chain, see Martinet (1955:59).

63 Vowels

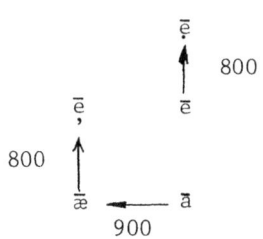

	selasnā	esmi
Fricative Weakening	selahnā	ehmi
1000 *1st Lengthening*	selānā	ēmi
900 *Fronting*	selǣnǣ	–
800 *Raising*	selẹ̄nẹ̄	ẹ̄mi

2.5.3 Raising of Long Mid Vowels in Dialects

Proto-Greek short mid vowels *e and *o became long mid vowels /ē/ and /ō/ by compensatory lengthening. These two merged with long Proto-Greek /ē/ and /ō/ in the 'peripheral' dialects (Arcado-Cypriot, Aeolic and Doric dialects). In the other Greek dialects (Attic-Ionic, North-West, Corinthian, Megarian and East Argolic) the resulting long mid vowels were raised and became half-close vowels /ẹ̄/ and /ọ̄/. As half-close vowels they remained distinct from the Proto-Greek vowels which were half-open. See Bartoněk (1966:172) for the traditional presentation (without diphthongs /ui, eu, au/).

Figure 2-12. Vocalic phonemes of Arcado-Cypriot, Aeolic and Doric dialects (after the 1st compensatory lengthening).

```
ī,i                    u,ū           ui         eu
   ē,e      o,ō                      ei,oi      ou
      ā,a                            ai         au
```

Figure 2-13. Vocalic phonemes of Attic-Ionic, North-West and Saronic dialects (after the 1st compensatory lengthening and raising of mid vowels).

```
ī,i                    u,ū           ui         eu
   ẹ̄          ọ̄
      e         o                    ei,oi      ou
   ē̜          ō̜
      ā,a                            ai         au
```

This kind of structural analysis is obviously problematic since Attic-Ionic, North-West and the Saronic group of dialects are overdifferentiated. It is well known that languages do not contrast half-close /ẹ̄,ọ̄/, half-open vowels /ḛ̄,ō̰/ and diphthongs /ei,ou/. As shown in 2.3, the diphthongs /ei,ou/ are best considered phonemic variants of half-close vowels /ẹ̄,ọ̄/. This means of course that even Proto-Greek and 'peripheral' dialects (Arcado-Cypriot, Aeolic and 'strict' Doric) can be phonemicized as a 4-grade system (or a 3-grade system with the diphthongs /ei, ou/).

Thus notations (1) and (2) are equivalent in terms of structural oppositions:

(1) ī,i   u,ū   ui   eu

     ē,e   o,ō   ei,oi   ou

        ā,a   ai   au

(2) ī,i   u,ū   ui   eu

   ẹ̄   ọ̄

     e   o   oi

  ḛ̄   ō̰

       ā,a   ai   au

Similarly there are two ways to phonemisize Mycenaean data:

		(1)	(2)
re-qo-me-no	(= λειπόμενος)	/leik\ʷomenos/	/lḛ̄kʷomenos/
me-no	(= μηνός)	/mēnos/	/mḛ̄nos/
qo-u-ko-ro	(= βουκόλος)	/gʷoukolos/	/gʷō̰kolos/
a-to-ro-qo	(= ἄνθρωπος)	/antʰrōkʷos/	/antʰrō̰kʷos/

Let us examine some phonemic notations from Classical dialects:

Proto-Greek		'strict' Doric		Attic-Ionic	
*keimai	'lie'	κειμαι	/keimai/	κεῖμαι	/keimai/
*patēr	'father'	πατηρ	/patēr/	πατήρ	/patḛ̄r/
*esmi	'I am'	ημι	/ēmi/	εἰμί	/ẹ̄mi/

After compensatory lengthening *esmi* ⟶ *ēmi*, /ē/ in /ēmi/ merged with /ē/ in /patēr/ in 'strict' Doric, but not in Attic-Ionic, where it was raised /ēmi/ ⟶ /ẹ̄mi/. If for argument's sake we assume that it merged with the Proto-Greek diphthong /ei/ we have to assume that [kēimai] is only a phonetic - not phonemic - transcription for Attic-Ionic. Consequently we would have to adopt phonemic notation (1) or (2) above:

Attic-Ionic	Phonetics	Phonemics (1)	Phonemics (2)
	[kēimai]	/keimai/	/kēmai/
	[patēr] or [patẹ̄r]	/patēr/	/patẹ̄r/
	[ēmi] or [ẹ̄mi]	/eimi/	/ẹ̄mi/

Thus a solution seems to be to assume underlying diphthongs /ei/ and /ou/ for 'peripheral' dialects (Aeolic, Arcado-Cypriot, 'strict' Doric) and underlying monophthongs /ẹ̄/ and /ọ̄/ for Attic-Ionic, North-West and Saronic dialects. In historical terms this means that in the second group of dialects Proto-Greek diphthongs /ei/ and /ou/ became phonemic variants of half-close mid vowels /ẹ̄/ and /ọ̄/ subsequent to compensatory lengthening and raising of Proto-Greek *e and *o in certain environments or through isovocalic contractions.6

2.6 VOWEL SEQUENCES IN DIALECTS

2.6.1 Height Dissimilation

In the Aeolic and Doric dialects (and also in Cypriot) a front mid vowel occurs subject to *regressive height dissimilation* in the environment before a back mid vowel:

Regressive Height Dissimilation A short front mid vowel becomes high in the environment before a back mid vowel:
e + o ⟶ i + o

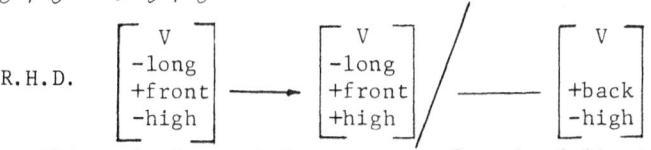

This rule is needed to account for the following data:

Lesbian	χρύσιος	Homeric	χρύσεος	'golden'
Thessalian	λίθιος	"	λίθεος	'made of stone'
Boeotian	ἰών	Attic	ἐγώ	'I'
Cypriot	ιοντα (Acc) but	Arcadian	εοντος (Gen)	'being'
Central Cretan	ποιιομενοι	Attic	ποιούμενοι	'made' (Pl)

Laconian, Argolic σιος   Attic θεός   'god'

In some dialects the environment of regressive height dissimilation included even a low vowel: e $\begin{Bmatrix} o \\ a \end{Bmatrix}$ ⟶ i $\begin{Bmatrix} o \\ a \end{Bmatrix}$. The appropriate class can be defined in negative terms: $\begin{bmatrix} -\text{front} \\ -\text{high} \end{bmatrix}$. We have evidence from Cypriot, Central Cretan and Boeotian (also Pamphylian, but I do not find any instances of the change eo ⟶ io in this dialect).

Cypriot Ϝεπιjα (but Arcadian Ϝετεα 'years') Attic ἔπη 'words'

κατεθιαν (but Arcadian συνεθεαν) Attic ἔθεσαν
'they put down'

Boeotian ἀνεθιαν 'they set up'

Central Cretan δόριαν 'gift' (Acc) Attic ἔτη (< ἔτεα) 'years'

Pamphylian Ϝετιια 'years'

The situation in Cretan dialects is quite complicated. Regressive height dissimilation before non-high back vowels *o, a* is documented in Central Cretan and in the eastern transitional region (Dreros and Latos) but this process did not take place in dialects spoken in western and eastern parts of the island. In both East and West Cretan dialects the *e* of contract verbs was syncopated before *o* in closed syllables e.g. κοσμοντες versus Central Cretan κοσμιοντες (κοσμιω 'be a member of the body of chief magistrates'), however, in open syllables *e + o* contract into *ō*, e.g. εὐχαριστωμες 'be thankful' (Allaria). The distribution is further complicated in some cities (Lappa, Phaselis) by the presence of *e + o* contracted into *ō* even in closed syllables. And finally, *e + o* in both open and closed syllables may remain unchanged (Itanos, East Cretan):[7]

	Closed syllable	Open syllable
East Cretan (Itanos)	-eo-	-eo-
Central Cretan	-io-	-io-
West Cretan	-o-	-ō-
West Cretan (Lappa, Phaselis)	-ō-	-ō-

	Central Cretan	
Regressive Height Dissimilation	kosmeontes	kosmeomes
	kosmiontes	kosmiomes
	West Cretan	
	kosmeontes	kosmeomes

67 Vowels

Assimilation	kosmoontes		kosmoomes
Syncopation	kosmontes	*Contraction*	kosmōmes
	(Lappa, Phaselis)		
	kosmeontes		
Assimilation	kosmoontes		
Contraction	kosmōntes		

According to Buck, (1955:22) regressive height dissimilation preceded the loss of intervocalic w, since e which appeared before another vowel with the loss of w was unaffected. This hypothesis is based on certain forms from Cretan, Laconian and Heraclean, where eo becomes regularly io, except where the eo goes back to *ewo:

<u>Cretan</u> καλιον 'calling' but υιεος 'son'(*$huiewos$ Gen)
<u>Heraclean</u> αδικιων 'doing wrong' but ρεοντα 'flowing'
(*$hrewonta$ Acc)

	adikeōn	rewonta
R.H.D.	adikiōn	-
$w \rightarrow \emptyset / V - V$	-	reonta

Another point regarding the relative chronology of R.H.D. can be made in connection with Boeotian ιων 'I' (= ἐγώ). Here e and o could have become adjacent only after the frication of the velar stop g (which could take place as early as the 4th B.C.), and palatal development $\gamma \rightarrow j$ after a front vowel. j could be felt only as an automatic glide. Thus the *regressive height dissimilation* should be later than these processes:

	egō
Frication	eγō
Palatalization	ejō
R.H.D.	ijō

In Ionic (and some Doric dialects) a back mid vowel is subject to a process of *progressive height dissimilation* in the environment after a front mid vowel:

<u>Progressive Height Dissimilation</u> A back mid vowel becomes high in the environment after a short front mid vowel:
$e + o \rightarrow e + u$

68 Phonological Interpretation of Ancient Greek

P.H.D. $\begin{bmatrix} V \\ -\text{long} \\ +\text{round} \\ -\text{high} \end{bmatrix} \longrightarrow \begin{bmatrix} V \\ -\text{long} \\ +\text{round} \\ +\text{high} \end{bmatrix} \Big/ \begin{bmatrix} V \\ -\text{long} \\ +\text{front} \\ -\text{high} \end{bmatrix} \underline{\hspace{1cm}}$

Buck (1955:40) cites evidence for progressive height dissimilation from:
(a) The texts of various early authors, e.g. Homeric μευ 'of me' (Attic μου), φιλεῦντας 'loving' (uncontracted φιλέοντας) Acc Pl.
(b) The spelling -ΕΥ- as a generalized phenomenon in Ionic inscriptions in the 4th c. B.C.
(c) The same spelling also occurring in many other areas like Rhodes and Cos, Thera and Cyrene, Megara, etc.
This indicates that progressive height dissimilation was a fairly common synchronic process existing in many dialects - Ionic, East Aegean Doric, Cyrenaean, Megarian. See e.g. Coan κυεοσα [kueosa], κυευσα 'pregnant' (Attic κυοῦσα [kuǫ̂sa]).

2.6.2 Height Assimilation

In various dialects a low vowel occurs subject to *progressive height assimilation* in the environment before a back mid vowel.

<u>Regressive Height Assimilation</u> A low vowel becomes front mid in the environment before a back mid vowel: $a + o \longrightarrow e + o$

R.H.A. $\begin{bmatrix} V \\ -\text{long} \\ +\text{low} \end{bmatrix} \longrightarrow \begin{bmatrix} V \\ -\text{long} \\ +\text{front} \\ -\text{high} \end{bmatrix} \Big/ \underline{\hspace{0.5cm}} \begin{bmatrix} V \\ +\text{round} \\ -\text{high} \end{bmatrix}$

There is both literary and inscriptional evidence from West Greek dialects for this process. Regressive height assimilation is followed by contraction in Rhodian and by regressive height dissimilation in Boeotian and Central Cretan but its product *eo* remains unchanged in Aetolian and Phocian.

<u>Attic</u>	τῑμῶντες	<u>Attic</u>	τῑμῶσα
<u>Rhodian</u>	τῑμουντες	<u>Rhodian</u>	τῑμουσα
<u>Aetolian</u>	τῑμεοντες	<u>Phocian</u>	τῑμεουσα
<u>Central Cretan</u>	τῑμιοντες	<u>Central Cretan</u>	τῑμιονσα
		<u>Boeotian</u>	τῑμιωσα

The difference between Attic τῑμῶσα /tīmǭsa/ and Rhodian τῑμουσα /tīmǭsa/ is the consequence of regressive height assimilation, which did not take place in Attic. Since in

69 Vowels

Attic one of the contracting vowels is low the resulting vowel must be low. In Rhodian after the regressive height assimilation both contracting vowels are non-low and the resulting vowel is non-low as well.

CONTRACTING DIALECTS

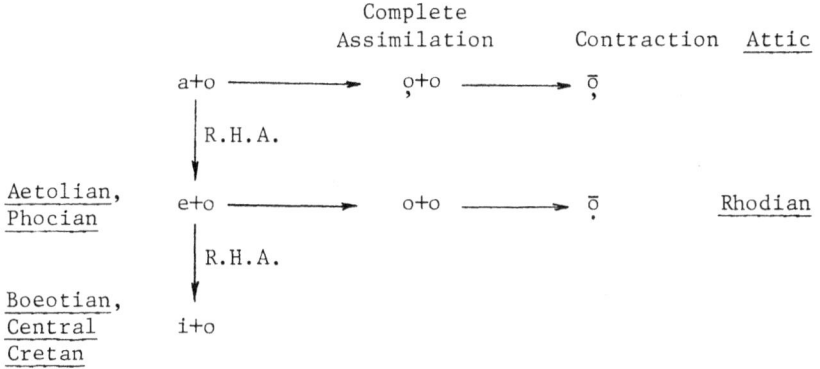

	Contracting dialects			
	Attic		Rhodian	
	tīmaontes	tīmaōsa	tīmaontes	tīmaōsa
R.H.A.	-	-	tīmeontes	tīmeōsa
Assimilation	tīmǫontes	tīmǫōsa	tīmoontes	tīmoōsa
Contraction	tīmǭntes	tīmǭsa	tīmǭntes	tīmǭsa

	non-contracting dialects			
	Aetolian	Boeotian	Cretan	
	tīmaontes	tīmaōsa	tīmaontes	tīmaonsa
R.H.A.	tīmeontes	tīmeōsa	tīmeontes	tīmeonsa
R.H.D.	-	tīmiōsa	tīmiontes	tīmionsa

2.7 CONTRACTIONS IN ATTIC AND OTHER DIALECTS

Attic - Ionic   Doric

a) ă + ŏ ⟶ ō̜   a + ŏ ⟶ ō
                                            ā + ŏ ⟶ ā

b) a + ĕ ⟶ ā   a + ĕ ⟶ ē also Aeolic and Arcado-Cypriot

   ā + ĕ ⟶ ē̜   ā + ĕ ⟶ ā also Aeolic

c)   e + ă⟶ ē̦   γένη 'kinds'
         but ā in ὀστᾶ

d)   o + ă ⟶ ō   αἰδώ   o + a ⟶ ō
              'shame' (Acc)
                                o + ā ⟶ ā sometimes in <u>Doric</u>
         but ā in ἁπλᾶ   and <u>Aeolic</u>

     ō + a ⟶ ō̦

e)   e + e ⟶ ē
                                e + ū ⟶ ō   <u>Cretan</u>
                                o + o ⟶ ō

Note: Anomalous contractions like ὀστᾶ (< ostea) 'bones' and ἁπλᾶ (<haploa) 'simple' (Neuter Pl) are best explained as due to analogy with neuters in -a.

For the traditional presentation of Attic rules of contractions see Lejeune (1972:260-3); the following generalizations can be made:
(1) A vowel resulting from the contraction is always long.
(2) If one of the contracting vowels is round the resulting vowel will be round.
(3) If one of the contracting vowels is low the resulting vowel will be low.

Figure 2-14. Attic rules of vocalic contraction

	Rule (2)
$e + \begin{Bmatrix} e \\ \bar{e} \end{Bmatrix} \rightarrow \bar{e}$	$o + \begin{Bmatrix} e & o \\ \bar{e} & \bar{o} \end{Bmatrix} \rightarrow \bar{o}$
	$e + \begin{Bmatrix} o \\ \bar{o} \end{Bmatrix} \rightarrow \bar{o}$
e + ē̦ ⟶ ē̦	e + ō̦ ⟶ ō̦
e + a ⟶ ē̦ (or ā)	o + a ⟶ ō̦ (but also ā!)

71 Vowels

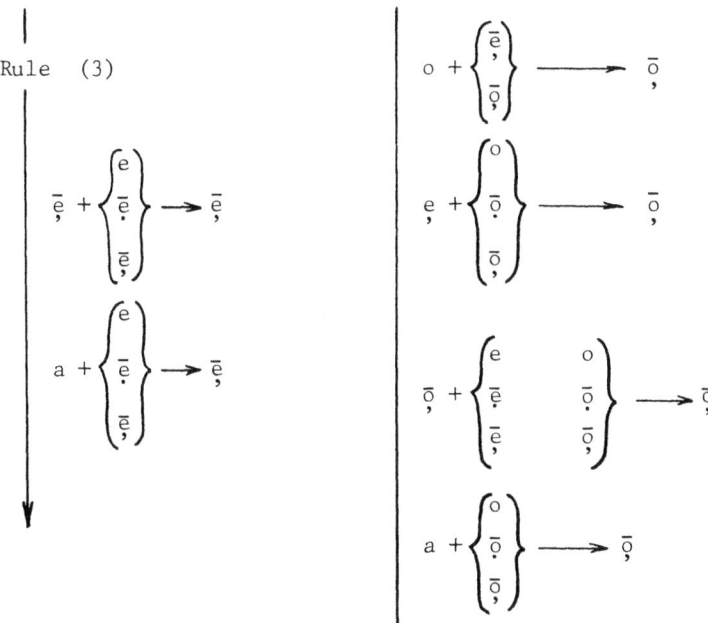

Rules (2) and (3) are not valid for other dialects (Doric, Aeolic and Arcado-Cypriot).

In the case of Doric, (2) suffices as an approximation but an additional regularity must be built in:

If one of the contracting vowels is $\bar{a}$, the resulting vowel will be $\bar{a}$.

Furthermore (3) must be replaced by the rule:

The contraction of $a + \bar{e}$ results in $\bar{e}$.

The most basic difference between the Attic and Doric type of contraction emerges from the case where one of the contracting vowels is $\bar{a}$. Whilst Doric vowels could be hierarchized $\bar{a}\ \bar{o}\ \bar{e}$ (the surviving vowel of a sequence of two will be that which occurs first in this series), the Attic scale would be $\bar{o}\ \bar{e}\ \bar{a}$. The feature 'round' is dominant in Attic, but in Doric it is the feature 'low'. This is clear from the examples below:

	Attic	Doric	
hāelios	ἥλιος	ἇλιος	'sun'
peināomen	πεινῶμεν	πεινᾶμες	'we are hungry'
kʰrūseā	χρυσῆ		'golden'

The results of contraction in Attic and Doric are the same only for $\breve{a} + \breve{o}$, since the progressive assimilation operates

72 Phonological Interpretation of Ancient Greek

in Attic-Ionic while regressive assimilation is observed in Doric.

	Attic-Ionic	Doric	
timá+omen	τιμῶμεν	τιμῶμες	'we honor'
timá+ete	τιμᾶτε	τιμῆτε	
peiná+omen	πεινῶμεν	πεινᾶμες	'we are hungry'
peiná+ete	πεινῆτε	πεινᾶτε	

Attic-Ionic /a/ + /o/
/ā/ + /o/ ⟶ /ō/ regressive assimilation
/a/ + /e/ ⟶ /ā/ progressive "
/ā/ + /e/ ⟶ /ē/ regressive "

Doric /a/ + /o/ ⟶ /ō/ regressive "
/ā/ + /o/ ⟶ /ā/ progressive "
/a/ + /e/ ⟶ /ē/ regressive "
/ā/ + /e/

	Attic-Ionic		Doric
	tīmáomen		tīmáomes
Regressive Assimilation	tīmǫ́omen	*Regressive Assimilation*	tīmóomes
Contraction	tīmȏmen		tīmȏmes
	tīmáete		tīmáete
Progressive Assimilation	tīmáȩte	*Regressive Assimilation*	tīméete
Contraction	tīmâte		tīmȇte
	peináomen		peináomes
Regressive Assimilation	peinǫ́omen	*Progressive Assimilation*	peináames
Contraction	peinȏmen		peinȃmes
	peináete		peináete
Regressive Assimilation	peinéȩte	*Progressive Assimilation*	peinȃate
Contraction	peinȇte		peinȃte

73 Vowels

The presence or absence of progressive and regressive assimilation preceding the contraction as well as the regressive height dissimilation simplified West Greek paradigms of contract verbs. Compare the 1st and 2nd Pl Ind of contract verbs in Attic and Doric:

Attic-Doric

	1st Pl		2nd Pl	
$a + o$	τῑμῶμεν	$a + e$	τῑμᾶτε	$\bar{\underset{.}{o}}$: $\bar{a}$
$e + o$	φιλοῦμεν	$e + e$	φιλεῖτε	$\bar{\underset{.}{o}}$: $\bar{\underset{.}{e}}$
$o + o$	μισθοῦμεν	$o + e$	μισθοῦτε	$\boxed{\bar{\underset{.}{o}} : \bar{\underset{.}{o}}}$
$\bar{a} + o$	πεινῶμεν	$\bar{a} + e$	πεινῆτε	$\bar{\underset{,}{o}}$: $\bar{\underset{,}{e}}$

Doric

$a + o$	τῑμῶμες	$a + e$	τῑμῆτε	$\bar{o}$: $\bar{e}$
$e + o$	(φιλίομες)	$e + e$	(φιλίετε)	io : ie
$o + o$	μισθῶμες	$o + e$	μισθῶτε	$\boxed{\bar{o} : \bar{o}}$
$\bar{a} + o$	πεινᾱ́μες	$\bar{a} + e$	πεινᾶτε	$\boxed{\bar{a} : \bar{a}}$

A typical feature of the North West dialects and Boeotian is the Middle Participle in -ειμενος (or -ημενος) from verbs in -e. Traditionally they are explained as due to analogy with forms where ει (or η) goes back to $e + e$ as the infinitive:

	Attic	North West, Boeotian	
Infinitive	φιλεῖσθαι	φιλεισθαι	↓ analogy
Participle	φιλούμενος	φιλειμενος	

In terms of processual analysis it can be said that Attic /ō/ results from $e + o$ by regressive assimilation, while North West and Boeotian /ē/ is the result of progressive assimilation:

	Attic		North West, Boeotian
	phileomenos		phileomenos
Regressive Assimilation	philoomenos	Progressive Assimilation	phileemenos
Contraction	philōmenos		philēmenos

Another example of analogical extension is a set of forms in -ήω and -ώω, where the long-vowel stem of other tenses (Future, Aorist) was extended to the Present. As a result of this the paradigmatic contrasts in contract verbs are distributed differently in Attic and West Greek. This is observable in the following data from Cretan and Phocian:

	-eo-	-oo-	-ao-			
Attic	φιλοῦντες	μισθοῦντες	τιμῶντες	ọ̄	: ọ̄	: ọ̄
Cretan	φιλιοντες	μισθωντες	τιμιοντες	io	: ō	: io
Phocian[8]	φιληοντες	μισθωοντες	τιμηοντες	ẹ̄o	: ǫo	: ẹ̄o

NOTES

1 Lupaş (1972:123-6) regards the diphthongs of Attic as sequences of two phonemes (not as monophonematic units). She identifies the first segments of these diphthongs with simple vowels which occur in other environments (= allophones of vocalic phonemes) and she considers the palatal [i̯] and velar glide [u̯] as realizations of archiphonemes /I/ and /U/. In this position [i̯] contrasts regularly with [i]; but [u] contrasts only with [ü], e.g. ἄιστος [áistos] 'unseen' versus αἰσχρός [aiskʰrós] 'disgraceful'; αὖτῶ [aüt͡ō] 'shout' versus αὐτός [autós] 'self'. As is obvious, this solution necessitates the introduction of the zero phoneme (= juncture) before all high vowels in hiatus: /â-istos/, /a-ūt͡ō/.

This problem is a trivial one in the framework of generative phonology, where forms like Διί [dií] would be derived from underlying /dyewi/, see Sommerstein (1973:114). However, difficulties would arise if dialectal forms like Cypriot πτόλιϝι (vs. πόλῑ<πόλιι in many dialects) were taken into account. In historical retrospective the intervocalic w was lost (this is duly repeated by the derivations of generative phonology):

			5th c.	4th c.
Systematic level	/awidtos/	/dyewi/	/druwinos/	/druwinos/
Autonomous level	/â-istos/	/di-í/	/drú-inos/	/drű-inos/
Phonetics:	[áistos]	[dií]	[drúinos]	[drűinos]

2 These generalizations are made on the basis of data in Lupaş (1972:101-2).
3 Allen (1974:77) points out that the concomitant factor of quality might exist in the case of /ōi/ versus /oi/, since it seems that one of the phonetic values of the phoneme /oi/ was [ö̈i]. Consequently, the opposition of /ōi/ versus /oi/ could be realized phonetically as [oi] versus [ö̈i]:

/lógōi/ Dat Sg versus /lógoi/ Nom Pl
[lógoi]   [lógöi]

This view may be supported by phonetic interpretation of spellings OE or OEI instead of etymological OI, found in various inscriptions older than 350 B.C., e.g. in Attic (Κροεσος Kretschmer, *Griech. Vaseninschr.* 129), Corinth αυτοπο(ε)ια = αὐτοποία, Schwyzer (1923:123,4).

4   Allen (1974:79) interprets the diphthong /ei/ in the environment before a vowel phonetically as [eyy] and thinks first of the reduction [eyy] ⟶ [ey] as a reason for the delayed monophthongization, when compared with /ei/ before a consonant, which can be interpreted only as [ey]. Some spellings in Homer apparently support this interpretation e.g. τελέω [teleyō] beside τελείω [teleyyō] etc. When later on [ey] was monophthongized into [ẹ̄] the second [y] became an automatic glide. Since there is a well-established parallelism between ει and ου Allen wonders whether a similarly delayed development applied to prevocalic ου /ou/. He hypothesizes that at some earlier period its value could have been [oww] and finds a support for this in Attic ἀκοή [akowẹ̄] beside Homeric ἀκουή [akowwẹ̄]. Later on the intervocalic [w] was lost in Attic [akowẹ̄] ⟶ [akoē], whereas in Homeric [ow] was monophthongized: [akowwẹ̄] ⟶ [akọ̄wẹ̄]. Similarly can be interpreted Attic ὠτός (<ὄατος < ὀϜατος) beside Homeric οὔατος.

5   Lejeune (1972:153,238) explains Attic χῑ́λιοι, μῑλῑ́χιος and ἱμᾱ́τιον by regressive assimilation. Similar examples are according to him βιβλίον (<βυβλίον), ἱστία (<ἑστία) etc. Notice that /i/ in εἱμάτιον is supposed to have assimilated initial /ẹ̄/ at a distance.

6   Bartoněk (1966:63) claims that 'in this way the second group of dialects became different from the presupposed proto-Greek condition, because the origination of new long ē- and ō- phonemes resulted in the transformation of the hitherto existing three-grade system into a four-grade system'.

However, it is obvious that we do not have to do with any 'revolutionary transformation' of the three-grade system. All that happened was that some Proto-Greek contrasts were redistributed and some new contrasts appeared. Using my examples:

Proto-Greek
        /keimai/   :   /patēr/   (esmi)
   or   /kẹ̄mai/   :   /patẹ̄r/
Attic-Ionic
        /kẹ̄mai/, /ẹ̄mi/   :   /patēr/
   or   /keimai/, /eimi/   :   /patẹ̄r/

'strict' Doric
/keimai/ : /patēr/, /ēmi/
or /kēmai/ : /patẹ̄r/, /ẹ̄mi/

Schematically:

Proto-Greek   after the 1st lengthening
(represented as the
4-grade system)

ī   ū   ī   ū
ei (=ẹ̄)   (ọ̄=)ou   ẹ̄   ọ̄

ē (=ę̄) (ǭ=) ō   ę̄   ǭ

        ā   ā

where $\frac{ei}{\bar{e}} = \frac{\bar{ẹ}}{\bar{ę}}$ where /ẹ̄/ = [ẹ̄] ∿ [ei]

7 See Thumb-Kieckers (1932:149) for data on West Cretan:
   πειρασώμεθα (Cydonia), ὠνωμένος (Hierapytna)
   εὐορκῶσι (Hierapytna) - notice that this form indicates
   underlying *euorkeōsi not *euorkeonsi; ἐπαινῶμεν (Aptera,
   Cydonia).
   παρακαλῶντι (Lappa), διατηρῶντες (provenance unknown)
   ἐξαιρῶντες (Phaselis).
   East Cretan: συνεσσέομαι προδωσέω (Itanos)
      There is also some evidence for regressive height
   dissimilation in both West and East Cretan (see M.
   Guarducci, *Inscriptiones Creticae* II and III, Roma 1939
   and 1942):

   Eleutherna (West) κἠπαινύομεν (= καὶ ἐπαινέομεν)
                     παρ' ἀμίων (= παρ' ἡμέων)

   Itanos (East) ὅρκον τελ ⎤ ιόντω

   if the reading is τελιόντω not τελειόντω
8 See Thumb-Kieckers (1932) for the actually documented
   Phocian forms:

   e+o: ποιήουσα
   o+o: μαστιγώων, ἀπαλλοτριώουσα (also Boeotian δᾱμιώοντες)
   a+o: σῡλήοντες and σῡλέοντες, ἐπιτῑμέοντες (also
        Aetolian τῑμέοντες).

3

Consonants

3.1 THE CONSONANTS OF ATTIC AND OTHER DIALECTS

3.1.1 *The Consonants of Classical Attic*

The phonological system of Classical Attic *obstruents* can be established on the basis of the following commutation tests:
(a) voiceless – voiced
(b) non-aspirated – aspirated or sibilant
(c) aspirated or sibilant – voiced
(d) short – long (geminated)
(e) aspirated or sibilant – glottal fricative
(f) labial – dental
(g) labial – velar
(h) dental – velar

Examples are mainly taken from Lupaş (1972:110-14):

(a) /p/ – /b/   πάθος   'experience' – βάθος   'depth'
    /t/ – /d/   τόμος   'slice, cut' – δόμος   'house'
    /k/ – /g/   κέρας   'horn'   – γέρας   'prize, reward'

(b) /p/ – /pʰ/   πόρος   'passage'   – φόρος   'tribute'
    /t/ – /tʰ/   τείνω   'stretch'   – θείνω   'strike'
    /k/ – /kʰ/   Κρόνος   'Cronos'   – χρόνος   'time'
    /t/ – /s/   τορός   'piercing' – σορός   'urn'

(c) /pʰ/ – /b/   φαίνω   'make appear' – βαίνω   'go'
    /tʰ/ – /d/   θάπτω   'bury'   – δάπτω   'devour'
    /kʰ/ – /g/   χεῦμα   'stream'   – γεῦμα   'taste'
    /s/ – /d/   σῶμα   'body'   – δῶμα   'house'

(d) /p/ – /pp/   ?
    /t/ – /tt/   πλάτει   'breadth'   – πλάττει   'form, shape'
                       (Dat)
    /k/ – /kk/   κάκη   'wickedness' – κάκκη   'human ordure'

78   Phonological Interpretation of Ancient Greek

                                             Ionic
  /s/ - /ss/   πρᾱ́σει 'sale' (Dat) - πρᾱ́σσει 'make' (West
                                                      Ionic)
               ἧσαι   'be seated'   - ἧσσαι   'defeats'
                       (2nd Sg)

(e) /pʰ/- /h/ φύσω   'beget' (Fut) - ὕσω   'send rain'
                                                  (Fut)
    /tʰ/- /h/ θύω   'sacrifice'   - ὕω   'send rain'
    /kʰ/- /h/ χώρα   'country'   - ὥρα   'season'
    /s/ - /h/ σός   'yours'   - ὅς   'who'

(f) /p/ - /t/ ποῖος   'of what sort'- τοῖος   'such'
    /b/ - /d/ βόλος   'net'   - δόλος   'wile,
                                                  treachery'
    /pʰ/-/tʰ/ φῶ   'say'   - θῶ   'put'
                       (Subj Pres)   (Subj Aorist)

(g) /p/ - /k/ πληρῶ   'make full'   - κληρῶ   'draw lots'
    /b/ - /g/ βοῶ   'shout'   - γοῶ   'wail'
    /pʰ/- /kʰ/ φόρτος 'load'   - χόρτος   'feeding-
                                                  ground'

(h) /t/ - /k/ τέρας   'wonder,   - κέρας   'horn'
                        marvel'
    /d/ - /g/ δέρων   'flay' (Part) - γέρων   'old man'
    /tʰ/- /kʰ/ θέω   'run'   - χέω   'pour'

Similarly the following minimal pairs can establish phonological system of *nasals* and *liquids*:
(a) labial nasal - labial obstruent
(b) dental nasal - dental obstruent
(c) labial nasal - liquid
(d) dental nasal - liquid
(e) short   - long (geminated)
(f) labial nasal - dental nasal
(g) trill   - lateral liquid
(h) liquid   - sibilant

(a) /m/ - /p/   μόνος 'sole'   - πόνος   'toil'
    /m/ - /b/   μαίνω 'drive mad'   - βαίνω   'go'
    /m/ - /pʰ/ μαίνω   - φαίνω   'make appear'

(b) /n/ - /t/   νόμος 'law'   - τόμος   'cut, slice'
    /n/ - /d/   νόμος   - δόμος   'house'
    /n/ - /tʰ/ νέα   'new' (Fem)   - θέα   'seeing, view'
    /n/ - /s/   νοῦ   'mind' (Gen)   - σοῦ   'yours' (Gen)

(c) /m/ - /r/   μαίνω   - ῥαίνω   'sprinkle'
    /m/ - /l/   μανθάνω 'learn'   - λανθάνω 'escape notice'

(d) /n/ - /r/   νέω   'swim'   - ῥέω   'flow'

			νεώς	'temple'	- λεώς	'people'
(e)	/m/ - /mm/	λῆμα	'will, desire'	- λῆμμα	'anything received'
	/n/ - /nn/	γενικός	'generic'	- γεννικός	'noble'
	/r/ - /rr/	πυρός	'fire' (Gen)	- πυρρός	'flame-coloured'
	/l/ - /ll/	ἄλη	'wandering'	- ἄλλη	'another' (Fem)
		μέλει	'song' (Dat)	- μέλλει	'intends to do'
(f)	/m/ - /n/	μάττω	'knead dough'	- νάττω	'pack close'
(g)	/r/ - /l/	ῥύμη	'swing'	- λύμη	'maltreatment'
(h)	/r/ - /s/	ῥαίνω	'sprinkle'	- σαίνω	'wag the tail'
	/l/ - /s/	λῆμα		- σῆμα	'sign'

3.1.1.1 Phonemic variants

(a) Clear and dark *l*

In Attic the lateral liquid was probably a clear variant in all environments (or more precisely, we do not possess any inscriptional evidence that /l/ was velarised before consonants). However, in some dialects - most notably in Central Cretan - there is evidence for the dark [ɫ] as is shown by these spellings:

καυχος and καλχος 'copper' (= χαλκός)
Ϝευμενος 'assembled' (= Ϝελμενος)
αδευπιος 'brother' (= Ionic ἀδελφεός)

On the basis of such spellings we may justify the phonetic reconstructions [kalkʰos] or even [kaɣkʰos] with over-dark [ɫ].

(b) The velar nasal [ŋ] occurs predictably in the environment before the velar stops $k, g, kʰ$. The usual spelling is with Γ: e.g. ἐγγύς 'near', but in certain archaic inscriptions, spellings with N are quite common: e.g. ενγυς (also ανφοτερος = ἀμφότερος). Obviously, the first spelling indicates the place of articulation (velar) and the second indicates the manner of articulation (nasal). Greek did not develop a special grapheme for this phonemic variant as Sanskrit and the Old Germanic Runic systems did.

The interpretation of the spellings ΓM and ΓN remains controversial. I assume with Lejeune (1972:146) and Lupas (1972:20-2) against Sturtevant (1940:64-5) and Allen (1974: 33-5) that the phonetic value of Γ before nasals was not a velar nasal [ŋ] but a velar stop [g]. The main reason for the reconstruction ΓM [ŋm] is a parallelism of certain forms like

τέτριμμαι (τρίβω 'rub') i.e. b + m ⟶ m + m
λέλεγμαι (λέγω 'talk')   g + m ⟶ ŋ + m

In my view this parallelism is irrelevant since the alleged change $g ⟶ ŋ$ does not exactly parallel the change $b ⟶ m$.

These two are homorganic sounds, but *g* and *m* are not. Similarly, there is no cogent reason for reconstructions like φθέγμα [pʰtʰeŋma]. The spelling ΓΜ represents here a graphic simplification for *φθέγγμα (cf. φθέγγομαι). Admittedly, the triadic cluster ŋgm could be simplified in two ways - either [ŋm] or [gm]. However, the analogy could restore [gm] easily in paradigms like ἔφθεγμαι, ἔφθεγξαι. My main reason for reconstruction with [gm] is the lack of positive evidence for [ŋm] - there are no examples of the spelling *NM* (instead of *ΓΜ*).

(c) The feature of voice was not contrastive in sonorants and sibilants. Voiceless [r̥] occurred in these environments:

  i) initially ῥύμη [r̥umē̄]

  ii) after *r* πυρρός [purr̥os]

  iii) after aspirates φρήν   [pʰr̥ēn]
                      θρόνος   [tʰr̥onos]
                      χρόνος   [kʰr̥onos]

According to the ancient grammarians *r* was 'aspirated' initially and in geminates, and this is supported by isolated dialectal spellings (Corcyrean ρhoFαισι), Latin transcriptions (*Pyrrhus*) and the Byzantine spellings ῥ and ῤῥ (Allen, 1974:39). Sturtevant (1940:62) interpreted correctly the varying spellings PH ∿ HP in the sense, that the aspiration was simultaneous with the articulation of *r*. Modern phonetics clarified the relationship between aspiration and voicelessness by relating the former to the state of the glottis during and immediately after the release of the stricture. Thus, according to Ladefoged (1971:9) 'in any aspirated sound the vocal cords are in the voiceless position during the release'. In other words, we may assume that *r* in the environment after p^h, t^h, k^h could have been partly unvoiced (or even voiceless, as in English *pray*). There are some Latin transcriptions of Greek words which evidently support this interpretation, e.g. χρύσιππος [kʰr̥üsippos] Latin *Crhysippus*.

Evidence for voiceless [l̥] is meagre, see Lejeune (1972: 144). In this sense can be interpreted isolated examples like λhαβōν [l̥abō̄n] from Aegina (Argolic dialect).

Voiceless nasal and lateral liquid may be postulated in the environment after aspirates for the same reason as in the case of [r̥] after aspirates, e.g. σταθμός [statʰm̥os] 'stable', αἰχμή [aikʰm̥ē] 'edge', θνητός [tʰn̥ētos] 'mortal', φλέγω [pʰl̥egō] 'burn' etc.

(d) Voiced sibilant [z] does not possess a phonemic status in Classical Attic and can be regarded as a phonemic variant of the voiceless sibilant /s/. It occurs only medially before voiced obstruents, and sonorants. Furthermore, the clusters of voiced sibilant plus dental nasal or liquid occur only in compound words.

		[zb]	πρεσβεύω	'be the elder'
		[zd]	τράπεζα	'table'
		[zg]	φάσγανον	'sword'
		[zm]	θεσμός	'law'
/s+n/	⟶	[zn]	προσνέμω	'assign'
/s+r/	⟶	[zr]	εἰσρέω	'stream into'
/s+l/	⟶	[zl]	προσλαμβάνω	'take besides'

We may safely assume that voicing was only optional in the last three cases and in the clusters of sibilant plus voiced stops or labial nasal in compound words:

/s+b/	⟶	[zb]	προσβολή	'attack'
/s+d/	⟶	[zd]	εἰσδέχομαι	'admit'
/s+g/	⟶	[zg]	δυσγενής	'low-born'
/s+m/	⟶	[zm]	δυσμενής	'hostile'

Notice that phonetic spellings like ψηφιζμα (= ψήφισμα) appear in the 4th c. B.C.

Classical Attic did not have a voiced affricate [dᶻ] in its phonemic inventory. /dᶻ/, as a phoneme, existed in earlier times in all dialects (it developed through palatalization and affrication of Proto-Greek *dj and *gj ⟶ d'z'j' ⟶ dz). However, before Classical times dz was metathesized in Attic and in most other dialects: dz ⟶ zd. That the letter Z represents the cluster /zd/ can be established by facts like these:

i) θύρας + δε 'to the door' (cf. οἶκόν+δε 'to home') is spelled θύραζε.
ii) The treatment of nasal before Z /zd/ corresponds to that before /st/. -n in συν is lost before st/d- but -n in ἐν is preserved:

συστέλλω   [sustellǭ]   'draw together'
συζεύγνυμι   [suzdeugnūmi]   'yoke together'
ἐνστέλλω   enstellǭ   'dress in'
ἐνζεύγνυμι   enzdeugnūmi   'yoke in'
                 sun+stellō   en+stellō
Cluster Simplification sustellō   —
                 sun+zdeugnūmi   en+zdeugnūmi
Cluster Simplification suzdeugnūmi   —

iii) The interpretation /zd/ not /dᶻ/ is favoured by various structural considerations. Contrast the inventory of initial and medial clusters of the type *sibilant + voiceless* and *sibilant + voiced obstruent*. There would be no symmetry of the inventory of voiceless and voiced clusters if there were a voiced affricate /dᶻ/ (or alternatively the pressure of

this subsystem could cause the preclassical metathesis
$dz \longrightarrow zd$):

sp-	-sp-	zb-	-zb-
st-	-st-	zd-	-zd-
sk-	-sk-	∅	-zg-
σπείρω	ἑσπέρα	σβέννυμι	πρεσβεύω
στόμα	ἐστί	ζέω	τράπεζα
σκότος	διδάσκω		φάσγανον

iv) Another systemic reason for the early metathesis $dz \longrightarrow zd$ can be seen in the distribution of dyadic clusters with a voiced obstruent as a first member:

bd	(bn)		br	bl	∅
gd	gm	gn	gr	gl	∅
∅	dm	dn	dr		dz

The voiced affricate /d^z/ in a pre-classical system was isolated (there was no voiceless counterpart and there were no clusters *bz and *gz). By its metathesis a certain symmetry was achieved because now there was a complete set of dyadic clusters bd, zd, gd, combining a voiced labial, dental and velar obstruent + voiced dental stop.

It should also be mentioned that consonant clusters with initial d- are extremely rare (there are two or three examples of /d/ + nasal δμώς 'slave', δνόφος 'darkness', δνοπαλίζω 'shake violently'), with the exception of dr-.

The voiceless aspirate /t^s/ existed as a phoneme in some dialects. Our evidence comes mainly from certain Arcadian and Central Cretan spellings. /t^s/ could be spelled in Arcadian with a special letter Ͷ as in Ͷις /$t^s$is/ 'who' (= τίς), οͶεοι /ot^{s}eoi/ 'to whomever' (cf. Homeric ὅτεῳ), or with a diagraph TZ (as in τζετρακατιαι /t^setra-/ 'fourhundred') or ZT (as in ζτεραιον, probably cognate with ζειρά 'upper garment'), or with Z as in οζις /ot^{s}is/ 'whoever' (cf. Homeric ὅτις). On the interpretation of Cretan οζοι see p.117, n.10.

3.1.1.2 *Phonological system*

The consonantal phonemes of Classical Attic may be tabulated by means of their features as in Figure 3-1. I have departed from the traditional three-term system (labial, dental, velar) in describing the Greek obstruents and will now be using (rather inconsistently) binary features *coronal - peripheral, anterior (front) - back* as is the common practice in phonology:

	labial	dental	velar
anterior	+	+	−
coronal	−	+	−

Figure 3-1. Distinctive features of consonantal phonemes of Classical Attic

	p	pp	b	pʰ	t	tt	d	tʰ	k	kk	g	kʰ	m	mm	n	nn	r	rr	l	ll	s	ss	h
consonantal	+	+	+	+	+	+	+	+	+	+	+	+	+	+	+	+	+	+	+	+	+	+	+
vocalic	-	-	-	-	-	-	-	-	-	-	-	-	-	-	-	-	+	+	+	+	-	-	-
sonorant	-	-	-	-	-	-	-	-	-	-	-	-	+	+	+	+	+	+	+	+	-	-	-
long	-	+	-	-	-	+	-	-	-	+	-	-	-	+	-	+	-	+	-	+	-	+	-
voiced	-	-	+	-	-	-	+	-	-	-	+	-	+	+	+	+	+	+	+	+	-	-	-
nasal	-	-	-	-	-	-	-	-	-	-	-	-	+	+	+	+	-	-	-	-	-	-	-
aspirated	-	-	-	+	-	-	-	+	-	-	-	+	-	-	-	-	-	-	-	-	-	-	+
continuous	-	-	-	-	-	-	-	-	-	-	-	-	-	-	-	-	+	+	+	+	+	+	+
anterior	+	+	+	+	+	+	+	+	-	-	-	-	+	+	+	+	-	-	-	-	+	+	-
strident	-	-	-	-	-	-	-	-	-	-	-	-	-	-	-	-	-	-	-	-	+	+	-

Lupaș (1972:133) prefers Jakobson-Halle (1956) features:

	labial	dental	velar
compact	−	−	+
grave	+	−	+

Binary features permit a certain economy of statement in phonotactic descriptions. The fact that Attic permits the clusters ps, pt, bd, p^ht^h, ks, kt, gd, k^ht^h can be described in two ways:

i) Labial and velar obstruents cluster with homorganic dental obstruents.
ii) Peripheral (i.e. non-coronal) obstruents cluster with homorganic coronal obstruents.

However, the consistent use of binary features becomes inconvenient in many cases and I will be using also the traditional ternary features.

3.1.1.3 Geminates

The category of geminates was still a living category in Classical Attic. There are eleven geminates occurring intervocalically (all voiceless obstruents and sonorants have a 'long' counterpart). However, minimal pairs especially with obstruents are extremely rare - I cannot find any example of $p: pp$, $p^h : pp^h$ and $k : kk^h$.

pp	pp^h		mm		
tt	tt^h	ss	nn	rr	ll
kk	kk^h				

There is a considerable literature concerning the problem of the alternations between /tt/ and /ss/ in Classical Attic.[1] Both can be considered as phonemes (as a matter of fact only as subphonemes since they can contrast only intervocalically as all other geminates). As well-known, words with /tt/ occur in 'colloquial' Attic (inscriptions, comedy) while the same words show /ss/ in tragedy and prose works up to Thucydides:

inscriptions, comedy	prose works, tragedy	
θάλαττα	θάλασσα	'sea'
πράττω	πράσσω	'make'
τέτταρες	τέσσερες	'four'

The geminate /ss/ is of Ionic origin due to the fact that the literary Attic was under strong influence from Ionic (epic poetry, historiography) and we may simply assume that literary Attic borrowed this particular phoneme. That colloquial Attic was most likely totally unaffected by this borrowing is obvious if we compare Attic inscriptions (and comedy), which use /tt/ almost exclusively. Of course, there are some words with /ss/ even in comedy, but these can be explained as borrowings from tragedy: ἄνασσα 'queen', λεύσσω 'look'. (See

Lupaş (1972:37) and Allen (1974:11) for details.) Using our examples, a minimal pair of colloquial Attic like πλάτει : πλάττει did not exist in literary Attic and vice-versa a pair from literary Attic like πράσει : πράσσει was non-existent in colloquial Attic (where 'genuine' Attic πράττει would be used).

Lupaş (1972:114) decided to include geminate aspirates among the phonemes of Attic; however, there are no minimal pairs of non-aspirated versus aspirated geminate and I know only of one example of non-geminated versus geminated aspirate /tʰ/ : /ttʰ/:

τίτθης	'nurse' (Gen)	–	τίθης	'you put'
[títtʰēs]		–	[títʰēs]	
ἔκχει	'pour out' (Imp)		ἔχει	'he has'
[ékkʰē̜]			[ékʰē̜]	

The latter example involves a compound word: /k+kʰ/ versus /kʰ/.

For these reasons I have decided to exclude all geminated aspirates from the table of consonantal phonemes of Attic. It means that I will ignore the isolated pair /tʰ/ : /ttʰ/, because the gemination in τίτθη 'nurse' is probably only expressive. On the other hand, I will include /pp/ among the Attic phonemes even if I do not know of a minimal pair /p/ : /pp/. This admittedly is an arbitrary treatment; however, it does not make any difference in our dialectal comparisons since /pp/ and /kk/ will figure in all dialectal inventories. See Bubeník (1976:164) for details.

There are isolated examples of the gemination of all obstruents in compound words or in external sandhi, mostly from Homeric dialect:

Homeric	/p+p/	κάππεσον	'I fell down' (= κατέπεσον)
	/p+pʰ/	καπφάλαρα	'cheek coverings' (= κατά φάλαρα)
	/t+t/	καττάνυσαν	'they drew tight' (= κατετάνυσαν)
	/t+tʰ/	κάτθανον	'they died' (= κατέθανον)
Attic	/k+k/	ἐκκινέω	'move out of'
	/b+b/	κάββαλε	'he cast down' (= κατέβαλε)
	/d+d/	καδδῦσαι	'sink' (= καταδῦσαι)
Attic	/g+g/	ἔκγονος	'child, offspring'

All examples taken from Homeric dialect result from the apocope of final /a/ in the preposition κατά (there is no evidence that another preposition μετά could undergo the apocope as well). Subsequently, the dental obstruent was assimilated completely to a following labial obstruent:

86 Phonological Interpretation of Ancient Greek

	kata+p	kata+b	kata+t	kata+d
Syncopation	kat+p	kat+b	kat+t	kat+d
Voice Assimilation	-	kad+b	-	kad+d
Complete Assimilation	kap+p	kab+b	-	-

3.1.1.4 *Aspirates*

According to Lupaş (1972:134) the opposition /pʰ, ppʰ, tʰ, ttʰ, kʰ, kkʰ/ vs /p, pp, t, tt, k, kk/ is *lax* vs *tense*. However, she regards the category lax - tense only as a subcategory of quantity (long - short). As she points out, the lack of tenseness is relative since geminates are generally more tense than the corresponding (voiceless) non-geminates. That is, if geminated aspirates /ppʰ, ttʰ, kkʰ/ are classified as lax it does not mean that they are more lax than corresponding voiceless /p, t, k/, which are classified as tense. It only means that they are less tense than corresponding voiceless geminates /pp, TT, kk/. Lupaş's classification of Classical Attic obstruents is as follows:

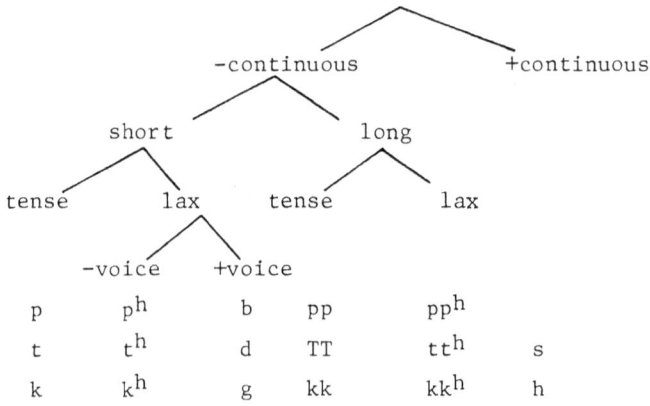

For reasons mentioned in 1.3, p. 17 I consider such an analysis as incorrect and believe that there are no good reasons to depart from the traditional ternary classification based on two binary features (voiceless - voiced, unaspirated - aspirated). From the point of voice onset - the feature specified by Ladefoged (1971:19) - aspirated versus unaspirated is the opposition between voicing starting considerably later and other types of voice onset:

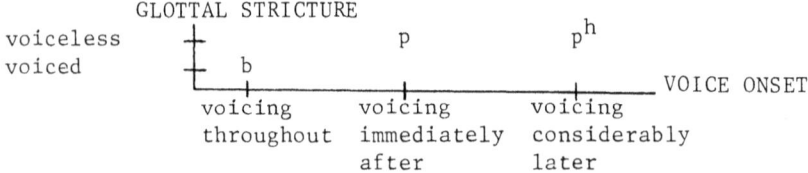

3.1.1.5 *Continuants and Sonorants*

The system of continuants was poor in all dialects. There was a sibilant /s/ (with a long counter-part in some dialects), glottal fricative /h/ and liquids /r/ and /l/.

I follow Ladefoged (1971:58) in using the term sonorant for liquids and nasals (= 'sounds with an auditory property which arises from their having a comparatively large amount of acoustic energy within a clearly defined formant structure'). In terms of articulatory phonetics, liquids possess both vocalic and consonantal features in that they 'combine closure and aperture either intermittently or by barring the median way and opening a lateral bypass', Jakobson et al. (1952:20). Nasals are articulated with a lowered velum; that is, their articulation combines the closure of the oral passage with the opening through the nose. There are only consonantal nasals in Ancient Greek dialects.

For the purpose of interdialectal comparisons the Classical Attic consonants will be presented by means of the following hierarchy of features:

Figure 3.2   Consonantal phonemes of Classical Attic.

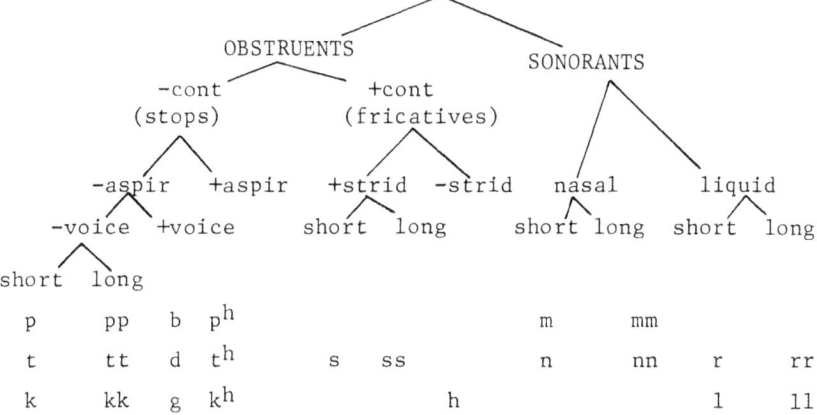

3.1.2 *The Consonants of the Greek Dialects*

The system of pre-Classical Attic-Ionic obstruents differed from its descendant by having two affricates. The term 'pre-Classical' refers to the period before the liquidation of a voiceless affricate /ts/ through assimilation (tt/ in Attic and /ss/ in Ionic) and before the metathesis of a voiced affricate *dz* ⟶ *zd*. In a system with two affricates the feature *strident* is necessary for a description of both stops and fricatives. It could well be that

88 Phonological Interpretation of Ancient Greek

this system survived until Classical times in Arcadian (if our analysis of Arcadian data is correct, see 3.6, p. 118).

Figure 3-3. Consonantal phonemes of pre-Classical Attic and Classical Arcadian.

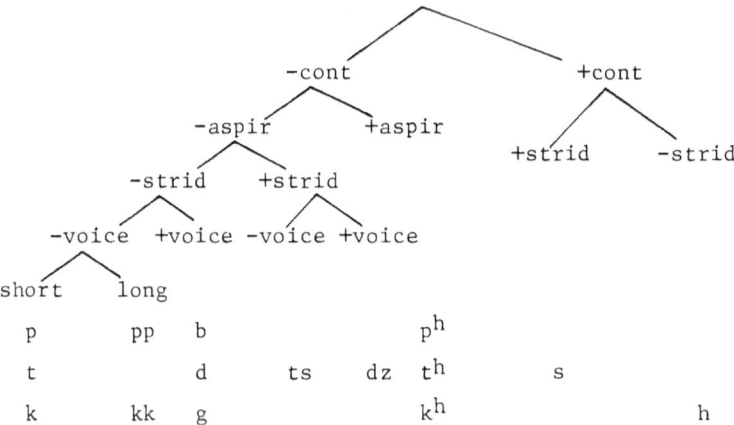

The phonological system of Boeotian and Central Cretan differed from other dialects in that the feature long was functional not only in voiceless but also in voiced stops. Boeotian has minimal pairs /tt/ : /dd/, μεττων 'middle' (Gen Pl) : μεδδων 'bigger' and /d/ : /dd/, μέδων 'guardian' (a Homeric word which I use only for the sake of exemplification). The difference between Attic and Boeotian (and Central Cretan) in terms of their minimal pairs can be expressed thus:

Figure 3-4. Consonantal phonemes of Boeotian and Central Cretan.

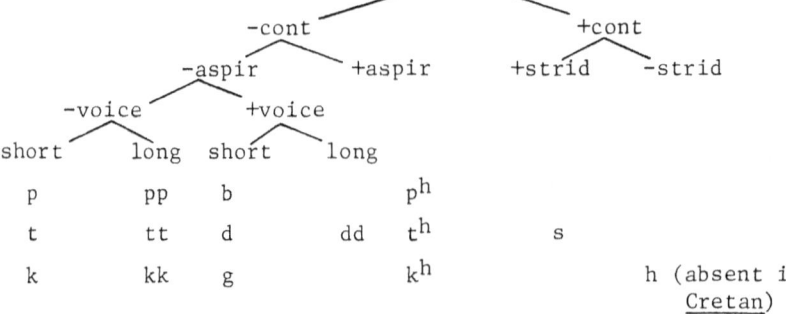

89 Consonants

In Ionic and Lesbian the contrast of length with dental stops does not exist (their phonological system knows only /pp/, /kk/ and /ss/). There is no glottal fricative.

Figure 3-5. Consonantal phonemes of Ionic and Lesbian.

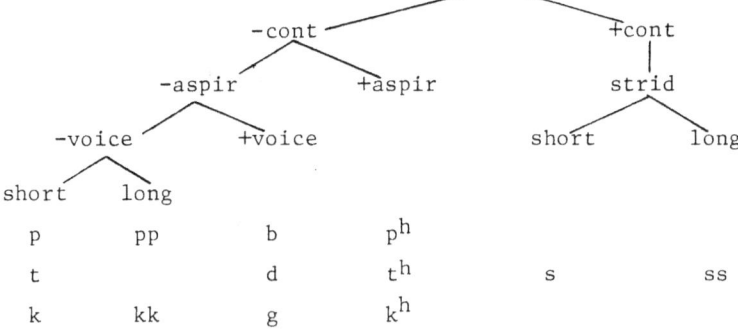

-voice		+voice	+aspir	short	long
short	long				
p	pp	b	p^h		
t		d	t^h	s	ss
k	kk	g	k^h		

3.1.3 Phonotactics of Classical Attic Consonants

3.1.3.1 Dyadic Clusters

Dyadic clusters of Classical Attic belong to one of four groups:

(I)   Obstruent + Obstruent   } occur both initially and
(II) Obstruent + Sonorant   } medially

(III) Sonorant + Obstruent   }
(IV) {Sonorant} + {Sonorant } } occur only medially
      {Sibilant} + {Fricative}

Clusters of type (I) and (II) occur both initially and medially. Those occurring only medially will be specified in the usual manner: -gd-; those occurring only across morpheme-boundaries will be marked with +.

Figure 3.6. Dyadic clusters (I) Obstruent + Obstruent

	pt	bd	p^ht^h	
	kt	-gd-	k^ht^h	
	k+p	k+b	k+p^h	
	k+t	k+d	k+t^h	k+s
	k+k	k/g+g	k+k^h	
s+b	sp	zb	sp^h	ps
s+d	st	zd	st^h	
s+g	sk	-zg-	sk^h	ks

These regularities of pattern can be observed:
i) Labial and velar stops cluster with homorganic dental stops (or in binary features: peripheral stops cluster with

coronal stops) initially and medially, but -gd- occurs only medially.
  ii) A voiceless velar stop clusters with all obstruents in compound words.
  iii) Sibilants cluster with all homorganic stops (i.e. voiceless + voiceless, voiced + voiced, voiceless + aspirated) initially and medially, but -zg- occurs only medially.
  iv) A voiceless sibilant clusters with voiced stops only in compound words.
  v) Only *ps* and *ks* occur finally.

Figure 3-7. Dyadic clusters (II) Stop + Sonorant.

	pn	pr	pl
tm	-tn-	tr	tl
-km-	kn	kr	kl
		br	bl
dm	dn	dr	
-gm-	gn	gr	gl
	-p^{h}n-	p^{h}r	p^{h}l
-t^{h}m-	t^{h}n	t^{h}r	t^{h}l
-k^{h}m-	k^{h}n	k^{h}r	k^{h}l

All stops cluster with sonorants both initially and medially. These clusters occur only medially:

  i) Aspirates plus labial nasal (i.e. $t^h m$, $k^h m$) and $p^h n$.
  ii) Velar stops plus labial nasal (i.e. *km*, *gm*, $k^h m$).
  iii) A voiceless dental plus dental nasal. In some dialects *tn* could occur both initially and medially, since the cluster $t^h n$ could be dissimilated /t^hn/ ⟶ [tn], see 3.2, p. 97.

Clusters of type (III) and (IV) occur only medially.

Figure 3-8. Dyadic clusters (III) Sonorant + Stop

-mp-	-rp-	-lp-
-nt-	-rt-	-lt-
-ŋk-	-rk-	-lk-
-mb-	-rb-	-lb-
-nd-	-rd-	-ld-
-ŋg-	-rg-	-lg-
-mp^h-	-rp^h-	-lp^h-
-nt^h-	-rt^h-	-lt^h-
-ŋk^h-	-rk^h-	-lk^h-

(IV) $\begin{Bmatrix} \text{Sonorant} \\ \text{Sibilant} \end{Bmatrix}$ + $\begin{Bmatrix} \text{Sonorant} \\ \text{Fricative} \end{Bmatrix}$

(-)mn-
-rm-   -rn-   -rs-

                    -lm-   -ls-
                  (-)sm-

i) *mn* and *sm* also occur initially.
ii) The following clusters occur only in compound words:
       n+h, r+h, s+h (and also *d+h*)
    r+l, s+n, s+r, s+l.

Classical Attic does not permit the following clusters:
a) Non-strident coronal stop + peripheral stop (*tp, *db, *t^hp^h; *tk, *dg, *t^hk^h)
b) Peripheral stop + peripheral stop (*kp, *gb, *k^hp^h; *pk, *bg, *p^hk^h with the exception of k+p in compound words).
c) Peripheral stop + strident (*k^hs, *gs; *p^hs, *bs with the exception of *ps* and *ks*)
d) Coronal stop + strident (*ts, *t^hs, *ds)
e) Labial stop + labial nasal (*pm, *bm, *p^hm)
   Voiced labial stop + dental nasal (*bn)
f) Voiced dental stop + lateral liquid (*dl)
g) Nasal + liquid (*mr, *ml, *nr, *nl)
h) Lateral liquid + dental nasal (*ln)
i) Nasal + sibilant (*ms, *ns) but *n+s* does occur across morpheme-boundaries
k) Homorganic clusters: Dental + labial nasal (*nm) - but *mn* does occur initially and medially; lateral liquid + trill (*lr) - but *rl* occurs medially.

3.1.3.2 *Triadic Clusters*

Triadic Clusters of Ancient Greek[2] may be tabulated as in Figure 3-9. For the purpose of phonotactic patterning they may be studied as belonging to one of these four groups:

(V) $\begin{Bmatrix} \text{Sonorant} \\ \text{Sibilant} \\ \text{Velar Stop} \end{Bmatrix}$ + Peripheral Stop + Coronal Obstruent

(VI) Peripheral Stop + Coronal Stop + Trill

(VII) $\begin{Bmatrix} \text{Sonorant} \\ \text{Sibilant} \\ \text{Velar Stop} \end{Bmatrix}$ + Stop + Sonorant

(VIII) $\begin{Bmatrix} k \\ n, r \\ s \end{Bmatrix}$ + Sibilant + Stop

Figure 3-9. Triadic clusters of Ancient Greek

	p	b	pʰ	t	d	tʰ	k	g	kʰ	s
p				r						
k				r						+p+k+m
kʰ						r				
k/g+	tnrls	rl	tʰrl	m	r	nrl	tnrls	rl	rl	ppʰtdkkʰ
s	ls		r	r		ml	ls		nr	
s/z+	tnrls	drl	tʰrl	r	r	nrl	tnrls	nrl	rl	ppʰtdkkʰ
m/n/ŋ	ts	rl	tʰ	rl	r	r	tls		tʰnr	
m/n/ŋ+	tnrls	drl	rl	mr	r	nrl	nrl	nrl	nrl	pbpʰtdkkʰ
r	tns		tʰn	r	n	m	ts	m	tʰn	
r+	tnrls	rl	rl	r	r	nr	rl		rl	ppʰtdkkʰ
l	ts		tʰ	r			tms	m	tʰ	

Figure 3-10. Triadic clusters (V)$\begin{Bmatrix}\text{Sonorant}\\ \text{Sibilant}\\ \text{Velar Stop}\end{Bmatrix}$ + Peripheral Stop + Coronal Obstruent.

mp+s	mp+t	mp^h+t^h	m+bd
rp+s	rp+t	rp^h+t^h	
lp+s	lp+t	lp^h+t^h	
s+ps	s+pt	s+p^{h}t^h	s/z+bd
k+ps	k+pt	k+p^{h}t^h	
ŋk+s	ŋk+t	ŋk^h+t^h	
rk+s	rk+t	rk^h+t^h	
lk+s	lk+t	lk^h+t^h	
s+ks	s+kt		
k+ks	k+kt		

  i) Clusters of the type $\begin{Bmatrix}sibilant\\ velar\ stop\end{Bmatrix}$ + *peripheral stop + coronal obstruent* occur only in compound words.
  ii) Only clusters of the type *sonorant + voiceless peripheral stop + voiceless coronal stop* occur in non-compound words (across morpheme-boundaries).
  iii) Undocumented are: *r+bd, *k+bd, *s+k^{h}t^h, *k+k^{h}t^h, i.e. the prepositions ὑπέρ, ἐκ, πρός, δυσ-, εἰς do not combine with a handful of rare words with initial *bd-* (βδάλλω 'milk', βδελλύζω 'bleed with leeches', βδελύττομαι 'feel a loathing') and *k^{h}t^h-* (χθόνιος 'beneath the earth').
(VI) Greek does not permit clusters of the type
    peripheral stop + coronal stop + $\begin{Bmatrix}nasal\\ lateral\ liquid\end{Bmatrix}$.
Only two exceptions may be reconstructed in compound words: ἐκθλίβω 'squeeze out' [ek^{h}t^{h}lībǭ], ἐκθνήσκω 'die out' [ek^{h}t^{h}nęskǭ].   See 3.2, p. 95.
The clusters of the type *peripheral stop + coronal stop + trill* are limited pt+r (or p+tr), kt+r and k^{h}t^h+r (e.g. σκῆπτρον 'staff', οἰκτρός 'pitiable', ἐχθρός 'enemy').
(VIII) See Figure 3-11.
  i) Clusters of the type *trill + stop + sonorant* are quite common in non-compound words (rp+n, rp^{h}n, r+tr, rd+n, r+t^{h}m, r+t^{h}r, rg+m, rk^{h}n); on the other hand there are only three examples with *l* (lk+m, lg+m, l+tr, e.g. Ἀλκμήνη, ἐξημελγμένος 'milked out', φίλτρον 'love-charm').

Figure 3-11. Triadic Clusters (VII) {Sonorant / Sibilant / Velar Stop} + Stop + Sonorant

m+pn			n+tm		n+tʰn	ŋ+kn	ŋ+gn	ŋkʰn
mpr	mbr	m+pʰr	ntr	ndr	ntʰr	ŋ+kr	ŋ+gr	ŋkʰr
mpl	mbl	m+pʰl	ntl		n+tʰl	ŋkl	ŋ+gl	ŋ+kʰl
					r+tʰm			
rp+n		rpʰn		rd+n	r+tʰn	lk+m	l/rg+m	rkʰn
r+pr	r+br	r+pʰr		r+dr	r+tʰr	r+kr		r+kʰr
r+pl	r+bl	r+pʰl	l/r+tr			r+kl		r+kʰl
					stʰm			
s+pn					s+tʰn	s+kn	s/z+gn	skʰ+n
s+pr	s/z+br	spʰr	str	s/z+dr	s+tʰr	s+kr	s/z+gr	skʰ+r
spl	s/z+bl	s+pʰl	stl		stʰl	skl	s/z+gl	s+kʰl
k+pn			k+tm		k+tʰn	k+kn		
k+pr	k+br	k+pʰr	kt+r	k+dr	k+tʰr	k+kr	g+gr	k+kʰr
k+pl	k+bl	k+pʰl			k+tʰl	k+kl	g+gl	k+kʰl

Certain clusters in compound words are undocumented: *r+tm, *r+dn, *r+kn, *r+gn, *r+tl, *r+t^{h}l, *r+gl (the preposition ὑπέρ does not combine with verbs like κνάω 'scrape', γνάμπτω 'bend', τλάω 'suffer', etc.).

ii) Clusters of the type *velar stop + stop + sonorant* exist only in compound words (with a single exception of kt+r). Undocumented are: *k+dm, *k+dn, *k+k^{h}n, *g+gn, *k+tl (the preposition ἐκ does not combine with verbs like δνοπαλίζω 'shake with', χναύω 'eat by little bits', δμηθείς 'tamed', γνάμπτω 'bend', etc.).

iii) Clusters of the type $\begin{Bmatrix} dental\ nasal \\ sibilant \end{Bmatrix}$ + *dental stop + nasal* do not occur in non-compound words (st^{h}m in ἄσθμα 'panting' excepted). Only n+tm and n+t^{h}n are documented in compound words (the prepositions εἰς, πρός and ἐν do not combine with the infrequent words starting with tm, dm, dn, t^{h}n).

Figure 3-12. Triadic clusters (VIII) $\begin{Bmatrix} k \\ n,r \\ s \end{Bmatrix}$ + Sibilant + Obstruent

ks+m		n+sb		
ks+p	k+sp	n+sp	r+sp	s+sp
	k+sp^h	n+sp^h	r+sp^h	s+sp^h
	k+st	n+st	r+st	s+st
	k+zd	n+zd	r+zd	s+zd
ks+k	k+sk	n+sk	r+sk	s+sk
	k+sk^h	n+sk^h	r+sk^h	s+sk^h

These clusters exist only in compound words with the boundary *before* the sibilant. The boundary is found also *after* the sibilant in three instances: ἑξμέδιμνος 'holding six medimni', ἑξκαίδεκα 'sixteen' (= ἑκκαίδεκα), ἑξπηχυστύ 'of six cubits'.

The following clusters are not found:

$\begin{Bmatrix} k \\ n \\ r \\ s \end{Bmatrix}$ + Sibilant + $\begin{Bmatrix} \text{Voiced labial obstruent} \\ \text{Dental aspirate} \end{Bmatrix}$

The prepositions ἐκ; ἐν, σύν; ὑπέρ; πρός, δυσ-, εἰς do not combine with the words with initial *sb*- and *st^h*-. (An exception is found in Dioscorides ἐνσβέννυμαι 'to be quenched in').

3.2 PHONOLOGY OF ASPIRATES

3.2.1 Phonotactics of Aspirates

As is shown in Figures 3-6, 3-7 and 3-8, aspirates cluster only with aspirates, sibilants and sonorants. We may examine these three groups:

(I)		$p^h t^h$	sp^h	$k+p^h$
			st^h	$k+t^h$
		$k^h t^h$	sk^h	$k+k^h$
(II)		$-p^h n-$	$p^h r$	$p^h l$
	$-t^h m-$	$t^h n$	$t^h r$	$t^h l$
	$-k^h m-$	$k^h n$	$k^h r$	$k^h l$
(III)		$-mp^h-$	$-rp^h-$	$-lp^h-$
		$-nt^h-$	$-rt^h-$	$-lt^h-$
		$-\eta k^h-$	$-rk^h-$	$-lk^h-$

These regularities of pattern can be observed:

i) A cluster of two aspirates may be only of the types *peripheral + coronal*. Phonotactically impossible in Greek are clusters such as *coronal + peripheral* aspirate $*t^h p^h$, $*t^h k^h$ (as is known such clusters exist in Georgian, e.g. *t'it'k'mis* 'almost') and clusters of two *peripheral* aspirates $*p^h k^h$, $*k^h p^h$ (again possible in Georgian, e.g. *p'k'vili* 'flour'). It could be, however, that the cluster $k^h p^h$ existed as a feature of external sandhi in cases like ἐκ φυλῆς [ek^{h}p^{h}ulḗs] (from the underlying /ek+p^{h}ulḗs/), see p. 98.

ii) Attic (like all other dialects) does not allow for the sequence *aspirate + sibilant*. (Similarly Modern Greek does not allow for the sequence *fricative + sibilant*).
γράφω, Fut * $grap^h+sō$ ⟶ $grapsō$ (deaspiration) 'I shall write'
τρέχω, Fut * $trek^h+sō$ ⟶ $t^h reksō$ (aspirate throw-back) 'I shall run'

The inventory of clusters *sibilant + aspirate* is thus poorer than the inventory of *sibilant + non-aspirate*:

sp^h	st^h	sk^h	versus	sp	st	sk
				s/zb	s/zd	zg
∅	∅	∅				
∅	∅	∅		ps	ts*	ks
					dz*	

*/ts/ and /dᶻ/ existed as phonemes in Arcadian and Central Cretan.

iii) Aspirates form clusters with all sonorants under these restrictions: all aspirates form clusters with liquids both initially and medially; with nasals only medially. There are only a few exceptions to this:

$t^h n$ occurs initially only in θνήσκω 'die'
$k^h n$ occurs initially in two or three roots (χνοάζω 'get the first down', χνόη 'iron box of a wheel, nave', χναύω 'eat by little bits').
$*p^h m$ is not found

In some dialects clusters *aspirate + nasal* or *nasal + aspirate + /r/* are sometimes spelled with KN, TN, NTP instead of XN, ΘN, NΘP:

Locrian	τεκνα 'art' (= τέχνη)
Cretan	τνατος 'mortal' (= θνητός)
	αντροπος 'man' (= ἄνθρωπος)
Pamphylian	ατροπος

If these spellings really correspond to the phonetic reality, they can be interpreted as demonstrating the *deaspiration* of an aspirate in the environment before a nasal (or after a nasal before a liquid).

iv) Sonorants form clusters with aspirates only medially.

v) Triadic clusters with two aspirates of the type *sonorant + $\begin{Bmatrix} ph_t h \\ kh_t h \end{Bmatrix}$* are quite common, see 3.1, Table (V). On the other hand clusters of the type $\begin{Bmatrix} ph_t h \\ kh_t h \end{Bmatrix}$ *+ sonorant* are extremely rare. There is only one example of $k^h t^h r$ in ἐχθρός 'enemy'. Notice, however, that clusters $k^h t^h l$ and $k^h t^h n$ can be reconstructed in internal sandhi, e.g. ἐκθλίβω 'squeeze out' [ekʰtʰlībǭ] from underlying /ek+tʰlībǭ/, ἐκθνήσκω 'die out' [ekʰtʰn̥eskǭ] from underlying /ek+tʰn̥eskǭ/.

There are two synchronic processes which can be identified on the basis of variation in the spelling of aspirates prevocalically or in clusters. These are metathesis and anticipation of aspiration.

Cretan	καυχος [kalkʰos] or [kaʋkʰos] 'copper' (= χαλκός)
Ionic	ἄχαντος 'acanthus' (= ἄκανθος)
Thessalian	Πετθαλος 'Thessalian' (= Boeotian Φετταλος, Attic Θετταλός)
Attic	ἐνθαῦθα 'here, there' (= ἐνταῦθα, Ionic ἐνθαῦτα)

	khalkos	akanthos	pʰettalos	enthauta
Metathesis of aspiration	kalkʰos	akʰantos	pettʰalos	entautʰa

In [kalkʰos] aspiration is actually carried over and in

[akʰantos] thrown back (cf. p. 96). Metathesis (with zero) is only a convenient label.

A phonetic reconstruction of the following examples is problematic:

Cretan θιθεμενος [tʰitʰemenos] 'placed' (= τιθέμενος)
  θυκα [tʰukʰa] or [tʰuka] 'fate' (= τύχη)
West Ionic (Cumae) θυφλος [tʰupʰlos] or [tʰuplos] 'blind'
  (= τυφλός).
Arcadian φαρθενος [pʰartʰenos] 'virgin' (= παρθένος)

Cretan θυκα looks like the metathesis of aspiration [tʰuka]. After the anticipation of aspiration in West Ionic [tʰupʰlos] even a deaspiration of an aspirate before a liquid could take place [tʰuplos].

3.2.2 *Phonetic Reconstruction of Clusters* ΦΘ *and* ΧΘ

The phonetic reconstruction of these two clusters remains problematic. According to Allen (1974:25) there is no phonetic improbability about both consonants of the clusters φθ and χθ being aspirated:
  ἐχθρός 'enemy' [ekʰtʰros]
  ὀφθαλμός 'eye' [opʰtʰalmos]
These two examples represent inherited voiceless aspirate stops. On the other hand, labial or velar stops are regularly aspirated when they appear before the dental aspirate stop (as in the suffix of the Aorist Passive -*tʰē* or in the suffix of the 2nd Pers Pl Perfect Middle -*stʰe*:
  λείπω 'leave' ἐλείφθη
  δέρκομαι 'see' ἐδέρχθη
  πεφύλακται 'was guarded' πεφύλαχθε
Many linguists claim that the spellings ΦΘ and ΧΘ were mere conventions for unaspirated /p/ and /k/. This might seem a convenient explanation in the second case; thus we may phonemisize:
  leip-ō   /eleíp-tʰēn/
  derk-omai   /edérk-tʰēn/
  pephulak-tai *pepʰúlak-stʰe ⟶ /pepʰúlak-tʰe/

However, Allen rightly points out that this hypothesis is rather unlikely since in the geminate groups /ppʰ/, /ttʰ/, /kkʰ/, where the first element was unaspirated, the spelling with Π, Τ, Κ is normal:
  ἀπφῦς   /appʰūs/ 'papa'
  τίτθη   /tittʰē/ 'nurse'
  κακχάζω /kakkʰadᶻō/ 'laugh aloud'

Recently, this problem was discussed by Lupaș (1972:16). According to her these spellings represent voiceless unaspirated lenis stops [p̥] and [k̥], which are allophones of

99 Consonants

voiceless stops /p/ and /k/ in the environment before an
aspirate or sibilant /s/.
  According to this proposal the phonetic reality masked by
the Attic spellings is the following:

   φθόνος   [p̥ʰonos]   'malice'
   ψῆφος   [p̥sēpʰos]   'pebble'
   ἐκφέρω   [ek̥ʰerǭ]   'carry out'
   ἐχθρός   [ek̥ʰros]   'enemy'
   ξένος   [k̥senos]   'guest-friend'

  This analysis is based on the observation that consonant
clusters /ps/ and /ks/ were spelled in several ways before
the adoption of the Ionic alphabet:

   ps   ΠΣ   ΦΣ   Ionic alphabet   Ψ
   ks   ΚΣ   ΧΣ   Ξ

  This is supposed to indicate that their first element contained some special voiceless unaspirated stops; since they
do not merge either with /p/, /k/ or with /pʰ/, /kʰ/ they are
taken for voiceless lenis stops [p̥], [k̥]. In this proposal
Lupaş followed Lejeune (1972:72), who discusses other details,
like spellings ΧΣ alternating with ΗΣ in Amorgos and Naxos
(7-6th c. B.C.), which seem to indicate the lax pronunciation
of /k/ before /s/.
  A certain arbitrariness of this solution is patent from
the fact that it attributes the value of a lenis voiceless
stop to [k̥] before a labial aspirate, but the value of a tense
voiceless stop to [k] before a velar aspirate, e.g. ἐκχέω
[ekkʰeǭ] 'pour out'.[3]
  On the other hand, the reconstruction of the lax [k̥] in
clusters with non-homorganic aspirate seems to be supported
by spellings like ἐχφέρειν, Ἔχφαντος, ἐχφορήσαντι,[4] where we
find ΧΦ instead of ΚΦ. The same spelling occurs also in the
preposition ἐκ before aspirates and s; witness the following
data from Attic inscriptions:

   εχ   φυλες   IG I²   45.7   /ek+pʰulēs/
   εχ   θετον   "   45.40   /ek+tʰetǭn/
   εχ   Σαμο   "   304.20   /ek+samǭ/ 'from Samos'
   εχς   Ροδο   "   218 I 11   /eks+rodǭ/ 'from Rhodes'

  If we examine both solutions closely it will become obvious
that the controversy is more or less terminological. Lupaş
postulates a 'lenition' (a voiceless velar or labial stop
becomes lenis in the environment before a voiceless lax
obstruent i.e. aspirate; notice that 'lenition' will not do
in the case of ps and ks since Lupaş does not specify s for
this feature). Allen postulates an 'assimilation in

aspiration' (i.e. assimilation in the manner of articulation, resulting from the contact of a voiceless labial or velar stop with a labial or dental aspirate):

	Lupaș	Allen
	[ekp^{h}ulḛ̄s]	[ek^{h}p^{h}ulḛ̄s]
	[ek̬t^{h}etǭn]	[ek^{h}t^{h}etǭn]
[exsamǭ] or	[ek̬samǭ]	
[eksrodǭ]	[ek̬srodǭ]	

Since the phonetic reconstruction [ek^{h}samǭ] and [ek^{h}srodǭ] cannot be justified by the 'assimilation in aspiration' [eksamǭ] and [eksrodǭ] might be preferred. Notice that the spelling ἐχ in this case does not need to be taken as indicating either lenition or aspiration of /k/ before /s/. The same ἐχ occurred also before k, p, t, - according to Meisterhans-Schwyzer (1900:160), ἐχ before k, p, t was abandoned in favour of ἐκ after 292 B.C. - and it could be that the spelling ἐχ was simply a convention. (Similarly the spelling ἐκ is another convention, which indicates the phonetic value of /k/ in ἐκτείνω but not in ἔκγονος).

Let us examine some more complicated forms like ἐθάλφθη 'warm' (Aorist Passive of θάλπω), ἐθέλχθη 'enchant' (Aorist Passive of θέλγω) and πρόσφθεγμα 'address, salutation'.

	Lupaș	Allen
	[et^{h}alp̥t^{h}ḛ̄]	[et^{h}alp^{h}t^{h}ḛ̄]
	[et^{h}elk̬t^{h}ḛ̄]	[et^{h}elk^{h}t^{h}ḛ̄]
	[prosp̥t^{h}egma]	[prosp^{h}t^{h}egma]

It can be argued that in colloquial Attic not everybody pronounced all three aspirates in *et^{h}alp^{h}t^{h}ḛ̄* or both aspirates after /s/ in *prosp^{h}t^{h}egma*. Even if such sequences certainly do not constitute a physiological impossibility in any actual languages, it could well be that speakers showing consistently both aspirates in [eleip^{h}t^{h}ḛ̄] would quite naturally dissimilate the first aspirate in the cluster after another aspirate [et^{h}alft^{h}ḛ̄]. Unfortunately, this statement implies that such speakers assimilated the final voiceless /p/ to a following aspirate /t^h/, and then dissimilated the resulting /p^h/ after the preceding /t^h/:

	et^{h}alp+t^{h}ḛ̄	eleip+t^{h}ḛ̄
Assimilation	et^{h}alp^{h}t^{h}ḛ̄	eleip^{h}t^{h}ḛ̄
Dissimilation	et^{h}alft^{h}ḛ̄	

So it is safer to claim, that in forms like *ethalpth̄ē* the assimilation in the manner of articulation did not take place. In this sense, there is no controversy between the above hypotheses. Of course, one may still wonder why these two forms were spelled in the same way ἐθάλφθη and ἐλεύφθη, if the first was presumably pronounced [et^{h}alpt^{h}ē] and the second one [eleip^{h}t^{h}ē].

3.3 GRASSMANN'S LAW

The well-known phenomenon of 'Grassmann's Law' (1863), stating basically that the leftmost of the two nonadjacent aspirates is deaspirated, has been the subject of various controversies in recent publications. My intention is to show that much of this controversy is simply due to the neglect to distinguish carefully between synchronic and diachronic descriptions and between *historical* and *underlying* forms. These confusions were already to be found in the Neogrammarians and are simply perpetrated in much of the contemporary writings of generative phonologists.

The biggest error, expressed quite clearly, is that Grassmann's Law is a synchronic rule of Greek (and of Sanskrit). Thus Kiparsky (1973:115) derives synchronically *tit^{h}ēmi* from underlying *t^{h}it^{h}ēmi*, *tétropha* from *t^{h}et^{h}rop^{h}a*. Derivations like these are based on the Neogrammarian assumption that there are underlying diaspirate roots like *$^*t^h$rep^h* in Greek (or *$^*bhudh$* in Sanskrit). Consequently, the simple form of the Present *tréphō* needs to undergo Grassmann's Law. This kind of reasoning is based on the observation of the occurrence of aspirates in forms like *trep^{h}ō* (Present) and *t^{h}repsō* (Future); hence by the simple cumulative method of Neogrammarian historical linguistics we obtain the underlying root *t^{h}rep^h*. The root-final aspirate is eliminated before *s* of the Future by a *Cluster rule* which deletes the aspiration immediately before obstruents. So according to Kiparsky the above two forms are derived like this:

	t^{h}rep^{h}ō	t^{h}rep^{h}sō
Cluster rule	-	t^{h}repsō
Grassmann's Law	trep^{h}ō	-

Kiparsky then proceeds to formalize Grassmann's Law which is restricted by the fact that it does not operate across a morpheme boundary.[5] The aspirate in the environment must be part of the root: that is, neither in Sanskrit nor in Greek does the aspirate in an ending have a dissimilatory effect on the aspirate in a root or in a prefix:

$$[\text{-vocalic}] \longrightarrow [\text{-aspirated}] / \_\_\_ X [\text{+aspirated}]$$

where X does not contain a + boundary.

This is supposed to explain why the initial segment of a double-aspirate root is not deaspirated when the ending begins with an aspirate. Thus the Passive Aorist $eth\hat{r}eph^{th}\bar{e}n$ is safely derived from underlying $eth\hat{r}eph^hth\bar{e}n$ by applying the cluster rule, but not Grassmann's Law, which is blocked by the intervening morphemic boundary.

In connection with Grassmann's Law Kiparsky postulates another synchronic rule of Greek s- *Aspiration*, which turns s into h in sonorant environments:

$$s \longrightarrow h \Big/ \left\{ \begin{array}{c} \# \\ [\text{-obstruent}] \end{array} \right\} \_\_\_ [\text{-obstruent}]$$

This 'synchronic' rule again is nothing more than a Neogrammarian account of forms like $ek^h\bar{o}$ (Present), $heks\bar{o}$ (Future): the root sek^h, which retains the s intact in the Aorist $\acute{e}sk^hon$ shows it as h in the future $h\acute{e}ks\bar{o}$; the underlying $s\acute{e}k^h\bar{o}$ becomes $h\acute{e}k^h\bar{o}$ by the s-Aspiration rule, and then $\acute{e}k^h\bar{o}$ by Grassmann's Law. In other words, two historical sound changes stated as synchronic rules are necessary to account for the simple form of the present $ek^h\bar{o}$. The derivations below are supposed to represent a synchronic process of Greek:

	$thet^hrop^ha$	$eth\text{reph}th\bar{e}n$	$thresph\bar{s}\bar{o}$	$sek^h\bar{o}$	$sek^hs\bar{o}$
s-Aspiration	-	-	-	$hek^h\bar{o}$	$hek^hs\bar{o}$
Cluster rule	-	$eth\text{rep}th\bar{e}n$	$threps\bar{o}$	-	$heks\bar{o}$
Grassmann's Law	$tetrop^ha$	-	-	$ek^h\bar{o}$	-
	τέτροφα	ἐθρέφθην	θρέψω	ἔχω	ἔξω

Since in Greek dialects diaspirate and monoaspirate roots, e.g. /t^hreph-/ versus /$treph$/, never contrast, any PIE root /C^hVC^h/ would be relexicalized as /CVC^h/. (The same is true about Sanskrit, since both languages show a neutralization process called Grassmann's Law).

This assumption does away with both s-Aspiration and Grassmann's Law from the derivations above. All we need to derive these forms synchronically is to keep the Cluster Rule, which must be reformulated as 'aspirate throw-back', conditioned by the following /s/ or /t^h/:

	$tetrop^ha$	$etreph+th\bar{e}n$	$treph+s\bar{o}$	$ek^h\bar{o}$	$ek^h+s\bar{o}$
Aspirate Throw-back	-	$eth\text{rep}+th\bar{e}n$	$t^hrep+s\bar{o}$	-	$hek+s\bar{o}$

Thus in my opinion all that is needed for synchronic

derivation is a) to assume *monoaspirate* underlying roots and
b) to evaluate *synchronically* the alternations
of the type $treph\bar{o}$ (Pres) $t^hreps\bar{o}$ (Fut), without any Neogrammarian bias.

As pointed out by Miller (1974:211) the 'aspirate throwback' was a very irregular phenomenon, which takes place only if the consonant to which the aspiration is thrown back is a voiceless dental stop followed by /r/ (with exceptions), and also in a few isolated roots where there is only a voiceless dental stop followed by a vowel. There are no cases of 'aspirate throw-back' to a velar stop followed by /r/ or in a prevocalic position and only isolated examples of 'aspirate throw-back' to a bilabial stop before /r/:[6]

$treph\bar{o}$ 'nourish'	$t^hreps\bar{o}$ (Fut)	but $teukh\bar{o}$ 'make'	
		eteuksa (Aorist)	
$trekh\bar{o}$ 'run'	$t^hreks\bar{o}$ (Fut)	but $trūkh\bar{o}$ 'waste'	
		$trūks\bar{o}$ (Fut)	
$trikhos$ (Gen Sg.)	t^hriks (Nom Sg) 'hair'		

Some isolated roots showing 'aspirate throw-back' are:

$tūph\bar{o}$ 'smoke' $t^hūpsai$ (Aorist Inf) Hesychius, Suidas

$takhus$ 'swift' $t^hatt\bar{o}n$ (Compar)

$etaph\bar{e}$ (Aorist Pass) $t^hapt\bar{o}$ 'bury'

There is no 'throw-back' in environments like:

$ekruph\bar{e}$ (Aorist Pass) $krupt\bar{o}$ 'hide'

$pakhus$ 'thick' $pass\bar{o}n$ (Compar) Homeric

$ebaph\bar{e}$ (Aorist Pass) $bapt\bar{o}$ 'dip in water'

$eskaph\bar{e}$ (Aorist Pass) $skapt\bar{o}$ 'dig'

$streph\bar{o}$ 'turn' $streps\bar{o}$ (Fut)

According to Miller (1974:214) 'aspirate throw-back' can be viewed only as a subrule of deaspiration. They are clearly the same synchronic process in the sense that they take place in the same environment - the contact of two continuous segments results in a manner dissimilation, where the first segment loses its aspiration:

<u>Deaspiration</u> $[+ \text{asp}] \longrightarrow [- \text{asp}] / \underline{\quad} [+ \text{asp}]$

Under special circumstances in the roots $trV \begin{Bmatrix} p \\ k \end{Bmatrix} h$, the aspiration is thrown back to the first consonant. The 'aspirate throw-back', furthermore, must be blocked if there is an /s/ preceding /t(r)/: $strep^h\bar{o}$ 'turn' forms the Future $streps\bar{o}$ (not $*st^hreps\bar{o}$). This form is derived simply by de-aspiration from underlying $strep^hs\bar{o}$. Obviously, no 'aspirate throw-back' can take place if the first consonant of the root is a voiced stop, since there are no voiced aspirates in Greek.[7]

According to Kiparsky (1973:122) the spelling ΦΘ in ἐθρέφθη does not indicate a cluster of two aspirates /p^ht^h/ but a cluster of the form non-aspirated stop + aspirated stop /pt^h/. I think that there are good reasons not to believe that this was the ordinary Greek convention. As pointed out by Allen it is difficult to see how such a convention could have come about, since in the geminate groups /pp^h, tt^h, kk^h/ the spelling ΠΦ, ΤΘ, ΚΧ is normal.

As a matter of fact, there is no point in insisting on the interpretation /pt^h/ since both /pt^h/ and /p^ht^h/ can be derived:

ἐτρέφθη 'he was turned' /$etrept^h\bar{e}$/ or /$etrep^ht^h\bar{e}$/
ἐθρέφθη 'he was nourished' /$et^hrept^h\bar{e}$/ or /$et^hrep^ht^h\bar{e}$/

	$trep^h$+$s\bar{o}$	$etrep^h$+$t^h\bar{e}n$	$etrep$+$t^h\bar{e}n$
Aspirate Throw-back	$t^hreps\bar{o}$	$et^hrept^h\bar{e}n$	−
Assimilation	−	$et^hrep^ht^h\bar{e}n$	$etrep^ht^h\bar{e}n$

That Grassmann's Law is not a synchronic rule of Greek dialects but a historical rule can be seen in the derivational history of words like

ταχύς 'quick' − θάσσων (Comparative) <u>Homeric</u>
ἐτάφην (Aorist Pass) − θάπτω 'bury'

Here Grassmann's Law must be ordered before palatalization which certainly is not a synchronic rule. Compare the derivational history of these two words with παχύς 'thick − πάσσων (Comparative) <u>Homeric</u>:

	$pak^hj\bar{o}n$		
	$pakj\bar{o}n$	$tak^hj\bar{o}n$	$tap^hj\bar{o}$
Grassman's Law	−	$t^hakj\bar{o}n$	$t^hapj\bar{o}$
Palatalization	$pak'j\bar{o}n$	$t^hak'j\bar{o}n$	$t^hap'j\bar{o}$
Affrication	$pat's'j\bar{o}n$	$t^hat's'j\bar{o}n$	$t^hapt'j\bar{o}$
Depalatalization	$pats\bar{o}n$	$t^hats\bar{o}n$	$t^hapt\bar{o}$
Regressive Assimilation	$pass\bar{o}n$	$t^hass\bar{o}n$	−

3.4 FRICATION OF CLASSICAL ASPIRATES

As shown by Modern Greek, the ancient aspirates /p^h/, /t^h/, /k^h/ changed into fricatives /f/, /θ/, /x/. The beginnings of this process of 'frication' are usually placed in the Greco-Roman period (starting circa 150 B.C.). However, certain spellings found in inscriptions from various dialectal areas seem to suggest that this process could have started much earlier in particular dialects. The best known examples are from the Laconian dialect. By the end of the 5th c. Attic writers (Aristophanes, Thucydides) transcribe Laconian /θ/ before vowels with Σ, e.g. σιός (= Attic θεός 'god'), ἀγασώς (= Attic ἀγαθούς 'good'), and the same spelling occurs in inscriptions from Sparta, beginning in the 4th c., ανεσηκε (= Attic ἀνέθηκε 'dedicated'). This apparently indicates that speakers of Attic noticed the difference between their voiceless dental aspirate /t^h/ and its Laconian counterpart, which was probably a voiceless interdental fricative /θ/. Consequently, the spelling with Σ representing a voiceless sibilant /s/ in Attic, was more convenient than the spelling with θ since acoustically /s/ and /θ/ are closer (qua fricatives), than /s/ and /t^h/ (fricative versus aspirated stop). The same kind of reasoning can be applied to evaluation of Laconian inscriptions from the 4th c., if they are compared with older inscriptions, which show the spelling with θ consistently. We can assume that a certain generation of speakers of Laconian became aware that their pronunciation of prevocalic dental aspirate /t^h/ of the older generation changed in direction to interdental fricative /θ/; consequently they duly tried to express this phenomenon in their inscriptions and the letter Σ was found as the most suitable. What is interesting is that this spelling disappears from later inscriptions, and shows up again in very late inscriptions from the 2nd c. A.D. As was pointed out in the Introduction, this certainly represents a good example of the discrepancy between the literary and colloquial usage of dialect. The scribes simply noticed that the spelling with Σ was a kind of 'provincialism' (which was the best possible representation for /θ/!) but since it did not occur elsewhere they chose to avoid it. In other words, after the sound /t^h/ changed to /θ/, let us assume in the 4th c., it did not change back to /t^h/ as it might seem judging on the basis of later inscriptions, and again to /θ/ judging on the basis of very late inscriptions - the sound /θ/ became probably a new phoneme of Laconian and has been used ever since. More evidence from other dialects may be found in Buck (1955:59) and Lejeune (1972:61).

However, it might be wrong to assume that a full scale

frication of all aspirates affected Hellenistic Koine as early as the 2nd c. B.C., even if the beginnings of such a change can be traced to these times. Certainly, if we want to think of a historical sound change in terms of quantitative drift we can imagine that there appeared fricative allophones of old aspirates in certain environments; this relationship was reversed probably not earlier than in the 1st c. of the Christian era when for the first time the whole system was analyzable as containing voiceless stops versus voiceless fricatives (p, t, k versus f, θ, x). The positive evidence for a fricative pronunciation of all aspirates (p^h, t^h, k^h) is from the 1st c. A.D. in Pompeian spellings, Dafne (= Δάφνη), lasfe λασφη (for λάσθη 'mockery'), see Schwyzer (1938:158).

The environment for the frication of aspirates which comes most readily to mind is in the clusters φθ and χθ /p^ht^h/, /k^ht^h/. These clusters could be affected first by the process of frication, and there could appear fricatives [fθ] and [xθ], first only as allophones of aspirates. What is meant by this is that it was perfectly possible for somebody to have an aspirate in prevocalic position in words like φαιδρός [p^haidros] 'bright', and θεός [t^heos] 'god', but to have fricatives in a cluster ὀφθαλμός [ofθalmos] 'eye'. [f] in such a case would be considered only as an allophone of /p^h/ and [θ] as an allophone of /t^h/. The same might be true about the clusters σφ, σθ, σχ /sp^h/, /st^h/, /sk^h/, which were quite difficult to pronounce (compare the situation in English, where /p/ in 'pit' is aspirated, but not /p/ in 'spit' - aspiration in English is, of course, only allophonic). A sequence *fricative* plus *aspirate* could be realized in two ways:
a) as a sequence *fricative* plus *stop* (= dissimilation in the manner of articulation): /st^h/ ⟶ [st]

Evidence for this can be seen in early inscriptions of the West dialects: <u>Elean</u> χρεεσται (= χρῆσθαι), λυσαστο (= λυσάσθω) and even elsewhere, in <u>Arcadian</u> εσκεθην, <u>Lesbian</u> υποσκεθην vs. <u>Homeric</u> σχεθέειν 'hold'.
b) as a sequence *fricative* plus *fricative* (= assimilation in the manner of articulation): /st^h/ ⟶ [sθ]

Inscriptional evidence can only be indirect since there was no grapheme for a voiceless interdental fricative [θ], so far as this sound only occurred as an allophone of an aspirate /t^h/. There are spellings like ΣΣ for ΣΘ found in late Elean (4 - 2nd c.) and spellings like θθ for the same cluster found in Central Cretan:

<u>Elean</u>	αποδοσσαι	(= ἀποδόσθαι)
	ποιηασσαι	(= ποιήσασθαι)

Central Cretan προθθα   (= πρόσθεν)

              αποϜειπαθθω (= ἀπειπάσθω)

Elean spellings can be interpreted as showing the fricative value of the second sound. In other words, a phoneme /t^h/ could be realized as an interdental fricative [θ] in the environment after /s/:
  $t^h \rightarrow \theta$ / s -
Given the inventory of Elean graphemes, the letter Σ would be the most suitable for this phonetic value. A counter-hypothesis might be a *complete assimilation* in the manner of articulation: $st^h \rightarrow st$, which I think is to be ruled out on the basis of other data from Elean and other West dialects showing a *dissimilation* in the manner of articulation: $st^h \rightarrow st$, since these two processes would be counter-acting:

Locrian   hελεσται   (= ἑλέσθαι)
Delphian   προστα   (= πρόσθεν)
Cretan   μιστος   (= μισθός)
Laconian   χρησται   (= χρῆσθαι)

The spelling θθ instead of Σθ is quite regular in Central Cretan and we find it also in Elean προθθα [prosθa] 'in front of'. On the other hand, there are also rare spellings with Τθ:

δεκετθαι   (= δέχεσθαι)
χρητθαι   (= χρῆσθαι)
απολογιττετθω (= ἀπολογιζέσθω)

If we take [dek^{h}esθai] for the most probable phonetic reconstruction it also appears that fricativity dissimilation sθ $\rightarrow$ tθ could take place and we may reconstruct [dek^{h}etθai], [k^{h}rētθai]. The situation is complicated by the fact that the spelling Σθ occurs also in the earliest inscriptions (in late inscriptions as well, here undoubtedly under the influence of Koine).

Summarizing the preceding discussion, we can assume that a long time before the change of aspirates into fricatives (taking place in the last pre-Christian and the first Christian century) Hellenistic Koine could have had fricative allophones [f], [θ], [x] of aspirate phonemes /p^h/, /t^h/, /k^h/ in certain environments such as clusters φθ and χθ after a sibilant /s/. Whoever wishes to view a historical sound-change in terms of a quantitative drift may claim that a historical process of frication started in these environments, and later on affected aspirates in other environments, namely the intervocalic position.

In terms of historical sound-change we can say that

108 Phonological Interpretation of Ancient Greek

fricative allophones of the aspirate phonemes, which occurred
in the older type of Hellenistic Koine became phonemes in later
Hellenistic Koine:

Hellenistic Koine
(before frication)   p   pʰ   [f]   b
                        t   tʰ   [θ]   d
                        k   kʰ   [x]   g

Hellenistic Koine
(after frication)   p   f   b
                        t   θ   d
                        k   x   g

It is more likely that the phonetic value of the fricative
allophone of bilabial aspirate was also bilabial [ɸ], rather
than labiodental [f]. The change ɸ ⟶ f took place later
on, as is demonstrated by Modern Greek.

In terms of our phonological features we may say that the
Classical Greek system *stop :aspirate :fricative* was trans-
formed into a system based on a binary opposition *non-
continuous :continuous*. The Hellenistic obstruents can be
classified in this way:

Figure 3-13. Obstruents of Hellenistic Greek

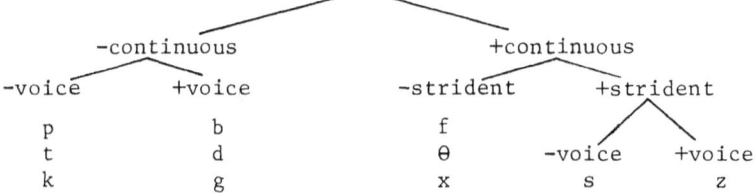

```
              -continuous              +continuous
          -voice     +voice        -strident      +strident
            p          b              f          -voice  +voice
            t          d              θ            s       z
            k          g              x
```

It is more difficult to establish at what period the fricative pronunciation of the old voiced stops /b/, /d/, /g/
developed. Authorities differ more widely than in the case of
frication of aspirates. According to Lejeune (1972:55) voiced
stops remained unchanged in Koine and developed fricative
values as late as in the Transitional Period from Old to
Modern Greek (ca. 3rd - 6th c. A.D.). /b/ seems to be the
first to develop the fricative value. Lejeune bases this
claim on the observation that about the beginning of the
Christian Era the Greek letter *B* could represent the Latin
voiced labiodental fricative /v/, which was spelled with
letter *U* in Latin:

      Latin Flauius [flavius]   Greek   Φλαουιος
                                       or   Φλαβιος

Whereas the first Greek rendering is a simple translitera-
tion (Latin *U* = Greek *OY*), the second rendering need not be
interpreted as evidence for a fricative value of Greek *B*

since even if we assume that the phonetic value represented by this letter in Greek was a stop [b], this letter still would be the most fitting representation of Latin [v]. Again given the graphemic inventory of Greek, the only other possibility could be the letter Φ, which by these times represented a voiceless labiodental fricative [f]. This, however, was rightly refused, since anyone attempting a phonetic transcription of Latin in Greek characters considered b (voiced stop) a better transcription of v (voiced fricative) than f (voiceless fricative). In other words, a voice distinction was more important than the distinction in the manner of articulation.

In terms of our distinctive features, we may say that it was as late as in the Transitional Period (300-600 A.D.) that the opposition of voice became fully functional in continuants:

Figure 3-14. Obstruents of Greek of the Transitional Period (300-600 A.D.)

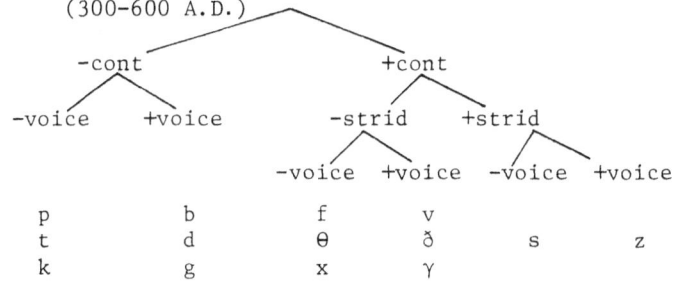

Again data from various dialects indicate that the process of frication could affect voiced stops much earlier than the suggested late period. In the later inscriptions of several Doric dialects (Cretan, Elean, Argolic and especially Laconian from the 4th to the 2nd c.), the old velar glide w spelled originally with digamma Ϝ (by these times w became labiodental fricative v) could now be spelled with Β. This undoubtedly indicates that the letter Β already represented a fricative [v] (or bilabial [β]) in certain environments and since then could be used interchangeably with digamma Ϝ:

Laconian   Βωρθεα or Βωρσεα beside   Ϝωρθεα 'Orthia'
                                      (='Ορθύα) [vōrθeā]
           προβειπαhας [proveipahās] 'having declared'
                                      (=προειπα(σα)ς)
Cretan   διαβειπαμενος 'having conversed with'
                                      (=διαειπάμενος)
Elean   βοικιαρ [voikiāɹ] 'house' (=οἰκίας Gen)

Sporadic omission of the letter Γ (or substitution of the letter Ι) in certain words in various dialects may be

interpreted as showing that g started being pronounced as a velar fricative [γ] (or better, g developed fricative allophones intervocalically):
<u>Boeotian</u> (Aristophanes, Corinna) ἰώ(ν) 'I' (=ἐγώ)
<u>Pamphylian</u> μhεɩαλαν 'big' (=μεγάλην Fem Acc)
<u>Arcadian</u> επιθιιανε 'touch lightly' (=ἐπιθιγγάνῃ Subj)
<u>various places</u> (late) ὀλίος 'little' (=ὀλίγος)

Puzzling Cypriot spellings with the letter Z instead of Γ ζα 'earth' (=γῆ) αζαθος 'good' (=ἀγαθός) seem to indicate spontaneous palatalization of /g/ before a velar vowel: [d^{z}ā], [ad^{z}at^{h}os].

3.5 DENTAL AND VELAR PALATALIZATION

<u>Dental Palatalization</u> - In Proto-Greek a dental obstruent /t/ in the environment before the palatal semivowel /j/ was palatalized. The palatalized dental obstruent was subsequently affricated $t'j \longrightarrow t's'j$; after the palatal glide had been lost this cluster was depalatalized $t's'j \longrightarrow ts$. At this stage Proto-Greek *tj merges with Proto-Greek *ts. The cluster ts could be subject to *progressive assimilation* in manner $ts \longrightarrow tt$ (as in Boeotian, Attic and Central Cretan) or to *regressive assimilation* $ts \longrightarrow ss$ (in other dialects).

<u>Velar Palatalization</u> - In Proto-Greek a velar obstruent /k/ in the environment before the palatal semivowel /j/ was palatalized. The palatalized velar obstruent was subsequently affricated $k'j \longrightarrow t's'j$. At this stage the Proto-Greek *kj merges with Proto-Greek *tj and all dialects with the exception of Attic-Ionic and Arcadian show the same reflexes for both *kj (or k^{h}j) and *tj (or t^{h}j):

	*tj	*kj
Palatalization	t'j	k'j
Affrication	t's'j	t's'j
Depalatalization	ts	ts
Progressive Assimilation	tt	tt
Regressive Assimilation	ss	ss

We may examine dialectal equivalents of Attic words μέσος 'middle', μέλιττα 'bee', and κηρύττω 'herald':

	*met^{h}jos	*melitja	*kārujkō
<u>Ionic</u>	μέσος	μέλισσα	κηρύσσω
<u>Arcadian</u>	μεσος		κᾱρυσσω
<u>Attic</u>	μέσος	μέλιττα	κηρύττω
<u>Lesbian</u>	μέσσος		κᾱρύσσω
<u>Central Cretan</u>	μεττος		
<u>Boeotian</u>	μεττος		κᾱρυττω

On the basis of reflexes of the Proto-Greek clusters *t(h)j, *k(h)j (and *tw, *ts and *ss) Classical dialects may

111 Consonants

conveniently be classified into three broad dialectal groups:
(a) On the one hand, Arcado-Cypriot and Ionic dialects
(Southern group) show consistently a geminate sibilant /ss/
for Proto-Greek *k(h)y and *tw and a sibilant /s/ for Proto-
Greek *ss, *ts and *t(h)j.
(b) On the other hand, Aeolic and West dialects (Northern
group) have only a geminate sibilant /ss/ for all these Proto-
Greek clusters.
(c) Attica, Euboea and Boeotia represent transitional areas -
Proto-Greek *k(h)j, *tw and partly even *tj developed into a
geminate dental obstruent /tt/. In Boeotian also the Proto-
Greek *ts gives the same result /tt/. According to Chadwick
(1969:92) the geminate tt may have been a genuine Aeolism,
surviving in Boeotian and extended to Attic,[8] but eliminated
partially in Thessalian and wholly in Lesbian. So far as
Attic and Euboic are concerned, it could be that the difference in the development *t(h)j had to do with the synchronic
recoverability of t(h). It was recoverable in words like
μέλιττα, κρείττων 'stronger', πλάττω 'form' (since there were
μέλιτ+ος 'honey', κράτ+ιστος 'strongest', κοροπλάθ+ος
'modeller of small figures'); but it was not recoverable in
words like μέσος or τόσος 'so much'.

Diverging developments of Proto-Greek *t(h)j and *k(h)j in
these groups can be represented by the derivational scheme on
p. 112.

The development of the voiced clusters *dj and *gj parallels
to a certain point the development of *tj and *kj (both groups
went through the affrication and depalatalization). However,
the parallel development is completed (with progressive
assimilation dz ⟶ dd, cf. ts ⟶ tt) only in Boeotian
and Central Cretan. *dj and *gj developed in the same way
also in Elean and Laconian (and maybe in Thessalian).

	*djeus	*psāpʰidjō *dikadjō	*megjōn	*gʷjōos
Boeotian	Δευς	φαφιδδω	μεδδονος	δωω
Elean		δικαδδω		
Central	Ζενι (6-5th)	φαφιδδω		ζοος (6-5th)
Cretan	Δηνα, (Τ)τηνα	δικαδδω		δοος (5-3rd)

Comparison of the derivation of Boeotian καρυττω and μεδδων:

	Boeotian		Central Cretan Elean
	kārukjō	megjōn	dikadjō
Palatalization	kāruk'jō	meg'jōn	dikad'jō
Affrication	kārut's'jō	med'z'jōn	dikad'z'jō
Depalatalization	kārutsō	medzōn	dikadzō
Progressive Assimilation	kāruttō	meddōn	dikaddō

	(c) Transitional areas			(a) Southern group		(b) Northern group	
	Attic	West Ionic	Boeotian	Central and East Ionic	Arcadian	Lesbian	West Dialects
			kārukjō				
Palatalization			kāruk'jō				
Affrication			kārut's'jō				
Depalatalization			kārutsō				
Progressive Assimilation	kāruttō	kāruttō	kāruttō *Regressive*	kārussō		kārussō	
Fronting	kæruttō	kæruttō		kærussō		—	
Raising	kēṛuttō	kēṛuttō		kēṛussō		—	
Fronting	kēṛüttō	—		—		—	
Deaspiration	melitja			methjos			
Palatalization	melit'ja			metjos			
Affrication	melit's'ja			met'jos			
Depalatalization	melitsa			met's'jos			
Progressive Assimilation	melitta		mettos *Regressive*	metsos		metsos Cretan	
Degemination	—		—	messos		messos	
				mesos		—	

Elsewhere (in Attic-Ionic and Lesbian) the voiced affricate dz was metathesized $dz \longrightarrow zd$ at quite an early date (it is impossible to specify more exactly at what time). For evidence regarding the Classical cluster zd, see under 3.1, p. 81. It is probable, however, that some dialects preserved the voiced affricate dz down to Classical times. The two most likely candidates are Arcadian and Central Cretan. The reason for the delayed metathesis of dz in Arcadian was apparently the fact that Arcadian had a voiceless counterpart /ts/ as a phoneme, consequently the voiced affricate had a support in the phonemic system, whereas elsewhere it was isolated. The same is true for the phonemic system of Central Cretan. Here also spellings like Ζένυ and ζόος in the 6-5th c. indicate that /dz/ was not yet liquidated by the progressive assimilation, which apparently took place in Classical times, since the same words are spelled Δηνα, (Τ)τηνα and δδος in the 5-3rd c.

<u>Arcadian</u>	μεζων	/medzōn/	δικαζω	/dikadzō/
<u>Ionic</u>	μέζων	/mezdǭn/	δικάζω	/dikazdǭ/
<u>Attic</u>[9]	μείζων	/mḙzdǭn/	"	"
	megjōn		dikadjō	
Palatalization	meg'jōn		dikad'jō	
Affrication	med'z'jōn		dikad'z'jō	
Depalatalization	medzōn		dikadzō	
Metathesis	mezdōn		dikazdō	

As a result of the metathesis $dz \longrightarrow zd$ the isoglosses linking the reflexes of *dj and *gj cut in a different way compared with the reflexes of *tj and *kj. This can be shown by the derivational history of *$psaph^{i}djō$, p. 114.

A consequence of the convergent development of the Proto-Greek clusters *dj and *gj was a restructuring in underlying representations of verbal stems in voiced dental stop. In Western dialects, Arcado-Cypriot, Thessalian and Boeotian there are Future and Aorist forms in -$k+s$-, while the same verbs in Attic-Ionic form their Future and Aorist in -s- (<ss<ts<$d+s$). The extension -$k+s$- from the stems in velar stop to the stems in dental stop occurs sporadically even elsewhere, e.g. in Homeric πολεμίξομεν (versus Attic πολεμίσομεν), but it remains a characteristic phenomenon in the above dialects.

        Attic
δικάζω 'judge' δικάσει   versus   δικαδδω - δικακσει
                                                           Cretan

	(a) Southern group		(b) North-East	(c) Transitional		(b) some West dialects
	Ionic	Arcadian	Lesbian	Boeotian	Central Cretan	
	Attic				Locrian	
					Elean	
Palatalization	———	———	psāpʰidjō	———		
Affrication	———	———	psāpʰid'jō	———		
Depalatalization	———	———	psāpʰid'z'jō	———		
Progressive Assimilation	———	———	psāpʰidzō			
Fronting	psāpʰidzō	—	—	psāpʰiddō		psāpʰiddō
Raising	psē̜pʰidzō	—	—			
Metathesis	psē̜pʰizdō	psāpʰizdō	psāpʰizdō			

κομίζω 'carry' ἐκόμισα versus κομιδδω - εκομιττα
                                              Boeotian
ψηφίζομαι 'vote' ἐψηφίσατο   ψαφιδδομαι - εψαφιξατο
                                              Thessalian

It seems hard to understand why the Proto-Greek cluster *tw developed in the same way as *t(h)j and *k(h)j since generally only a palatal glide has a palatalizing and affricating effect. Allen (1973b:114) assumes that the palatalization of the Greek dental obstruent /t/ could be inherent and that this could lead to an assimilation of the velar /w/, via a front rounded [ɥ] to the palatal glide /j/. Lejeune (1972:66) explains the palatalization of /t/ before a velar /u/ by "l'attaque prépalatale' of /u/ after a dental consonant: $tʲu \longrightarrow t^su \longrightarrow su$. He also notices that the cluster *tw is palatalized in dialectal groups where /t/ had the 'weakest' articulation and was generally 'assibilated' before /i/. Thus we can assume that the sequence of phonetic changes from Proto-Greek *tw parallels the palatalization of *tj and *kj:

	tw	tj	kj
Assimilation	t'ɥ	tj	kj
Palatalization	t'j	t'j	k'j
Affrication	t's'j	t's'j	t's'j
Depalatalization	ts	ts	ts
Assimilation	ss	ss	ss

Attic-Ionic ἥμισυ 'half' (*sēmitu-) versus Cretan
Arcadian   hεμισυ
Lesbian   αιμισεων (Gen Pl)

Also its thematic doublet:

Arcadian ημισσον (*sēmitwon)
Thessalian, Delphian hεμισσον
East Cretan ημισσον

Personal Pronoun of the 2nd Sg:

	Attic-Ionic, Lesbian	versus	Doric, Boeotian
Nom	σύ		τυ
Dat	σοῦ, τοι (enclitic)		τιν
Acc	σέ		τε

Attic-Ionic and Lesbian σε must be derived from *twe whereas Doric and Boeotian τε goes back to *te; i.e. the velar glide was lost in West dialects but it was assimilated to the palatal /t/ elsewhere:

116 Phonological Interpretation of Ancient Greek

	Arcadian Thessalian East Cretan	Attic-Ionic Lesbian	Doric Boeotian
Fricative Weakening	sēmitwon hēmitwon	twe	twe
Assimilation	hēmit'ʮon	t'ʮe *w-Loss*	te
Palatalization	hēmit'jon	t'je	
Affrication	hēmit's'jon	t's'je	
Depalatalization	hēmitson	tse	
Regressive Assimilation	hēmisson	sse	
Degemination	-	se	

Dialect reflexes of all Proto-Greek clusters discussed in 3.5 are surveyed in Figure 3-15.

3.6 REFLEXES OF PROTO-GREEK LABIOVELARS IN CLASSICAL DIALECTS

We may safely assume that Greek continued Proto-Indoeuropean labiovelars and that their labial and palatal development is a relatively recent phenomenon. This probably started in post-Mycenaean times since Mycenaean Greek has preserved the labiovelars as phonemes and the evidence for the labial development, typical above all of Classical Aeolic dialects, is insufficient in Mycenaean: see Vilborg (1960:46).

The evidence for labiovelars in Mycenaean is based on several words with plausible IE etymologies, which are written in Mycenaean with special syllabograms different from the graphemes for labial, dental and velar series:

Mycenaean		Classical Attic
a-to-ro-qo	/ant^{h}rōk^{w}os/ 'man'	ἄνθρωπος /ant^{h}rōpos/
qo-u-qo-ta	/g^{w}oug^{w}otās/ 'herdsman'	βουβότης /bǫbotē̜s/

The following data from Mycenaean and Classical Greek dialects will illustrate the labial and palatal development of Proto-Greek labiovelars:

	*k^{w}is	*k^{w}ēl	*k^{w}ol-	*g^{w}el- / g^{w}ol-
Mycenaean	k^{w}is	k^{w}ēle-	amp^{h}ik^{w}olos	
Lesbian		πήλοθεν		
Thessalian	κις			βελλομαι
Ionic	τις	τηλόθεν	ἀμφιπόλος	βούλομαι
Arcadian	ϻις			
West Dialects				δηλομαι

Figure 3-15. Dialect geography of reflexes of Proto-Greek clusters *ss, *ts, *t(h)j, *k(h)j, *tw, *dj and *gj

	*ss	*ts	*t(h)j		*k(h)j	*tw	*dj	*gj
Ionic	s	s	s	ss	ss	ss	zd	
Arcadian	s	s	s	ss	ss	ss	dz	
Attic	s	s	s	tt	tt	tt	zd	
Boeotian	ss	tt	tt		tt	tt	dd	
Lesbian	ss	ss	ss		ss	ss	zd	
West Dialects (Laconian)	ss	ss	ss		ss	ss	dd	
Central Cretan (6-5th)		ts	ts				dz	
Central Cretan (5-4th)[10]		tt	tt		tt		dd	

[After Lejeune (1972:106,112)]

According to Allen (1973:115) a probable phonetic development of Proto-Greek labiovelars in the environment before front vowels began with the palatalization of the labial feature to labio-palatal: k^w ⟶ $k^ɥ$, which entailed a fronting of the velar obstruent $k^ɥ$ ⟶ $k'^ɥ$ ⟶ $č^ɥ$. This is supposed to be an essential stage since plain velar obstruents are not palatalized. In later development the labial component of the palatal affricate was lost.

In Arcado-Cypriot the affricate undergoes the same development as the affricate resulting from the dental and velar palatalization of Proto-Greek clusters *t(h)j and *k(h)j, i.e. the palatal affricate was depalatized $t's'$ ⟶ ts, and the dental affricate could furthermore undergo a fricative development. The affricate stage is probably documented by Arcadian Ϻις /tsis/ 'who', written by the special grapheme of the Arcadian epichoric alphabet or by the diagraph TZ as in τζετρακατιαι /tsetra-/ 'fourhundred' (Attic τετρακόσιαι).

In Cypriot the affricate lost its closure completely σις /sis/ 'who'. Ionic dialects diverge at the affricate stage by losing the fricative component of the affricate. An interesting document is Thessalian κις 'who', which can be interpreted in the sense that Thessalian lost the labial component of Proto-Greek /k^w/ before /i/ without undergoing the palatal development:

	Arcado-Cypriot	Attic-Ionic	Thessalian
	$k^w$is	$k^w$is	$k^w$is
Palatalization	$k'^ɥ$is	$k'^ɥ$is	–
Affrication	$č^ɥ$is	$č^ɥ$is	–
Delabialization	čis	čis	kis
Depalatalization	tsis	tsis	
Frication	sis	*Deaffrication* tis	

Proto-Greek voiced labiovelar *g^w apparently underwent the same kind of development as the voiceless *k^w in Arcado-Cypriot.

δελλω   'throw' (Hesychius ζέλλω), Attic-Ionic βάλλω
δερεθρον 'pit' (Strabo ζέρεθρον), Attic-Ionic βάραθρον

That the palatal development could take place even in West dialects is demonstrated by Heraclean δηλομαι, Delphian and Locrian δειλομαι which correspond to the forms with labial development of other dialects: Boeotian βειλομαι and Thessalian βελλομαι 'will, wish' (other dialects have a different root-vowel: Lesbian βολλαμαι, Cretan βωλομαι, Attic-Ionic βούλομαι).

	Arcadian	West Dialects
	gʷel	gʷel
Palatalization	g'ɥel	gɥ'el
Affrication	ǰɥel	ǰɥel
Delabialization	ǰel	ǰel
Depalatalization	dᶻel	dᶻel
Deaffrication	del	del

	Boeotian Thessalian	Lesbian Attic-Ionic
	gʷel	gʷol
Labialization	bel	bol

In Aeolic dialects Proto-Greek labiovelars in the environment before non-high vowels /e, o, a/ lost their velar component but kept their closure i.e. they are reflected as labial stops. The same happened in all other dialects in the environment before back non-high vowels /o, a/. A labial obstruent before a front vowel, where other dialects show a dental obstruent, is a distinct characteristic of the Aeolic dialects, e.g. Lesbian πήλοθεν versus Attic τηλόθεν 'from afar'.

Proto-Greek labiovelars before a back round vowel /o/ could also be delabialized according to the evidence of various dialects, e.g. Mycenaean *gʷoukolos*, Homeric βουκόλος 'cowherd' (versus Mycenaean *ampʰikwolos*, Homeric ἀμφίπολος 'handmaid'); in the texts of Ionic authors there are forms κῶς 'how', κότερος 'which of two' (versus inscriptional and Attic πῶς, πότερος).

	Aeolic	Ionic
	kʷēlotʰen	kʷoteros
Labialization	pēlotʰen	poteros (inscriptional)

	Ionic	
	kʷēlotʰen	kʷoteros
Palatalization	k'ɥēlotʰen	–
Affrication	čɥēlotʰen	–
Delabialization	čēlotʰen	koteros (literary)
Depalatalization	tᶳēlotʰen	
Deaffrication	tēlotʰen	

There is some evidence for the reconstruction of Proto-Greek (or rather PIE) labiovelar /gʷ/ in the environment before a dental nasal. Lejeune (1972:78) believes that the cluster -g^wn- existed in Mycenaean times. However, there is no direct evidence in LB texts and the reconstruction is guaranteed only by external evidence. Thus the labiovelar may be postulated for Proto-Greek ancestors of Classical ἀμνός 'ram' (cf. Latin *agnus*), σεμνός 'revered' (cf. σέβομαι 'worship' and Sanskrit *tyaj-* 'abandon'), μνάομαι 'court' (cf. γυνή, Boeotian βανα). The labiovelar before /n/ was labialized (= lost its velar component) but the resulting cluster *bn did not survive anywhere in dialects (or expressed synchronically, in Greek a voiced bilabial stop does not cluster with nasals). The voiced bilabial stop was assimilated completely in the manner of articulation to the following dental nasal and became a bilabial nasal:

	ag^{w}nos	tjeg^{w}nos	g^{w}na-
Labialization	abnos	sebnos	bna-
Assimilation	amnos	semnos	mna-

The derivational history of the word τέτταρες 'four' is quite complicated due to the variety of dialectal forms. The possibility of glide dissimilation in *k^{w}etwVr must be taken into account. We need several proto-forms to account for all the dialectal variants: *k^{w}etwer, *k^{w}etwar and *k^{w}etwur.

Ionic	τέσσερες	*k^{w}etwer
Homeric	τέσσαρες	
Attic	τέτταρες	*k^{w}etwar Arcadian τζετρα - /t^{s}etra/
Boeotian	πετταρες	
West dialects	τετορες	
Lesbian	πέσυρες	*k^{w}etwur
Homeric	πίσυρες	

A possible sequence of sound-changes (palatalization precedes the delabialization) to account for all the dialectal variants is given on p. 121.

3.7 DEVELOPMENT OF PROTO-GREEK SONORANT CLUSTERS IN CLASSICAL DIALECTS

The development of Proto-Greek sonorant clusters is particularly important for the classification of Classical dialects, especially for the establishing of a dichotomy between Aeolic (North-East group) and all other dialects. These clusters can be divided into four groups:

(1) Sonorant + Sibilant: *ms,   *ns,   *rs,   *ls   *ws
(2) Sibilant + Sonorant: *sm,   *sn   *sr,   *sl,   *sw
(3) Lateral + Dental nasal: *ln
(4) Sonorant + Palatal glide: *nj,   *rj,   *lj

See some data representative of the main groups of dialects:
(1) Sonorant + Sibilant

	*ms	*ns	*rs	*ls
Aeolic	ἔνεμμα	ἔκριννα 'judged'		ἔστελλα
Doric		εφᾱνα	εκαθᾱρα	εστηλα

	Ionic	Attic	West Dialects		Boeotian	Lesbian
Glide Dissimilation	kʷetwer	kʷetwar	kʷetwor		kʷetwar	kʷetwur
Palatalization	kʷetjer	kʷetjar	kʷetor		kʷetjar	kʷetjur
Affrication	k'ɥet'jer	k'ɥet'jar	k'ɥetor		kʷet'jar	kʷet'jur
Delabialization	čɥečer	čɥečar	čɥetor		kʷečar	kʷečur
Depalatalization	čečer	čečar	četor	Labialization	pečar	pečur
Deaffrication	tˢetˢer	tˢetˢar	tˢetor		petˢar	petˢur
	tetˢer	tetˢar	tetor	Arcadian	—	—
Regressive Assimilation	tesser	—	—		—	pessur
Progressive Assimilation	—	tettar	—		pettar	—
Degemination	—	—	—		—	pesur

122 Phonological Interpretation of Ancient Greek

Ionic   ἔνειμα   ἔφηνα   ἐκάθηρα   ἔστειλα
         'I distributed'   'showed'   'cleansed'   'sent'

(2) Sibilant + Sonorant
              *sm   *sn   *sr   *sl
Aeolic   ἔμμι   σελάννᾱ   χέρρας   χέλλιοι
                                               (Acc Pl)

Doric   ημι   σελᾱνᾱ   χηρ   χηλιοι
Ionic   εἰμί   σελήνη   χείρ   χείλιοι
          'I am'   'moon'   'hand'   'thousand'

(3) Lateral liquid + Dental nasal
                              *ln
Aeolic   στάλλᾱ
Doric   στᾱλᾱ
Ionic   στήλη
                          'stele'

(4) Sonorant + Palatal glide
                              *nj   *rj   *lj
Aeolic   κτέννω   φθέρρω   στέλλω
Ionic   κτείνω   φθείρω   στέλλω
Arcadian   φθήρω
                          'kill'   'destroy'   'send'

(1) Sonorant + Sibilant
    In Aeolic dialects a sibilant in the environment after a
nasal or lateral liquid (there is no evidence regarding *rs)
occurred subject to the *progressive sibilant assimilation*:
A sibilant is assimilated completely to a preceding nasal or
lateral liquid.
    In other dialect groups a sibilant in the environment after
a nasal or liquid was lost and the loss was accompanied by
compensatory lengthening of the preceding vowel:
     V̆ nasal s V ⟶ V̄ nasal V
Almost all of our examples are sigmatic Aorists.

                          Aeolic dialects

                          enemsa   ekrinsa   estelsa
Voice Assimilation   enemza   ekrinza   estelza
Sibilant Assimilation   enemma   ekrinna   estella

                          Other dialect groups

                          enemsa   epʰansa   ekatʰarsa   estelsa
Voice Assimilation   enemza   epʰanza   ekatʰarza   estelza
Compensatory Lengthening enēma   epʰāna   ekatʰāra   estēla Doric
Fronting   epʰæna   ekatʰæra   -
Raising   enẹma   epʰẹna   ekatʰẹra   estẹla Ionic

    In Attic-Ionic, the clusters Sonorant + Sibilant in other

environments (not in the sigmatic Aorist) are treated differently. If *s* belongs to other inflectional and derivational morphemes it is never lost, but the preceding nasal can be lost and *r* can cause complete progressive assimilation of the following sibilant. Those morphemes include:
i) Dat Pl of athematic nouns -*si*
ποιμέσι 'shepherds' (< ποιμέν+σι)
ῥήτορ+σι 'public speakers'
ἁλ+σί 'lumps of salt'
The cluster *n+s* is regularly simplified. /n/ is sometimes preserved in dialects, e.g. <u>Arcadian</u> ἱερομναμονσι 'ministers of religion'. The cluster -*ns*- is quite common here and can be of two other origins: *ntj/i* as in πανσα 'all' (Attic πᾶσα) and *nt+s* as in φερονσι 'carrying' (Part) (Attic φέρουσι), see p. 201.
ἅλες is the only nominal stem in -*l*; there are also other forms of Dat Pl: ἅλεσσι (Homeric) and ἅλασι, where the cluster -*ls*- is 'avoided'.
ii) 2nd Sg Perf Middle -*sai*
πέφαν+σαι 'appear'
ἔσπαρ+σαι 'be scattered'
ἔσταλ+σαι 'be sent'
iii) Derivational suffix -*sis*
κλύσις 'bending' (< κλίν+σις)
but θέρμαν+σις 'heating'
ἔγερ+σις 'awaking' (ἐγείρω)
ἅλ+σις 'leaping' (ἅλλομαι)

The cluster *n+s* is exceptionally simplified in the environment after /i/. Thus there is κλίσις, κρίσις, 'decision' (κρίνω), but on the other hand θέρμαν+σις, πρᾶυν+σις 'appeasing'. *n+s* is preserved in ἀπόφαν+σις 'declaration' (ἀποφαίνω) since it could be confused with ἀπόφασις 'denial' (ἀπόφημι). Similarly there is a late ἔκφανσις 'making clear' (Synesius) versus ἔκφασις 'declaration'. However, *n+s* is not preserved in ἐπίφασις or ἔμφασις 'outward appearance' (-φαίνω).

In Homeric the clusters *l+s*, *r+s* in the Aorist remain unchanged:
κέλσαι 'drive in' (κέλλω)
ἔκερσεν 'shear' (κείρω)
ὦρσε 'stir up' (ὄρνῡμι)

In Attic the complete assimilation *rs* ⟶ *rz* ⟶ *rr* took place (unassimilated *rs* in early Attic writers is of Ionic origin):
<u>Homeric</u> ἄρσην 'male' <u>Ionic</u> ἔρσην versus <u>Attic</u> ἄρρην
<u>Old Attic</u> θάρσος 'courage' <u>New Attic</u> θάρρος

In Attic writers both *tʰars*- and *tʰarr*- and metathesized *tʰras*- can be found.

124 Phonological Interpretation of Ancient Greek

	NOUN	VERB	ADJECTIVE	VERB
tʰars-	θάρσος	θαρσέω	θαρσύς	θαρσύνω
tʰarr-	θάρρος	θαρρέω	∅	θαρρύνω
tʰras-	θράσος	∅	θρασύς	θρασύνω

(2) Sibilant + Sonorant

In <u>Aeolic</u> dialects a sibilant in the environment before a nasal or liquid occurred subject to the *regressive sibilant assimilation*: A sibilant is assimilated completely to a following nasal or liquid.

In other dialect groups a sibilant in the environment before a nasal or liquid became a glottal fricative (as before a vowel). The glottal fricative was lost and the loss was accompanied by *compensatory lengthening* of a preceding vowel:

V̆ h Sonorant ⟶ V̄ Sonorant

<u>Aeolic dialects</u>

	esmi	selasnā	kʰerras	kʰeslioi
Voice Assimilation	ezmi	selaznā	kʰezras	kʰezlioi
Sibilant Assimilation	emmi	selannā	kʰerras	kʰellioi

<u>other dialect groups</u>

	esmi	selasnā	kʰesr	kʰeslioi	
Voice Assimilation	ezmi	selaznā	kʰezr	kʰezlioi	
Fricative Weakening	ehmi	selahnā	kʰehr	kʰehlioi	
Compensatory Lengthening	ēmi	selānā	kʰēr	kʰēlioi	<u>Doric</u>
Fronting	-	selǣnǣ	-	-	
Raising	ēmi	selḗnḗ	kʰḗr	kʰḗlioi	<u>Ionic</u>
Raising	-	-	-	kʰīlioi	<u>Attic</u>

In <u>Attic</u> there are quite a few examples of the cluster -nn- and only some of these go back to Proto-Greek *sn:

ζώννῡμι   'gird' (*jōsnūmi)
σβέννῡμι   'extinguish' (*sgʷesnūmi)
ἕννῡμι   'put clothes on' (*wesnūmi) <u>Homeric</u> εἵνῡμι (hapax)

These forms underwent the 'Aeolic rule' of sibilant assimilation. Notice, however, that Homeric εἵνῡμι shows the non-Aeolic development (fricative weakening and lengthening):

	Homeric		Attic
	wesnūmi		wesnūmi
Voice Assimilation	weznūmi		weznūmi
Fricative Weakening	wehnūmi	*Sibilant Assimilation*	wennūmi
Lengthening	wēnūmi		
Raising	wēnūmi		

Other <u>Attic</u> forms like κεράννῡμι 'mix', στορέννῡμι

'spread' (older form στόρνῡμι) may be explained as having been formed recently from the stems in -s (Aorist, Future):

στόρνῡμι < *stor+nūmi
στορέννῡμι < stores+nūmi

It seems that in Aeolic dialects the sibilant could undergo sibilant assimilation even before a velar glide:

Lesbian (gloss) εὐέθωκεν probably [ew(w)éthōken]
Ionic ἔωθα
Homeric, Attic εἴωθα

	Aeolic
	sesweth-
Fricative Weakening	hesweth-
Voice Assimilation	hezweth-
Sibilant Assimilation	hewweth-
Psilosis	ewweth-

In other dialects a sibilant before a velar glide underwent the 'regular' development.

Cretan τελnος 'perfect' (*teles+wos), Attic-Ionic τέλειος (<*teles+jos)

East Aegean Doric (Cos) τελεως

	Homeric, Attic	Doric
	seswōtha	teleswos
Voice Assimilation	sezwōtha	telezwos
Fricative Weakening	hehwōtha	telehwos
Compensatory Lengthening	ēwōtha	telēwos
$w \rightarrow \emptyset / V - V$	ēōtha	teleos (Cretan)
Raising	ẹ̄ọtha *Metathesis of length*	teleōs (Cos)

(3) Lateral liquid + Dental nasal

In Aeolic dialects a dental nasal in the environment after a lateral liquid (there is no evidence regarding *rn) occurred subject to the *nasal assimilation*: A dental nasal is assimilated completely to the preceding lateral liquid.

In other dialect groups a lateral liquid in the environment before a dental nasal was lost and the loss was accompanied by a *compensatory lengthening* of a preceding vowel:

$$\breve{V} \; l \; n \; V \longrightarrow \bar{V} \; n \; V$$

	Aeolic dialects		
	stalnā	ophelnō	bolnā
Nasal Assimilation	stallā	ophellō	bollā
	other dialect groups		
	stalnā	ophelnō	bolnā

126 Phonological Interpretation of Ancient Greek

Compensatory Lengthening	stālā	opʰēlō	bōlā	Doric
Fronting	stǣlǣ	–	bōlǣ	
Raising	stẹ̄lẹ̄	opʰẹ̄lọ̄	bọ̄lẹ̄	Ionic

Note: We do not know if Aeolic βολλᾱ goes back to Proto-Greek *bolnā or *bolsā.

Attic form (ἀπ)όλλῡμι 'destroy' shows the Aeolic development through the nasal assimilation from *olnūmi ⟶ ollūmi (instead of predicted *ọlūmi).

(4) $\begin{Bmatrix} \text{Dental nasal} \\ \text{Liquid} \end{Bmatrix}$ + Palatal glide

In <u>Aeolic</u> dialects a palatal glide is assimilated completely to a preceding liquid or a dental nasal in the environment after front and high back vowels /i, e, u/. A *glide assimilation* restricted to the environment after a lateral liquid is common to all dialects (with exceptions found in Cypriot and Elean).

In all dialects a *metathesis* of palatal glide in the case of clusters *rj and *nj took place. The metathesis in Aeolic dialects took place only after back non-high vowels /o, a/.

Metathesis: $V \begin{Bmatrix} r \\ n \end{Bmatrix} j V \longrightarrow V i \begin{Bmatrix} r \\ n \end{Bmatrix} V$

	Aeolic dialects			
Glide Assimilation	ktenjō	pʰtʰerjō		
	ktennō	pʰtʰerrō		
	all dialects (with the exception of Aeolic)			all dialects
Metathesis of glide	ktenjō	pʰtʰerjō	banjō	morja
	kteinō	pʰtʰeirō	bainō	moira
	all dialects			
Glide Assimilation	aljos	steljō		
	allos	stellō		

In Cypriot and Elean there is some scanty evidence that the metathesis of palatal glide could take place even in the case of the cluster *lj:

<u>Cypriot</u> αιλος 'another' (elsewhere in Doric αλλος)
      Απειλων 'Apollo' (Doric 'Απέλλων)
<u>Elean</u> αιλοτρια 'alien' (= ἀλλότρια)

	Cypriot, Elean	
Metathesis of glide	aljos	apeljōn
	ailos	apeilōn

	other Doric dialects	
	aljos	apeljōn
Assimilation of glide	allos	apellōn

An item of direct evidence for a non-metathesized cluster -rj- comes from Mycenaean spellings with syllabograms ra$_2$ /rja/ and ro$_2$ /rjo/ in words like a-ro$_2$-e /arjohes/ 'better' (cf. Superlative ἄριστος), tu-ro$_2$ /turjos/ 'cheese' (Diminutive, cf. τῡρός). See Lejeune (1972:156).

Another solution instead of metathesis of palatal glide would be to assume compensatory lengthening, as in (1), (2) and (3), with the loss of palatal glide:

	ktenjō	pʰtʰerjō		
Compensatory Lengthening	ktēno	pʰtʰēro	Arcadian	φθηρω
Raising	ktẹ̄no	pʰtʰẹ̄ro	Attic-Ionic	φθείρω

The result is the same in both cases since phonologically /ẹ̄/ = [ẹ̄] ∿ [ei]. However, this solution may be regarded as preferable in the case of high vowels: *urjV (no evidence for *irjV)

Aeolic ὀλοφύρρω 'lament'
Attic-Ionic ὀλοφύρομαι

	Aeolic		Attic-Ionic
	olopʰurjō		olopʰurjomai
Glide Assimilation	olopʰurro	*Compensatory Lengthening*	olopʰūromai

NOTES

1 In Lupaș's analysis (1972:144ff) phonemes /tt/ and /ss/ are interpreted as stylistic variants of a single archiphoneme /TT/. The archiphoneme /TT/ is realized as [ss] in elevated style (tragedy) and [tt] in colloquial style (comedy and inscriptions). She proposes to indicate the presence of elevated style [+emph] as a triggering device for the phoneme /ss/. In the absence of this mark the archiphoneme /TT/ is realized as [tt].

2 Lupaș's corpus is not representative of Classical Attic in the sense that she did not include any prose (it includes only the three great tragedians, Aristophanes, and inscriptions from the same time published in IG I^2). For a description of the phonotactics even the time limit seems to be detrimental since if we include writers of the 4th c. (Plato, Aristotle, Xenophon, Theophrastus, Demosthenes) we can add to her triadic clusters examples like: s+kt,

k+ks, n+tm, n+t^{h}l, r+bl, r+rk^{h}r, s+kn, s+gl, k+p^{h}l, k+tm, k+t^{h}l, k+kn, k+kr, k+kl, g+gl, k+k^{h}r, k+sk^h, r+sk, s+sp, ks+p. Many other clusters can be found in authors of Helenistic and Graeco-Roman period. I included even those in order to obtain a more exhaustive picture of the phonotactics of Ancient Greek.

The following clusters are not found in Lupaş's corpus (1972:138):

$\begin{Bmatrix} \text{Sibilant} \\ \text{Velar Stop} \end{Bmatrix}$ + Peripheral Stop + Coronal Obstruent

s/z+bd	εἰσβδάλλω	Galen
k + ps	ἐκψύω	Hippocrates
s + kt	προσκτάομαι	Xenophon
k + ks	ἐκξυλόομαι	Theophrastus
k + kt	ἐκκτυπέω	Pollux

$\begin{Bmatrix} \text{Sonorant} \\ \text{Sibilant} \\ \text{Velar Stop} \end{Bmatrix}$ + Obstruent + Sonorant

n+tm	ἔντμημα	Xenophon
n+t^{h}l	ἐνθλίβω	Aristotle
ŋ+kn	ἐγκνώσσω	Moschus (200 B.C.)
r+pr	ὑπερπράξιον	C.I.
r+bl	ὑπερβλαστής	Theophrastus
r+p^{h}l	ὑπερφλεγμαίνω	Hippocrates
r+kr	ὑπερκρεμάννυμι	Pindar
r+kl	ὑπερκλύζω	Strabo
r+k^{h}r	ὑπέρχρεως	Demosthenes
s/z+br	προσβρέχω	Hippocrates
s+p^{h}l	ἐσφλάω	"
s+kn	προσκνάομαι	Xenophon
s/z+gl	προσγλύχομαι	Aristotle
k+p^{h}l	ἐκφλέγω	Atistophanes
k+tm	ἔκτμησις	Aristotle
k+t^{h}l	ἐκθλίβω	"
k+kn	ἐκκνάω	Herodotus
k+kr	ἐκκρέμαμαι	Plato
k+kl	ἐκκλίνω	"
g+gl	ἐκγλύφω	"
k+k^{h}r	ἐκχράω	Sophocles
k+k^{h}l	ἐκχλοίομαι	Hippocrates

$\begin{Bmatrix} k \\ n,r \\ s \end{Bmatrix}$ + Sibilant + Obstruent

k+sp^h	ἐκσφραγίζομαι	Euripides
k+sk^h	ἐκσχίζω	Aristotle

n+sb	ἐνσβέννυμαι	Dioscorides
n+sph	ἐνσφηνδομαι	Dioscorides
r+sp	ὑπερσπουδάζω	Lucian
r+sph	ὑπερσφριγάω	Gregorius Nyssenus
r+sk	ὑπερσκελής	Plato
s+sp	προσσπάομαι	Aristotle
s+sph	προσσφάζω	Plutarchus
s+zd	προσζεύγνυμι	Lucian
s+sk	προσσκοπέω	Strabo
s+skh	προσσχεδιάζω	Josephus
ks+k	ἑξκαίδεκα	Phrynichus
ks+p	ἐξπηχυστί	Sophocles

3   In her phonological analysis Lupaș (p. 109) notes correctly that the lenis allophones [p̥k̥] appear only in the context which does not tolerate the presence of [p b pʰ k g kʰ] (i.e. the opposition voiceless: voiced: aspirate is neutralized before [s] and [tʰ]). And this induces the tantalizing question for any structuralist – to which phonemes should the lenis allophones [p̥k̥] be assigned? They resemble /pʰkʰ/ in being voiceless and lax, /p k/ in being voiceless and finally /b g/ in being lax. Since there is no criterion available, she prefers to set up two archiphonemes /P K/.

In a more dynamic theoretical framework which allows for low-level phonological rules the problem of setting up an archiphoneme in similar circumstances would not arise. Furthermore, it is possible to analyze Ancient Greek without the feature tense-lax which forced Lupaș to set up an archiphoneme. Lupaș's analysis:
   /pʰkʰ/   -voice, -tense
   /p k/   -voice, +tense
   /b g/   +voice, -tense
Traditional analysis (adopted in the present monograph):
   /pʰkʰ/   -voice, +aspirated
   /p k/   -voice, -aspirated
   /b g/   +voice, -aspirated
Thus in my analysis [p̥] in [grap̥sǫ] etc. is assigned automatically to /p/ with which it shares two features (-voice, -aspirated) and the relationship of [p̥] and /p/ is of course captured by a low-level phonological rule:
/p/ ⟶ [p̥] / — [s].

4   But there are also spellings Ἔκχφαντος, ἐκχφορᾶς. All these examples are taken from Dow (1967:213).

5   There are quite a few exceptions showing that the deaspiration of the leftmost aspirate could operate across a morpheme boundary; however, they comprise mostly personal names where it can be argued that the morpheme boundary is lost. Examples given by Schwyzer (1939:261):

Delos ἀρκεθέωρος 'chief ambassador' (= ἀρχεθέωρος)
       κρεοφυλάκιον 'the office in which the register of
                     public debtors is kept'
                     (= χρεοφυλάκιον)

                Εκεσθενης
Aetolian   Αρκεφων
Delphian, Laconian   Εκεφυλος
Cretan   Τευφιλος
Attic   Κρυσόθεμις
                             Πωσφόρος
                             Ἀντεσφόρος

An aspirate in the ending does not have a dissimilatory effect on the aspirate in the root; however, the opposite phenomenon of progressive dissimilation is sometimes observed:
σώθητι (Aorist Pass) not *σώτηθι (< *sōth$\bar{e}$+thi)
ἐπιστράφητι (LXX) (< *epistraph$\bar{e}$+thi)
but γράφηθι (< *graph$\bar{e}$+thi)

	k^{h}reop^{h}ulakion	sōth$\bar{e}$thi	graph$\bar{e}$thi
Regressive Dissimilation	kreop^{h}ulakion	-	-
Progressive Dissimilation	-	sōth$\bar{e}$ti	

6 Those examples are:
φροῦδος 'gone, departed' (< προ + ὁδοῦ)
φρουρός 'watcher, guard' (< προ + ὁράω)
φροίμιον 'opening, introduction' (< προοίμιον, οἶμος 'road, path')

	pro+horos	pro+hodos
Aspirate Throw-Back	p^{h}ro+oros	p^{h}ro+odos
Contraction	p^{h}rō̄ros	p^{h}rō̄dos

7 The 'aspirate throw-back' rule is quite a costly mini-rule which captures the 'regularity' in behaviour of not more than a handful of forms. Two verbs: τρέφω 'nourish' and τρέχω 'run' (but there are also the forms δραμοῦμαι (Fut) and ἔδραμον (Aorist) and the isolated noun θρίξ 'hair', plus the three other above mentioned isolated forms. The rule has been formalized by Miller as follows:

Aspirate Throw-Back

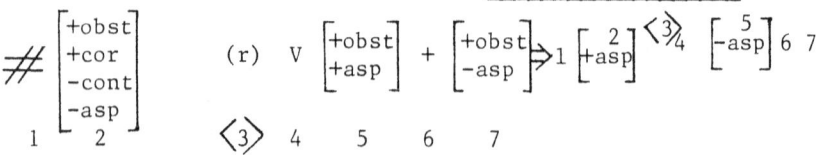

Of course, relevant roots must be marked in the lexicon for undergoing this subrule. Where /r/ is present, the subrule

131   Consonants

will apply normally; and a rule will be needed to interpret the lexical marks: M for /tVCh/ means that the subrule applies, U means it does not apply; and the same marks for /trVCh/.

8   Chadwick (1969:92) regards Attic as a mixed dialect in the sub-Mycenean period. The evidence seems to be the cultural unity of the Cycladic area and Eastern Attica, which suggests that the Eastern Attic was a dialect identical with Cycladic (= Proto-Ionic), while Western Attic was a different dialect, influenced by a dialect of the Boeotian type.

9   According to Lejeune (1972:113) 'le vocalism de l'attique μείζων comme celui de κρείττων est analogique et a été introduit secondairement dans la vulgate homérique'. The source of analogy is supposed to be the comparative χείρων 'worse' - however, no cogent reasons are given to believe that this was really the case.

Ionic	κρέσσων	Attic	κρείττων
	μέζων		μείζων
			χείρων
			ὀλείζων

This kind of conceptual analogy of course cannot be ruled out a priori; nevertheless it could be that the forms κρείττων and μείζων represent non-analogical formations, since depalatalization of the cluster $t's'j \longrightarrow t^s$ could be preceded by the metathesis of the palatal glide:

	kretjōn	megjon
Palatalization	kret'jōn	meg'jōn
Affrication	kret's'jōn	med'z'jōn
Metathesis of glide	kreit's'ōn	meid'z'ōn
Depalatalization	kreit^{s}ōn	meidzōn
Assimilation	kreittōn	-
Metathesis	-	meizdōn

10 There are various difficulties connected with the phonetic reconstruction of Central Cretan reflexes of Proto-Greek clusters *ts, *t(h)j and *k(h)j; those spellings of θθ occurring between the 4th - 2nd c are especially hard to explain.

		Central Cretan			
Proto-Greek	*ss	*ts	*t(h)j	*k(h)j	*tw
6-5th c.	?	δαζαθαι	οζοι	?	?
			μεζατος		
5-4th c.	?	δατταθθαι	οποττοι	φυλαττην	?
			μεττον	φυλαδην	
			ιατταν	(East Cretan)	
4-2nd c.			οθθακιν	?	ημιτθον
	Fετεθθι	Αρκαθθι	ιαθθαν		ημισσον
					(East Cretan)

Probable phonetic values of Central Cretan reflexes are given below:

Proto-Greek	*ss	*ts	*t(h)j	*k(h)j	*tw
Central-Cretan					
6-5th c.	?	ts	ts	?	?
5-4th c.	?	tt	tt	tt	?
4-2nd c.	ss	θs	θs	?	tθ

οθθος probably does not represent [ossos], since in Central Cretan the cluster /ts/ (primary or secondary) was subject to the progressive assimilation of sibilant as in Boeotian. ss would be a result of the regressive assimilation which is quite common in all other dialects.

In my analysis Central Cretan spellings like οθθακιν represent [oθsakin] or [oθθakin] which can be explained phonologically as follows: Primary or secondary /ts/ occurred subject to the complete assimilation of sibilant in 5 - 4th c., and later on in 4 - 2nd c. to the fricativity assimilation, when the dental obstruent was assimilated in manner to the sibilant and became an interdental fricative. Complete assimilation of the sibilant to the preceding interdental fricative could subsequently take place:

                                         otsos
(Regressive) Fricativity Assimilation   oθsos
(Progressive) Complete Assimilation   oθθos

On the other hand, this interpretation of the spelling does not fit examples like Fετεθθι or Πολιθι (Attic ἔτεσι or πόλισι), since it is hard to imagine something other than [wetes(s)i] and [polisi].

```
   grapheme            sound
      θ    ────────────  θ
           ╲     ╱
            ╳
           ╱     ╲
      Σ    ────────────  s
```

This is just the opposite of the Laconian pattern:

Laconian before the 5th c.

```
   grapheme            sound
      θ                  tʰ

      Σ                  s
```

Laconian after 5th c.

```
   grapheme            sound
      θ                  θ

      Σ                  s
```

During the 5th C., when the new interdental fricative [θ] developed from pre- or intervocalic /tʰ/, the phonetic value [s] represented by the grapheme Σ became closer to the [θ] and could be conveniently used for it. Thus the Laconian gloss βεσορ (= ἔθος) can be reconstructed phonetically as [weθoɹ] (or [weθo̞ɹ]).

4

The Accentual System

4.1 THE GENERAL LIMITING RULE

The Attic accent was in a sense 'free', in other words, its position was not phonologically predictable. However, inside of various inflectional paradigms phonological constraints apply which limit the number of positions in which the accent could occur. The most important of these is a *rule of recession* which limits the distance from the end of the word. This rule is common to all Greek dialects - Ionic, Aeolic and West (Doric) dialects.

As is generally known, the accentuation rules and graphic notations for different types of the accent were elaborated by Aristophanes of Byzantium (about 200 B.C.), in order to teach foreigners the 'correct accent' in pronouncing the Attic Koine. Statements of the Attic *rule of recession* found in various school grammars, based on the work of Aristophanes, are unnecessarily involved and complicated.

Thus Goodwin (1894:24) gives the following account:

> The acute can stand only in one of the last three syllables of the word, the circumflex only on one of the last two, and the grave only on the last. The circumflex can stand only on a syllable long by nature. The antepenult, if accented takes the acute. But it can have no accent if the last syllable is long either by nature or by position. An accented penult is circumflexed when it is long by nature while the last syllable is short by nature. Otherwise it takes the acute.

R. Jakobson (1937/1962:263) simplified considerably the rule of recession by introducing the concept of *mora* 'The span between the accented and the final mora cannot exceed one syllable'.[1] The economy of statement achieved by

Jakobson is, however, counterbalanced by the fact that his formulation operates with two distinct notions, which are not easy to define: mora and syllable.

Allen (1966:13) further simplified the rule by getting rid of the syllable, but he introduced the new concept *'contonation'* (= the combination of high pitch + falling glide). Thus he produced the following statement: 'Not more than one mora may follow the contonation'.

A binary accentual opposition in Attic was recognized from the time of Plato (e.g. Cratylus 399 A). A term ὀξύς 'acute' was applied to the positive, culminative feature, occurring only once in each full word (= high pitch). A term βαρύς 'grave' was applied to the negative, non-culminative feature, occurring predictably on all other syllables with the exception of the syllable immediately following the high pitch in the same full word (= low pitch).

The syllable immediately following a high pitch did not bear a low pitch, but a falling glide, starting at a high pitch and finishing low. Since such a glide was automatic in the environment after the high pitch, it must be considered structurally as a contextual variant of the low pitch.

In Attic (and apparently in all other non-Doric dialects i.e. Ionic and Aeolic) when a syllable contained a long vowel or diphthong it could carry a falling melodic pattern without any preceding high pitch. Syllables like that are marked with the circumflex (instead of the acute). It can be said that on the level of phonetics this independent falling glide is identical with the dependent glide following a high pitch.

In Allen's theory, we may consider the falling glide as a feature of the phonetic realization of the accent. The combination of high pitch + falling glide can thus be envisaged as a single unit, which is termed by Allen contonation.

The *phonological opposition* between the falling melodic pattern and the high pitch without falling glide (= between circumflex and acute) existed only in the case of long vowels (or diphthongs) *in final syllables* and *only in Attic* (and apparently in other Ionic dialects, but *not* in Aeolic). Below are listed some minimal pairs in Attic:

φῶς	'light'	φώς	'man'
οἷ	'whither'	οἵ	'who'
ᾗ	1) 'which way, how' 2) Subj. of ἵημι 'send'	ᾕ	'who' (Dat Sg Fem)
εἷς	'one'	εἵς	Aor Part of ἵημι 'send'

λυπηρᾶς 'painful' (Gen Sg)   λυπηράς (Acc Pl)

θεᾶς   'goddess' (Gen Sg)   θεάς   (Acc Pl)

etc.

In other words, the alternation of acute and circumflex is in certain cases synchronically unpredictable and acute and circumflex are to be considered as lexical properties of these items. These are not too many and they include grammatical forms. Consequently it might be argued, in terms of more abstract phonology, that the alternation of acute and circumflex on the ultima is predictable as in the case of the alternation on the penult, which is determined by the morphological structure of the word. This would mean that circumflex in φῶς 'light' is predictable, since the underlying representation is *$ph^{a}os$ – all what matters now is if we consider the contraction /a/ + /o/ as a synchronic process. Admittedly, this cannot be ruled out – Attic tragedy knows both φῶς ∿ φάος, φωσφόρος 'giving light' ∿ φαεσφόρος 'light-bringing'.

In Aeolic the variation between acute and circumflex is automatic on the penult (as in Attic) according to the general limiting rule e.g. θῦμος, θύμου (= Attic θυμός). Since in Aeolic the accent of all full words recedes to its full limit, we do not find the change in contour from acute to circumflex on the thematic vowel that is found in Attic e.g. πόταμος, ποτάμου (= Attic ποταμός, ποταμοῦ) 'river', σόφος, σόφου (= Attic σοφός, σοφοῦ) 'wise'. Thus it can be said with Garde (1968:148), that in Aeolic the mora is irrelevant and only syllables are necessary to accentual description. Consequently, the accent in Aeolic was not contrastive as in Attic. The following Attic pairs, see Vendryes (1938:149 ff), would be homophonous in Aeolic:

a) noun of action   noun of actor or instrument
   τόμος 'a cut'   τομός 'cutting'
   τρόχος 'a running, course'   τροχός 'a runner, wheel'
b) noun   adjective
   ἔχθρα 'hatred'   ἐχθρά 'hated' (Fem)
   λεύκη 'leprosy; the white   λευκή 'white' (Fem)
          poplar'
c) concrete noun   abstract noun
   ἁρπάγη 'a hook, rake'   ἁρπαγή 'seizure; rapacity;
d) in nominal inflection:
   βόλων (Gen Pl) of βόλος 'a net'   βολῶν (Gen Pl) of βολή
                                                    'a throw'
e) proper name   common noun
   Φαῖδρος   φαιδρός 'bright'

f) in compounding: passive   active
   πατρόκτονος 'killed by the   πατροκτόνος 'parricide'
              father'
   θηρότροφος 'feeding on   θηροτρόφος 'feeding wild
              beasts'   beasts'

It is not easy to answer the question whether there was a phonological opposition between the falling melodic pattern and the high pitch (or rather rising melodic pattern) in the case of long vowels (or diphthongs) in penultimate syllables. In the overwhelming majority of examples the occurrence of the circumflex or acute on penultimate long vowels or diphthongs is determined automatically by the length of the final vowel:

δῶρον 'present' vs δώρων (Gen Pl)
παῖδες 'boys'   παίδων (Gen Pl)

Metatony in δῶρον (as contrasted with δώρων) and παῖδες (as contrasted with παίδων) is found in Attic (and Aeolic) only, it does not exist in Doric (δώρον, παίδες). This metatony is stated traditionally as a 'final trochee' rule: if the high pitch occurs on a penultimate syllable containing a long vowel or a diphthong it must occur on the first mora if the final vowel is short (i.e. the accent will be circumflex and not acute). If the final vowel is long, then by the general three mora rule the high pitch must occur on the second mora. In other words, there is no phonological opposition of acute and circumflex on penultimate syllables.

However, in Attic there are minimal pairs such as the following:

οἴκοι (Nom Pl) 'houses' vs οἴκοι (Loc Sg) 'in the house'
λῦσαι (Inf Aor) 'loose'   λύσαι (Opt Aor) 'may he loose'

In terms of autonomous phonology the above examples would suffice to prove that there was a phonological opposition between the falling and rising melodic pattern on penultimate syllables in Attic. However, in terms of more abstract phonology the above examples could be explained by grammatical rules which would assign different mora values to the final diphthongs /oi/ and /ai/.

This solution is in perfect agreement with the data of historical phonology. Prepausal diphthongs /oi/ and /ai/ are considered for accentual purposes as monomoric units (i.e. as V̆C): /oi/ = /oj/ and /ai/ = /aj/. Contrary examples, like the above, contain morphemic boundary in underlying representations: /oi/ = /o + i/ and /ai/ = /a + i/. This entails that the location of the high pitch is specified by the general limiting rule and the alternation between two pitch contours (falling and rising) is automatic, determined by the fact that the prepausal diphthongs /oi/ and /ai/ count as monomoric or dimoric units.

οἶκοι /oîkoi /, underlying representation *óikoj
οἶκοι /oíkoi /,   *oíko+i
λῦσαι /luûsai /,   *lúusaj
λῦσαι /luúsai /,   *luúsa+i

Processual description of Attic is given below:

	oíkoi	dooron	oíko+i	dooroon
Metatony (= Final Trochee)	oîkoi	dôoron	-	-
Loss of morphemic boundary	-	-	oíkoi	-
	οἶκοι	δῶρον	οἶκοι	δώρων

The principal objection which might invalidate this analysis (not to mention that the whole approach recapitulates only the historical sequences and hardly represents anything psychologically real) concerns the concept of the mora. Martinet (1954:51) points out that the concept of the mora does not correspond to a phonetic reality, it is only an analytical device occurring in our descriptions (unlike the vowel or syllable). It is unlikely that speakers of Attic were aware of the fact that the prepausal diphthong /oi/ was monomoric in the Nom Pl but dimoric in the Loc Sg. However, they may have been aware of the morphemic boundary in the Loc Sg (this of course is tantamount to saying that they were aware of the fact that the diphthong /oi/ was not a diphthong but a sequence of two vowels /o/ and /i/, something which is counterdicted by the phonetic evidence). Supporting evidence for this statement can, however, be sought in reference to grammatical (morphological) criteria. The meaning of the final /i/ in the Loc Sg could be recovered synchronically on the basis of the following juxtapositions:

οἶκοι /oíko+i/ 'at home' versus οἴκοθεν /oíko+then/ 'from home'

χαμαί /khama+í/ 'on the earth'   χαμᾶθεν /khamâ+then/ 'from the earth'

Some problematic divisions:

ἄλλοθι /állo+t^{h}i/ or /álloth+i/ 'elsewhere'   ἄλλοθεν /állo+t^{h}en/ 'from elsewhere'

Ἀθήνησι /ath$\bar{\underline{e}}$n$\bar{\underline{e}}$s+i/ or   Ἀθήνηθεν /ath$\bar{\underline{e}}$n$\bar{\underline{e}}$-t^{h}en/
/Ath$\bar{\underline{e}}$n$\bar{\underline{e}}$+si/
'at Athens'   'from Athens'

There are some difficulties involved in this approach. First of all, there is also a form οἴκοθι /oíko+t^{h}i/ or /oíkot^h+i/ 'at home', with problematic division. Second, οἴκοι means not only 'in the house' but also more commonly 'at home'. The phrase 'in the house' would rather be constructed as a prepositional phrase ἐν τῷ οἴκῳ or κατ' οἴκον. Third, synchronically in these examples there is not a postposition -*i* meaning 'at, on', but -*t^{h}i*, cf. many examples like οὐρανόθι 'in heaven', Ἰλιόθι πρό 'before Ilium', etc. Relics of the original locative case in -*i* are found mostly with toponyms: Ἰσθμοῖ 'at the Isthmus', Πυθοῖ 'at Pytho', etc. These forms can be classified synchronically as adverbs. In other words, the crucial semantic juxtaposition of οἴκοι 'houses' and οἴκοι 'at home' yielding the meaning of locative postposition -*i* is not psychologically very likely; all speakers, however, were aware of the opposition (*t^h*)*i* versus *t^{h}en* = 'at' versus 'from'.

(1)   pó+i   oíko+i
(2)   pó+t^{h}i   oíko+t^{h}i   állo+t^{h}i
(3)   pó+t^{h}en   oíko+t^{h}en   állo+t^{h}en

(1), (2) 'whither'   'at home'   'elsewhere'
(3)   'whence'   'from home'   'from elsewhere'

Notice also that οἴκοι was later used in metaphoric expressions like τὰ οἴκοι 'one's domestic affairs', ἡ δ' οἴκοι 'one's own country', where the concrete meaning of 'house' disappeared completely. This might be the reason why we find two forms for 'at home': οἴκοι (older) and οἴκοθι (later), where /t^h/ comes probably from /t^{h}en/ and /i/ is the old locative ending /i/:

(older)   oíko + i

(later)   oíko+ t^h + i

(resegmentation) oíko+ t^h+ en

Kiparsky (1967:124) tried to remove some of these difficulties. The most important argument used by him bears on the problem of whether speakers of Attic were aware of the fact that the prepausal diphthong /oi/ was monomoric in the Nom Pl but dimoric in the Loc Sg. Kiparsky's answer is positive and it is based on a 'striking parallelism' between the accentuation pattern of οἴκοι and οἴκοθι. The accent pattern of the locative in -*t^{h}i* is given by the rule that the

accent stays in its original place if the stem is disyllabic
(as in our case), but shifts to the penultimate mora in
stems of more than two syllables e.g. Κόρινθος ∿ Κορινθόθι.
But this happens to be identical with the accent pattern of
the locative in -i, which follows the accent of the stem if
it is disyllabic (as in our case) and gets a circumflex on
the -oi in the case of polysyllables e.g. Μέγαρα ∿ Μεγαροῖ.
These facts suggest to Kiparsky that the above locatives are
synchronically related. The way to relate them is the
metathesis rule which inverts word-final -i with preceding
dental consonants. By this rule he can derive forms like
2nd Sg Ind λέγεις and 3rd Sg Ind λέγει from Proto-Indoeuropean
*$légesi$ and *$légeti$. The word-final -t or -t^h is deleted
by the Greek loss of word final-obstruent stops (as in
*$sōmat$ → σῶμα)

	*legeti	*oikot^{h}i
Metathesis	legeit	oikoit^h
obstruent stop → ∅ /-#	legei	oikoi

In other words, the derivation of the locative in -i from
the locative in -t^hi is supposed to account for the shared
accent pattern, and also for the accentual peculiarity of
the locative in -i, namely the dimoric value of the final
'short' diphthong.

I feel somewhat uneasy about this derivation. The left
column represents the historical sequence of sound changes
from PIE down to Greek; the rules here are simply labels for
sound changes which took place in the history of more than
a thousand years. The right column represents presumably
some synchronic 'mental' process by which speakers of Attic
attributed a dimoric value to the final diphthong /oi/.
According to this proposal locative like Μεγαροῖ is to be
derived from underlying *$megaróthi$ → $megaróith$ → $megarói$.
This proposal does not lack a certain ingenuity, but is
completely void of any cogent evidence. Ultimately,
Kirparsky refutes himself when he recognizes the double
source of the Greek locative - PIE *dhi would not be the
only source of the *-i locative in Greek, this could be
derived also from PIE *-i with which the *-dhi locative
merged phonologically and thus imposed on it its accentual
pattern.

Another difficulty - why there are still locatives in
-thi, and even side by side with the locative in -i, as in
οἴκοι ∿ οἴκοθι - is to be obviated by the ambiguous syntactic
status of -thi, which is interpreted as either a suffix or
as an enclitic. Since the suffixes are preceded by morpheme
boundaries but enclitics by word boundaries, Kiparsky can
derive both οἴκοι and οἴκοθι from a single underlying *oikothi:

	*oĩko+thi	*oĩko#thi
Metathesis	oíkoith	–
tʰ - Deletion	oíkoi	–

Again there is no cogent reason for undertaking this derivation given the double source of the Greek locative – the underlying form of οἴκοι is much more probably *oíko-i*.

Finally it should be mentioned that the parallelism between the accent patterns of οἴκοι and οἴκοθι did not escape the grammarian Herodian, who listed these two side by side in his treatise on Greek accentuation.

This might corroborate the hypothesis that speakers of Attic were really aware of the morphemic boundary in οἴκοι on the basis of synchronic juxtaposition of *oíko+i* with *oíko#thi*.

4.2 MINOR RULES AND ENCLISIS OF ACCENT

4.2.1 Minor Rules

There are three other rules, which exist only in the Attic dialect:

a) The *'Final Trochee'* rule (a misleading label, since the rule refers to vowel lengths, not to syllable quantities): If the high pitch occurs on a penultimate syllable containing a long vowel (or a diphthong), it must occur on the first mora (i.e. the accent will be circumflex and not acute) if the final vowel is short.
This rule did not exist elsewhere. Contrast:

Attic		Doric		
	παῖδες		παίδες	'boys'
	γυναῖκες		γυναίκες	'women'
	τιμῶμεν		τιμῶμες	'we honour'

b) *'Wheeler's Law'*:
Original polysyllabic oxytones become paroxytones if the vowel of the penult is short and the vowel of the antepenult is long (= if the word has a dactylic ending).
This rule did not exist elsewhere. Contrast:

Attic		Aeolic		
	πατροκτόνος		πατρόκτονος	'parricide'
	ποικίλος		ποίκιλος	'many-coloured'
	ἀγκύλος		ἄγκυλος	'crooked'

For the original accent of composite words like *πατροκτονός, see words which do not have a dactylic ending: ἱπποφορβός 'horse-keeper', στρατηγός 'commander'.

The original final accent of trisyllabic adjectives in -ι/-υλος is reconstructed mainly on the basis of external evidence (Vedic pesắlắs, aŋkurắs).

However, quite a few analogical extensions obliterate the original conditions under which this rule operated, e.g. οἰκοδόμος 'architect', οἰκονόμος 'housekeeper'; see Lejeune (1972:298).

c) *'Vendryes' Law'*:

A word with properispomenon accent, as ἐρῆμος 'desert', retracts the accent to the preceding syllable if this is light. Thus we have in Attic ἔρημος against ἀνδρεῖος 'manly' where the first syllable is heavy.

According to Lejeune (1972:298) 'Vendryes' Law' operates also across word boundaries: ἐγώ#γε → ἔγωγε, ἐμού#γε → ἔμοιγε.

It means that in this case 'Vendryes' Law' operates on the output of 'final trochee' rule:

	egó # ge	emoí # ge
Final Trochee	egôge	emôige
Vendryes' Law	égōge	émoige

That Greek grammarians refer to an Old Attic τροπαῖον which was later accented (according to 'Vendryes' law') τρόπαιον, seems to indicate that 'Vendryes' Law' could be a synchronic rule of (Old) Attic. Presumably, in terms of relative chronology it was a later phenomenon than the Attic isovocalic and anisovocalic contractions (like φιλέομεν → φιλοῦμεν, φιλέετε → φιλεῖτε). Unfortunately, the chronology of isovocalic contractions is impossible to establish; see Bartoněk (1966:71). If this is so, the problem seems to be why the contracted forms, where the circumflex originates from contraction, do *not* retract their accent according to 'Vendryes' Law'.

Why did speakers of Attic not retract the accent in the case of the circumflex arising from contractions? In other words, how to explain that the rule of accent retraction (= Vendryes' Law) does not apply if it is ordered after the contraction? Schematically:

	erêmos	philéomen
Contraction	-	philômen
Vendryes' Law	érēmos	-

According to Sommerstein (1973:126) the rule of accent retraction must come *before* the contraction, since if after the contraction the rule would incorrectly generate *φίλουμεν from φιλοῦμεν. It can be pointed out that (for some speakers at least) uncontracted forms were psychologically real in the sense that they occurred in historical orthography (e.g. Homeric poems). Second, since uncontracted forms occurred in many other dialects it can be said that they existed as 'surface' forms in native dialects of many bidialectal speakers. We can imagine speakers of 'mild' Doric dialects from the Saronic Gulf or speakers of the Boeotian dialect adjusting their dialects to 'standard' Attic Koine. They could not fail to realize the relationship between Attic φιλοῦμεν and their native φιλέομεν, φιλέομες or φιλίομεν, φιλίομες (with *height dissimilation* /eo/ → /io/) and consequently could 'analyze' their learnt Attic φιλοῦμεν as φιλέομεν. This might indicate that there is not much point in reordering the above rules, at least so far as we have in mind our main purpose of interdialectal comparisons. Since the 'final trochee' rule is not found in Doric dialects, we may order the contraction before this rule in the derivative schema:

	Attic			Doric
	erémos	tīmáomen	phīléomen	tīmáomes
Contraction	-	tīmǿmen	phīlǿmen	tīmǿmes
Final Trochee	erêmos	tīmômen	phīlômen	-
Vendryes' Law	érēmos	-	-	-
Raising	-	-	phīlômen	-

What is spurious in this derivation is that the contraction in Attic yields an acute accent, which is changed into a circumflex by the 'final trochee' rule. If we derive the circumflex immediately, we cannot explain why the same is not good for Doric, and furthermore it becomes obvious that there is no point in bringing Vendryes' Law into the discussion. In other words, the question as to why not *φιλούμεν instead of φιλοῦμεν, and the problem of ἔρημος versus φιλοῦμεν, are more or less pseudoproblems. Especially in the latter case we are comparing incomparables in the sense that the 'final trochee' rule deriving érēmos from *erêmos is a historical rule (i.e. the change from *erémos into érēmos by the final trochee rule and Vendryes' Law is a historical change), while the contraction tīmáomen → tīmômen is a synchronic process.

4.2.2 *Enclisis of Accent*

Full words with enclitics following form a phonological unity which manifests itself in the enclisis of accent of the enclitic. The accent of the full word serves now as the accent of the resulting phonological word. Thus in Attic we get combinations like ἀνήρ τις where the accent of the full word ἀνήρ serves as the only accent of the combination ἀνήρ τις 'a man'.

Where the accent of the full word, if applied to the resulting phonological word, would be in disagreement with the general limiting rule, a secondary accent is added to make the phonological word comply with this general rule: e.g. underlying ἄνθρωπος becomes ἄνθρωπός τις.

It can be said, that the general rule of recession operates, with notable exceptions, across word boundaries (in contrast with the 'final trochee' rule). The exceptions are:

a) It is impossible to add a secondary accent in combinations like

καλῶς πως
καλοῦ τινος
καλῶν τινων
οὕτω πως

since the prepausal syllable carries a falling glide.

b) There is a secondary accent added in combinations like

οἶκοί τινων

but the general limiting rule still does not apply, since there is a long vowel in the final syllable of the enclitic τινων. As is well-known, the same happens in the inflection of words like πόλις 'city', Gen Sg πόλεως, where there is an explanation for this anomaly, namely metathesis of vowel-length *$pol\bar{e}jos$ → πόλεως. It is usually said that the length of the final vowel of the enclitic is irrelevant. This seems to be a very likely explanation, which is tantamount to saying that (colloquial) Attic neutralized the contrast of vowel length in the final syllable of enclitics, consequently for the purpose of accentual description καλοῦ τινος and καλῶν τινων behave in the same way: [kalô # tinos] and [kalôn # tinon]. So there is a complete parallel with the accentual pattern of πόλις

(Dat Pl) πόλεσι(ν) - καλοῦ τινος
(Gen Sg) πόλεως   - καλῶν τινων

Alternatively, we may hypothesize that the enclisis of accent was governed by the 'three syllable' rule (see under 4.3.2).

On the other hand, the Attic 'final trochee' rule does not apply across word boundaries. Thus the phonological word φώς τις 'a man' is not turned into φῶς τις (which would be homophonous with φῶς τις 'a light') by this Attic rule. Only when the word boundary is really erased and the full

word and its enclitic constitute a real semantic unit will
the 'final trochee' rule apply. This observation has already
been made in antiquity – according to Herodian, the combination of τούς and enclitic δε, after they merged to form the
demonstrative pronoun τοῦσδε, is to be accented τοῦσδε,
according to the 'final trochee' rule. The word boundary
is equally erased in the combination like ἐγώγε which merges
into a single semantic and phonological unit ἔγωγε 'I (at
least)'. On the other hand, in the combination τοῦτόγε
'this (at least)' the word boundary has not been erased and
the demonstrative pronoun receives its secondary accent.
Since the 'final trochee' rule is limited to Attic it might
be expedient to compare Attic and (reconstructed) Doric forms:

Attic	egṓ # ge	anḗr # tis	ánthrōpos # tis
Antepenult	–	–	ánthrŏpós # tis
Boundary Erasure	egṓge	–	–
'Final Trochee'	egôge	–	–
'Vendryes' Law'	égōge	–	–
Doric	egṓ # ge	anḗr # tis	anthrópos # tis
Boundary Erasure	egṓge		

Disyllabic enclitics represent an exception to the general
rule that enclitics are unaccented. According to the ancient
tradition, there is a secondary accent placed on the final
syllable of enclitics. However, there arises a difficulty
if we compare forms like

       καλοῦ τινος   versus   μεγάλου τινός
       καλῶν τινων   μεγάλων τινῶν

One may wonder why the tradition does not show forms like
καλοῦ τινός or καλῶν τινῶν. Allen (1973:241) tried to
obviate this difficulty by assuming a rule that not more
than two unaccented syllables may follow the syllable containing the high pitch; admission of syllabic criteria into
a mora-based accentual system is legitimate – syllabic
criteria are being admitted into mora-systems in Lithuanian
and Serbo-Croatian.

So if the combinations like ἄνθρωπός τις, ἄνθρωποί τινες
are accented according to the general limiting rule, the
combination like μεγάλου τινές follows the above rule for-
bidding more than two unaccented syllables after the high
pitch. This kind of reasoning may have been based on the
observation of actual usage in contourless dialects – we may
hypothesize that this was the rule governing the

accentuation of enclitics in 'syllable-counting' Doric dialects. Finally, notice that this rule is actually the 'three-syllable rule', which I will postulate as a pre-historic ancestor of the general limiting rule (under 4.3.2).

Attic	Doric
καλοῦ τινος	καλῶ τινος
μεγάλοι τινές	μεγάλοι τινές
ἄνθρωποί τινες	ἀνθρώποι τινές

4.3 HISTORICAL ORIGINS OF THE GREEK ACCENT PATTERN

4.3.1 *Vedic and Greek*

As recognized long ago, the Greek and Vedic accentual systems go back to a common Indo-European source. This is obvious for reasons such as the following:

a) There are numerous correspondences regarding the location of high pitch (Greek ὀξύς 'acute' = Vedic *udātta* 'raised') on the ultima, on the penult (and more rarely even on the antepenult). A long list is given in Schwyzer (1938:380-1).

b) There are close parallels in the accent pattern of nominal and verbal paradigms, which are best explained by assuming a common origin.

Compare for example movable stems in Vedic and Greek:

		Vedic			Greek
Sg Nom	pā́t	'foot'			πούς
Gen		padás			ποδός
Loc		padí		Dat	ποδί
Acc		pā́dam			πόδα
Sg Nom		pitā́	'father'		πατήρ
Gen		pitúr			πατρός
Loc		pitári		Dat	πατέρι
Dat		pitré		Dat	πατρί
Acc		pitáram			πατέρα
Voc		pítar			πάτερ

c) Even more impressive is the fact that both Vedic and Greek accent possess the distinctive properties of PIE 'free' accent. Thus the similar permutations of accent can in both branches distinguish between the lexical meaning of a noun of action and that of an actor (or the grammatical meaning of a noun versus adjective):

Vedic

ápas	'work'	apás	'active'
váras	'choice, wish'	varás	'suitor, lover'
táras	'quickness'	tarás	'quick'
mánas	'mind'	durmanás	'evil-minded'

Greek (Attic)

τόμος	'a cut, slice'	τομός	'cutting, sharp'
τρόχος	'running'	τροχός	'runner, wheel'
ἔχθρα	'hatred'	ἐχθρά	'hatred, hateful' (Fem)
μένος	'mind'	δυσμενής	'evil-minded'

The main difference is that in Vedic there are no phonological constraints (regarding either the number of the preceding or following syllables or moras) which would limit the distance of the accent from the end of the word (contrast the 'recession' rule of Attic verbs and of both nouns and verbs in Lesbian). The accent in Vedic could occur on the 2nd, 3rd, 4th or 5th syllable from the end of the word. The rules of compounding could place the accent on the initial syllable as far as the 7th, 8th or 9th syllable from the end of the word:

Vedic		Greek	
bhárāmaṇas		φερόμενος	'carried'
ánapahitas		ἀνεπίθετος	'admitting no addition'
ábubodhiṣāmahi	'we wanted to learn'		
híraṇyavāśīmattamas	'wielding a golden axe'		

The list of accentual discrepancies regarding the location of the high pitch would be equally long (see again Schwyzer (1938:381)). Quite typical examples are cases where Vedic preserves the original final or penultimate accent, whereas Greek shifts the accent to the antepenult:

Vedic		Greek	
saptamá	'seventh'	ἕβδομος	'seventh'
ajríya	'pertaining to field'	ἄγριος	'wild'
katará	'which (of two)?'	πότερος	'which (of two)?'
anudrá	'waterless'	ἄνυδρος	'waterless'
subhára	'dense, abundant'	εὔφορος	'easily borne, bearing well'
paričará	'companion, servant'	περίπολος	'watchman'

The Accentual System

Thematic verbs in PIE could be accented in one of two ways: the accent could be located either on the root or on the thematic vowel. (Athematic verbs had mobile accents throughout the inflection of the Present - on the root in the singular and on the ending in the dual and plural).

In the first case (= Vedic Class I), the accent is located columnarly on the root throughout the inflection of the Present regardless of the number of following syllables. In the Imperfect the accent is retracted to the augment (regardless of the 2, 3 or 4 following syllables).

In the second case (= Vedic Class VI), the accent is located columnarly on the thematic vowel; consequently the number of following syllables does not exceed 2. In the Imperfect again the accent is retracted to the augment (regardless of the 2, 3 or 4 following syllables).

It can be said that the innovation of the Hellenic branch in the case of thematic verbs consists in the redistribution of these two PIE patterns. In Greek the Present Middle is root-accented with the exception of the 1st Pl (which is accented on the thematic vowel)-thus the accent of

    3 Sg   φέρεται   corresponds to *bhárate* (Class I)

but the accent of

    1 Pl   φερόμεθα   corresponds to *viśámahe* (Class VI).

Likewise the accent of the Imperative

    2 Pl   φέρετε   corresponds to *bhárata* (Class I)

but the accent of

    3 Sg   φερέτω   corresponds to *viśátām* (Class VI) not *bháratām*, which is root-accented.

THEMATIC VERB

	Vedic (Class I)	Greek		PIE
a) Present Active				
Pl 3	bháranti	φέροντι	(Doric)	bhéronti
1	bhárāmas	φέρομες	(Doric)	bhéromes
b) Imperfect Active				
Pl 3	ábharan	ἔφερον	(Attic)	ébheron
1	ábharāma	ἐφέρομεν		ébheromen
c) Present Middle				
Pl 3	bhárante	φέρονται		bhérontei
1	bhárāmahe	φερόμεθα		bhéromeCV

d) Imperfect Middle

    Pl 3   ábharanta   ἐφέροντο   ébheronto
        1   ábharāmahi   ἐφερόμεθα   ébheromeCV

                Vedic (Class VI)

a') Present Active

    Pl 3   viśánti   'enter'
        1   viśámas

b') Imperfect Active

    Pl 3   áviśam
        1   áviśāma

c') Present Middle

    Pl 3   viśánte
        1   viśámahe

d') Imperfect Middle

    Pl 3   áviśanta
        1   áviśāmahi

If we believe that the Vedic columnar accent in the above finite verbal forms continues the PIE accent pattern, these examples would show that Greek moved the PIE accent in thematic verbal forms from the augment to the root, or elsewhere from the augment or the root to the thematic vowel, so that the high pitch in Proto-Greek was always located on the antepenultimate syllable. We can formalize these data using the following abbreviations:

R - monosyllabic root
T - thematic vowel
s - monosyllabic suffix
ss - disyllabic suffix
a - augment

	Proto-Indo-European		Greek
a)	Ŕ T s	a') R Ť s	R̀ T s
	Ŕ T s		R Ť s
b) = b')	á R s		á R s
	à R T s		a R̀ T s
c)	Ŕ T s	c') R Ť s	R̀ T s
	R̀ T s s		R Ť s s
d) = d')	á R T s		a R̀ T s
	à R T s s		a R Ť s s

The Accentual System

Another innovation of Greek is the accent pattern of the Imperfect (if of course Vedic continues the PIE accent pattern). In Proto-Greek the accent pattern of the Imperfect was the same as that of the Present, i.e. it was subject to the same phonological constraint which locates the high pitch on the antepenultimate syllable. On the other hand, in Vedic (and presumably in PIE) the augment was always accented, the augment belonged to a class of 'accentable' morphemes. This statement, of course, needs a further clarification; it seems to be true in many cases, but there are some notable 'exceptions'. First of all, it presupposes the reconstruction of the Proto-Greek thematic paradigm of the Present as follows:

    *phérōmi φέρω
    *phéresi φέρεις
    *phéreti φέρει

with endings like those of the athematic verb:

    *dídōmi δίδωμι
    *dídōsi δίδως
    *dídōti δίδωτι West Greek
         δίδωσι East Greek

The problem here is that -*mi* in the 1st Pers might be only an innovation of Vedic; there is no direct evidence for this reconstruction in Greek dialects to justify *phérōmi* as a Proto-Greek form. Even the reconstruction of the 2nd and 3rd is not universally accepted in traditional books. The reason is that Proto-Greek *phéresi* should yield φέρει, by the 'laws' governing sound changes in Greek ($s \rightarrow h \rightarrow \emptyset$), and Proto-Greek *phéreti* should yield φέρεσι in East Greek ($t \rightarrow s$ in the environment between vowels) and remain unchanged in West Greek. However, such forms are not to be found. This problem was discussed by Kiparsky (1967:109), who argued quite convincingly for Proto-Greek forms *phéresi* and *phéreti* by showing that the 'laws' of sound change did not work inside of this particular paradigm, and derived the historical Greek forms by metathesis (see 5.1, p. 188 ff):

    *-esi → -eis
    *-eti → -eit → -ei

A real 'exception' to the above statement that Greek thematic verbal forms show the high pitch on the antepenultimate syllable is represented by forms with long suffixes, where the accent in non-Aeolic dialects occurs always on the penult, in agreement with historical rule of 'recession'. It is not without interest to realize that all these suffixes (with a single exception) belong to forms of extremely low frequency. These forms are: Imperatives in the 3rd Pers (in both voices and all numbers - Sg, Dual, Pl) and Dual in the 3rd Pers (in both voices) of all historical (augmented) forms. The exception, so far as the frequency count goes, is represented by the 1st Pers Sg in Middle Voice of all historical (augmented) forms, and also Optatives. Here are some examples with corresponding Vedic forms:

Imperfect Act Dual 3rd Pers				ἐφερέτην	ábharatām
"	Mid	"	"	"	ἐφερέσθην	ábharetām
Imperative Act Sg 3rd Pers				φερέτω	bháratu
"	" Dual	"	"	?	bháratām
"	" Pl	"	"	φερόντων	bhárantu
"	Mid Sg	"	"	φερέσθω	bhárantām
"	" Dual	"	"	} φερέσθων	bháretām
"	" Pl	"	"		bhárantām
Imperfect Mid Sg 1st Pers				ἐφερόμην	ábhare
Optative	"	"	"	"	φεροίμην	bháreya
Aorist	"	"	"	"	ἐδειξάμην	ádikṣi 'point'
Optative Aorist Mid Sg 1st Pers				δειξαίμην	vídeya 'find' (asigmatic)

The following conclusions may be drawn from this data:

a) It is obvious that a PIE reconstruction is reasonable in two or three cases only:

<u>Imperfect Active Dual 3rd Pers</u> *ébheretāN
<u>Imperative Active Plural 3rd Pers</u> *bhérontu (Proto-Indic)
                                        *bhéronto (Proto-Greek)

The reconstruction of Proto-Greek is based on the Aeolic (Lesbian) form φέροντον (the final -n is a Greek innovation).

<u>Imperative Active Singular 3rd Pers</u> *bhéretu (Proto-Indic)
                                          *bhéreto (Proto-Greek)

On the basis of Vedic *bhárantām* (Imperative Middle Plural 3rd Pers) the PIE *bhérontāN can be reconstructed. The same PIE form could yield (?) Attic φερόντων (Imperative Active Plural 3rd Pers). However, there is another

The Accentual System

explanation, possibly more convincing. Buck (1955:114) proposed that the ending -ντων, with double pluralization, is a blend of -των (formed from the singular -έτω by the addition of -ν) and -ντω (formed after the 'analogy' of 3rd Pl Indicative -ντι). So it can be said that all the above forms, with the exception of ἐφερέτην and Aeolic φέροντον are innovations of the Hellenic branch, without any direct PIE origin. The same is true about the ending -νμην (1st Pers Sg Middle Voice of all historical forms and optatives). Vedic *ábhare* goes back to PIE *ébherei*.

b) Aeolic dialects are closer to Proto-Indoeuropean in the sense that they did not replace the original short suffix in the 3rd Pers Pl Imp (Aeolic φέροντον = Vedic *bhárantu* = PIE *bhérontu/o*) whereas other dialects replaced this short suffix by the long one, e.g. Attic φερόντων (final -ν in Aeolic, as well as in Attic, represents an East (?) Greek innovation; the *n*-less form φερόντω is well documented by Arcadian, Boeotian, Locrian and Doric dialects).

Aeolic (Lesbian) shows the short suffix even in the 3rd Pers Pl Imp of Middle Voice φέρεσθον (versus Attic φερέσθων); however there is no PIE source for this form (the corresponding Vedic form is *bhárantām*).

In discussing monsyllabic versus disyllabic suffixes, and monosyllabic short versus monosyllabic long suffixes, it is quite interesting to see the long monosyllabic suffix of the 3rd Pers Pl Imp (in both voices) being replaced by a disyllabic suffix. This happened in the period of the spread of the Attic-based Koine through the addition of the Aorist suffix -σαν to the singular ending. This process is observable in later inscriptions in various dialects after about 300 B.C. when φερόντων was replaced by φερέτωσαν (more rarely by φερόντωσαν with double pluralization) and φερέσθων was replaced by φερέσθωσαν.

		Vedic	Greek	PIE
c)	Imperative			
	Dual 2	bháratam	φέρετον	bhéretoN
	3	bháratām	?	bhéretāN(?)
d)	Imperfect			
	Dual 2	ábharatam	ἐφέρετον	ébheretoN
		ábharatām	ἐφερέτην	ébheretāN

s̄ = long suffix

c)

Proto-Indoeuropean	Greek
Ŕ T s	Ŕ T s
Ŕ T s	R T́ s̄

152   Phonological Interpretation of Ancient Greek

d)   á R T s   a Ŕ T s
                      á R T s̄   a R T s̄

The same shift of the PIE columnar accent to the antepenultimate syllable in Proto-Greek occurred also in nominal thematic paradigms. Again, we presuppose that the accent pattern in the following Vedic words represents the original state of things. It should also be noted that the examples given below of nominal inflection are adjectives, where more regularities are to be expected than in nouns.

		Vedic	Homeric Greek	PIE
c)	Sg Nom	úttaras	ὕστερος	útteros
	Gen	úttarasya	ὑστέροιο	útterosjo
c')	Sg Nom	aj́ríyas	ἄγριος	agríos
	Gen	aj́ríyasya	ἀγρίοιο	agríosjo
d)	Sg Nom	bháramānas	φερόμενος	bhéromenos
	Gen	bháramāṇasya	φερομένοιο	bhéromenosjo

We can formalize these data using numbers this time to indicate syllables from the end of the word:

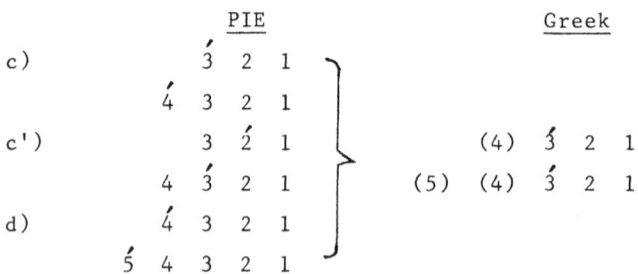

4.3.2 *Three Syllable Rule*

If we evaluate all the preceding data we may formulate the prehistoric ancestor to the general limiting rule, which could be labelled the 'three syllable' rule:

The accent (in polysyllabic verbal and nominal forms) is placed on the antepenultimate syllable.

Or we can reword this rule according to Jakobson's formulation of the historical limiting rule:

The span between the accented and the final syllable cannot exceed one syllable.

All that is meant by this rule is that there was a certain stage in the prehistory of Greek dialects when the location of the accent would be describable (with some exceptions) by the 'three syllable' rule not by its historical descendant

153   The Accentual System

(= general limiting rule). There is a fairly general
agreement among various textbooks on the historical grammar
of Greek as to what this stage looked like. I will give
some well-known examples (reconstructed forms are marked
with an asterisk; double-asterisked forms are controversial,
but essential for my reconstruction of the 'three syllable'
rule):

Proto-Greek ancestor of historical Greek dialects

Thematic Declension	Sg Nom	pʰerómenos	Pl	pʰerómenoi
		pʰeroménoio		**pʰeroménoōn
		*pʰeroménoei		*pʰeroménosi
		pʰerómenon		pʰerómenons
Thematic Conjugation	Sg 1	**pʰérōmi	Pl	pʰéromen/s
	2	*pʰéresi		pʰérete
	3	*pʰéreti		pʰéronti

Later development (*haplology*, *contraction* and *metathesis*)
of these prehistoric forms obliterated the original state of
things and the resulting forms are describable by the
historical limiting rule. We can imagine the sequence of
historical changes from PIE to Greek as shown below:

	Gen Sg	Dat Sg
	pʰéromen+o+sio	pʰéromen+o+ei
Three Syllable rule	pʰeroménoio	pʰeroménoei
Haplology	–	–
Contraction	pʰeroménō	pʰeroménoi
Metathesis	–	–
Raising	pʰeroménǭ	–

	Gen Pl	Dat Pl
	pʰéromen+o+ōn	pʰéromen+o+si
Three Syllable rule	pʰeroménoōn	pʰeroménosi
Haplology	pʰeroménōn	–
Contraction	–	–
Metathesis	–	pʰeroménois(i)
Raising	–	–

Doric forms² compared with Attic show the effects of
analogical levelling of paradigms:

Attic	Doric		
ἐλάβομεν	ἐλάβομεν	'we took'	
ἔλαβον	ἔλαβον	'they took'	
φερόμενοι	φερομένοι	'carried'	(Masc Pl)
φερομένη	φερομένᾱ	'carried'	(Fem Sg)

154   Phonological Interpretation of Ancient Greek

We may imagine the sequence of historical changes
(= metatonies) as follows:

	élabomen	élabon(t)	
Three Syllable rule	elábomen	-	
General Limiting rule	-	-	
Accent Levelling	-	elábon	Doric
	pʰéromenoi	pʰéromenā	
Three Syllable rule	pʰéromenoi	pʰerómenā	
General Limiting rule	-	pʰeroménā	Attic
Accent Levelling	pʰeroménoi	-	Doric

In the case of contracted stems there is no need for the
'three syllable rule', or, rather in this case the 'three
syllable rule' is the same as the general limiting rule.
This can be demonstrated by the derivational history of the
following forms:

	Attic	Doric	
Sg Nom	δοῦλος	δῶλος	'slave'
Gen	δούλου	δώλω	
Pl Nom	παῖδες	παίδες	'boys'
Gen	παίδων	παιδῶν³	

	dówelos	dóweloio		
General Limiting rule	-	dowéloio		
$w \to \emptyset / V - V$	dóelos	doéloio		
Contraction	dóolos	doóloo	Attic /dô̹los/	/dô̹lō̹/
Accent Levelling	doólos	doóloo	Doric /dǒ̹los/	/dǒ̹lō̹/
	páwides	páwidoon		
General Limiting rule	-	pawídoon		
$w \to \emptyset / V - V$	páides	paídoon	Attic /pâides/	/paídō̹n/
Accent Levelling	paídes	paidóon	Doric /paídes/	/paidǒ̹n/

Summarizing this discussion, I suggest the following
tentative sketch of the historical development of the Greek
accent pattern in terms of the sequence of metatonies from
PIE:

	Attic-(Ionic) (mora accent)	Aeolic (syllable accent)	Doric (syllable accent)
(1)	three syllable rule	three syllable rule	three syllable rule
(2)	general limiting rule	general limiting rule	general limiting rule
(3)	minor rules		accent levelling⁴

PIE ancestor of Greek	*élabomen	*élabont
	*phéromenoi	*phéromenā

prehistoric 'three syllable' rule

Proto-Greek	elábomen	élabon
	pherómenoi	*pherómenā

general limiting rule

Historical Greek Dialects	elábomen	élabon	Attic-Ionic	ἐλάβομεν–ἔλαβον
	pherómenoi	pheroménā	Aeolic	φερόμενοι–φcρομένη

analogical accent levelling

ἐλάβομεν–ἐλάβον   Doric
φερομένοι–φερομένᾱ

4.3.3 Analogical Accent Levelling

The phenomenon of analogical accent levelling, which presumably was so important in the formation of Doric paradigms, is also well-documented in Attic in both *nominal* and *verbal* inflection of contracted forms. One may contrast the inflection of ἄξιος 'worthy' with the inflection of contracted εὔνους 'well-disposed', and the inflection of Imperfect ἔλυον 'I unbound' with the inflection of contracted ἐφίλουν 'I loved':

			contracted forms	uncontracted forms
Sg	Nom	ἄξιος	εὔνους	εὔνοος
	Gen	ἀξίου	εὔνου	εὐνόου[5]
	Dat	ἀξίῳ	εὔνῳ	εὐνόῳ[5]
	Acc	ἄξιον	εὔνουν	εὔνοον
Sg	1	ἔλυον	ἐφίλουν	ἐφίλεον
	2	ἔλυες	ἐφίλεις	ἐφίλεες
	3	ἔλυε	ἐφίλει	ἐφίλεε
Pl	1	ἐλύομεν	ἐφιλοῦμεν	ἐφιλέομεν
	2	ἐλύετε	ἐφιλεῖτε	ἐφιλέετε
	3	ἔλυον	ἐφίλουν	ἐφίλεον

The question which arises is why speakers of Attic retracted the accent in εὔνου (from εὐνόου), but did not in ἐφιλεῖτε (from ἐφιλέετε); the form *ἐφίλειτε does not exist.

In other words, if we claim that speakers of Attic could synchronically recover ἐφιλέετε (or that ἐφιλεῖτε was for them underlyingly ἐφιλέετε, see under 4.2.1), we have to explain why they failed to do the same in the case of Gen Sg εὔνου since if they did not the resulting form would be *εὐνοῦ. As demonstrated by Kuryłowicz (1945-49) — and more recently by Antilla (1972:88-108) — examples like this

necessitate the introduction of some principle which would
be independent of phonology; a principle which is well-known
in traditional grammar under the label of analogical levelling
and whose effects are usually termed paradigm coherence.
Notice that this principle presupposes the notion of
'paradigm' as something psychologically real, the operational
locus of analogical levelling.

	Uncontracted forms	phonologically 'proper' forms		analogical levelling
Sg Nom	εὔνοος	εὔνους		εὔνους
Gen	εὐνόου	*εὐνοῦ	⟶	εὔνου
Dat	εὐνόῳ	*εὐνῷ	⟶	εὔνῳ
Acc	εὔνοον	εὔνουν		εὔνουν

Given the nature of our documents it is hard to say
whether the phonologically 'proper' forms εὐνοῦ and εὐνῷ were
actually prevented from occurring or whether they really
resulted and were leveled out by analogy with other members
of the paradigm (Nom and Acc) and other disyllabic adjectives.
The same situation obtains in plural where forms such as Gen
*εὐνῶν and Dat *εὐνοῖς are not found. It may be noted that
the actually documented form εὔνοων breaches the general
limiting rule. Put shortly, εὔνους behaves like any other
disyllabic uncontracted paroxytone in that it keeps the
accent columnarly in all forms on the penult (e.g. φίλος
'dear', Gen Sg φίλου).

A more abstract solution could require a reconstruction
of the thematic vowel (as in thematic nouns) and both Gen
and Dat Sg would then be derived from *eúno+ojo and *eúno+oei
by haplology.

	Sg Nom	Sg Gen	Sg Dat	Sg Acc
		eúnoojo	eúnooei	
Haplology	eúnoos	eúnojo	eúnoei	eúnoon
Contraction	eúnōs	eúnō	eúnōi	eúnōn
Raising	eúnọ̄s	eúnọ̄	-	eúnọ̄n

It should also be noted that the phonologically 'proper'
forms would be homophonous with some forms of the verb
εὐνῶ (<εὐνάω) 'send to sleep':

*εὐνῷ   'well-disposed' (Dat Sg) versus εὐνῶ 'I send to sleep'
*εὐνῶν   "   (Gen Pl)   εὐνῶν (<εὐνάων)   "
                                                  (Participle)

Thus it could be that the proportional analogy with disyllabic adjectives prevented forms which would be accented on the ultima from occurring (the accent in disyllabic adjectives remains on the initial syllable even in the Gen Pl Fem):

$$\frac{ph\acute{i}los}{ph\acute{i}lo\bar{\empty}} = \frac{e\acute{u}n\bar{o}s}{x}$$

The case of contract verbs is just the opposite. The application of the limiting rule would cause anomaly in the sense that the accent would be distributed columnarly in all forms of the Imperfect. This would contradict the accent pattern of Attic, which shows a characteristic regressive accent in the Imperfect, Perfect and Aorist Active, where a dissyllabic ending appears. The shift of accent one place to the end characterizes the plural paradigm versus the singular paradigm (1st and 2nd Pers):

	Singular	versus	Plural
1	ἔλυον		ἐλύομεν
2	ἔλυες		ἐλύετε
1	ἐφίλουν		ἐφιλοῦμεν
2	ἐφίλεις		ἐφιλεῖτε

This pattern of course would be blatantly breached by forms (which in a sense are 'proper' phonologically): *ἐφιλούμεν and *ἐφιλεῖτε. The same was probably true of Doric. Compare the reconstructed Doric paradigms:

2nd Aorist

	Attic	Doric	Hellenistic
Sg 1	ἔλαβον	ἔλαβον	ἔλαβον
2	ἔλαβες	ἔλαβες	ἔλαβες
3	ἔλαβε	ἔλαβε	ἔλαβε
Pl 1	ἐλάβομεν	ἐλάβομεν	ἐλάβομεν
2	ἐλάβετε	ἐλάβετε	ἐλάβετε
3	ἔλαβον	ἐλάβον	ἐλάβοσαν[6]

Contract Verbs – Imperfect

	Attic	Doric	Hellenistic
Sg 1	ἐφίλουν	ἐφίλιον	ἐφίλουν
2	ἐφίλεις	ἐφίλιες	ἐφίλεις
3	ἐφίλει	ἐφίλιε	ἐφίλει
Pl 1	ἐφιλοῦμεν	ἐφιλίομες	ἐφιλοῦμεν
2	ἐφιλεῖτε	ἐφιλίετε	ἐφιλεῖτε
3	ἐφίλουν	ἐφιλίον	ἐφιλοῦσαν[6]

As seen from the paradigms, Attic ἔλαβον was ambiguous (it could mean either 'I took' or 'they took'). In Doric dialects the 1st Pers Sg was accented on the antepenult but the 3rd Pers Pl on the penult ἐλάβον 'they took'. The situation

in contract verbs is similar. In Attic verbal inflections
the accent always recedes to its full limits but in Doric
dialects the accent is typically 'progressive' in the 3rd
Pers Pl. It may be noted that both situations are anomalous
for different reasons. Attic paradigms are regular phonologically (in that the accent always recedes to its full
limits) but irregular morphologically since the plural
paradigms have mobile accent. On the other hand, Doric
paradigms are regular morphologically in that the accent is
immobilized (on the augment in singular and on the root in
plural), but irregular phonologically (the accent could still
recede one syllable leftwards in the 3rd Pl).

Hellenistic Greek solved anomalies of both Attic and Doric
systems by borrowing the ending of the sigmatic Aorist -san.
The extra-syllable in ἐλάβοσαν made it possible to keep the
accent on the root (as in Doric plural paradigms) satisfying
in the same time the recessive accent of verbal system (as
in Attic).

It is of interest to observe a similar tug of war between
phonology and morphology in Modern Greek. In Modern Greek
past tenses the augment is lost if unstressed - this happens
in the 1st and 2nd Pl but there are two forms in the 3rd Pers:

Sg 1   égrafa   'I wrote'   Pl   gráfame
   2   égrafas   gráfate
   3   égrafe   égrafan or gráfane

The phonologically proper 3rd Pl *égrafan* with its mobile
accent (see Attic ἔλαβον) is paradigmatically irregular.
This irregularity can be liquidated only by the adoption of
an extra-syllable *(e)gráfan-e* (as in Hellenistic ἐλάβο-σαν),
which allows all plural forms to have accent on the root.
The elaboration of the same data in derivational terms
results in various difficulties; the starting point is
élabōnt:

	Attic	Doric
	élabōnt	élabōnt
Osthoff's Law	élabont	-
$t \to \emptyset\ /\ -\#$	élabon	élabōn
Metatony	-	elábōn
Shortening	-	elábon

First of all, *'Osthoff's Law'* (= a long vowel is shortened
in the environment before a liquid, nasal or glide followed
by an obstruent) must be invoked. This will apply in Attic
but not in Doric. Second, a shortening of the long vowel in
elábōn must be assumed. It might seem that there is some

evidence for such a shortening - see the 3rd Pl of Passive
Aorist ἐλύθην (Homeric), ἐλύθεν (in dialects) versus Attic
ἐλύθησαν - however, these forms can be derived by *Osthoff's
Law* and the *loss of final -t* as well:

	Homeric	dialects
	elúth$\bar{\text{e}}$nt	elúth$\bar{\text{e}}$nt
Osthoff's Law	-	elúthent
$t \rightarrow \emptyset\ /\ -\ \#$	elúth$\bar{\text{e}}$n	elúthen

If we prefer to get rid of '*Osthoff's Law*', we can start,
as Kuryłowicz[7] does, with *élab$\bar{\text{o}}$n:

	Attic	Doric
	élab$\bar{\text{o}}$n	élab$\bar{\text{o}}$n
Metatony	-	elább$\bar{\text{o}}$n
Shortening	élabon	elábon

However, there is no evidence whatever for such a shortening.

That the processual description can be remote from both
synchronic and historical (= metachronic) reality can be
demonstrated when it comes to the derivation of forms with
the Aorist ending -σαν. Here are some more data:

Attic	Homeric	Doric
ἔλυσαν		ἔλυσαν
ἔφασαν		ἔφασαν
ἔστησαν	ἔσταν	ἐστάσαν
ἐφιλήθησαν	ἐφιλήθην	ἐφιλάθεν

Note also the derivation of ἔστησαν 'they stood':

	Homeric	Attic	Doric
	éstānt	éstāsānt	éstāsānt
Osthoff's Law	éstant	éstāsant	-
$t \rightarrow \emptyset$	éstan	éstāsan	éstāsān
Metatony	-	-	está́sān
Shortening	-	-	está́san
Fronting	-	éstǣsan	-
Raising	-	estēsan	-

As shown by Homeric ἔσταν, the ending -σαν was adopted
later on (note however Homeric ἔσαν, Attic ἦσαν 'they were'
versus West Greek ἦν). In other words, the processual
description above is clearly fallacious since it only
repeats the history of Aorist ending -σαν (<*sānt). Synchronically, however, -σαν was adopted as a new unanalyzed marker
of the 3rd Pl of historical tenses. What is most remarkable

is the fact that this adoption took place several times in
the history of Greek, in preclassical times and Hellenistic
times, and as we have seen, a similar adoption of an extra
syllable in the 3rd Pl is known also in Modern Greek.

  West Greek ἦ+ν   Attic   ἔλαβο+ν
  Attic-Ionic ἦ+σαν   Hellenistic ἐλάβο+σαν

Here the reason for the adoption of the new ending −σαν seems
to be pretty obvious. The Homeric form ἔσταν 'they stood'
was quite inconvenient since if used without the augment
it was homonymous with the Neuter Participle στάν (Masc στάς).
The same is true about West Greek ἦν 'they were' which would
be homonymous with 'I was' and 'he was' in Attic.

 Thus it might be argued that the processual description
given below is more adequate in that it corresponds more
closely to what really happened in the history of Greek:

	Attic	Doric
	éstānt+san	éstānt+san
Osthoff's Law	éstantsan	éstantsan
$t \rightarrow \emptyset$	éstansan	éstansan
$n \rightarrow \emptyset$		
+ Compensatory Lengthening	éstāsan	éstāsan
Metatony	−	estā́san
Fronting	éstæsan	−
Raising	éstẹsan	

 Notice that in this derivational schema the metatony in
Doric is not due to the operation of the general limiting
rule, but it is simply a result of the analogical levelling
with other members of the plural paradigm (ἐστάσαμεν,
ἐστάσατε).

  4.4 CIRCUMFLEX IN FINAL SYLLABLES OF THEMATIC NOUNS

 Many linguists would agree that the circumflex on the
penult results from prehistoric contractions. On the other
hand, there is a considerable disagreement in older literature regarding the origin of the circumflex in final syllables. The classical theory, found in Schwyzer (1939:382),
goes back to Brugmann and Hirt and is a back-projection of
the Greek or Lithuanian situation to Proto-Indoeuropean −
the difference between acute and circumflex existed already
in the proto-language, subsequently it was lost everywhere
with the exception of Greek and Balto-Slavic branches.

 As was known long ago, there are correspondences in accent
contours in final syllables between Greek (Attic) and
Lithuanian. However, the phonetic values of the 'acute' and
'circumflex' are exactly reversed:

The Accentual System

	'acute'	'circumflex'
Attic	rising	falling
Lithuanian	falling	rising

Note the following data:

	Lithuanian		Attic	
Sg Nom	mergá	/-á/	τῑμή	/-eé/
Gen	mergõs	/-oós/	τῑμῆς	/-ées/
Pl Gen	mergų̃	/-uú/	τῑμῶν	/-óon/
Acc	mergàs	/-ás/	τῑμάς	/-aás/

In the older literature there was considerable disagreement as to which represents the more original state of things: the Lithuanian or the Attic pattern. Proponents of the distinction acute ~ circumflex in the final syllable in Proto-Indoeuropean alternatively explained both branches from PIE by assuming that either Lithuanian or Greek underwent a sound change (= metatony), which reversed the original accent contour in final syllables.

Kuryłowicz (1958) demonstrated that such an assumption is wholly unnecessary, since both Greek and Balto-Slavic accent contours are of secondary origin, and he views the original Proto-Indo-European system as a Vedic-like system without any distinctive oppositions of contour.

According to Kiparsky (1973:830) the correspondence of Greek falling to Lithuanian rising accent is not due to any metatony, but to the shift from central to marginal mobility. He demonstrates it in the moraic analysis of Lithuanian, where his starting point is a system like that of Attic with the IE rules producing contour accents.[8]

However, it is quite obvious that the circumflex accent in the final syllable of $\bar{a}$ - stems is a Greek innovation resulting from early contraction processes (as in the case of contractions taking place inside the word), which are distinct from the later Greek contractions. Compare the following Greek and Sanskrit forms with hypothetical reconstructions of Proto-Greek:

	Greek (Attic)		Proto-Greek	Vedic	
Sg Nom	τῑμή	contraction	tīmá	kanyá̄	'girl'
Gen	τῑμῆς	←	tīmájes	kanyá̄yās	
Dat	τῑμῇ	←	tīmájei	kanyá̄yai	
Acc	τῑμήν		tīmán	kanyá̄m	
Pl Nom	τῑμαί			kanyá̄s	
Gen	τῑμῶν	←	tīmáōn	kanyá̄nām	
Dat	τῑμᾶσι	(Early Attic)	tīmási	kanyá̄su	(Loc)
Acc	τῑμάς		tīmáns	kanyá̄s	

The traditional assumption that the circumflex in Greek inflections originates from prehistoric contractions is undeniably correct. As the Vedic evidence indicates, the Proto-Greek ancestor of the Attic inflections with circumflex was always disyllabic: *ᾰ́es → ᾶs, *ᾰ́ei → ᾶi; thus the resulting circumflex is the only possible accent. While the contractions in Gen and Dat Sg are prehistoric (i.e. the disyllabic forms of endings are prehistoric forms, which are not synchronically recoverable), the contraction of the disyllabic form in the Gen Pl Fem was a contemporary process in many of the Greek dialects.[9]

It is most unfortunate that we do not know enough about the accentuation of thematic inflections in other dialects. If on the basis of what we know about the accent pattern of Lesbian and Doric we undertake the reconstruction of the paradigm in these two dialectal groups, we might hypothesize that the split in contour accent between the strong and weak cases (Nom, Acc versus Gen, Dat) existed only in Ionic dialects:[10]

	Ionic		Aeolic		Doric	
Sg Nom	τεή	τῑμή	τεή	τίμη	τεά	τῑμά
Acc	τεήν	τῑμήν	τεήν	τίμην	τεάν	τῑμάν
Gen	τεῆς	τῑμῆς	τεῆς	τίμης	τεᾶ	τῑμᾶς
Dat	τεῆι	τῑμῆ	τεῆι	τίμη	τεᾶι	τῑμᾶι

It is worth mentioning in this connection that even Attic had paradigms which do not show the split in contour accent - these are paradigms of contract nouns like μνᾶ 'mina', σῡκῆ 'fig-tree':

	Attic		uncontracted
Sg Nom	μνᾶ	σῡκῆ	σῡκέα
Acc	μνᾶν	σῡκῆν	σῡκέαν
Gen	μνᾶς	σῡκῆς	σῡκέας
Dat	μνᾷ	σῡκῇ	σῡκέαι

Other dialects have uncontracted forms:

Ionic   μνέα, σῡκέη
Doric   σῡκία (with height dissimilation eā → iā).

On the basis of dialectal evidence we may assume that contractions responsible for the circumflex in Attic contract nouns (and adjectives) took place in historical times.

Thus the thematic oxytones with their accent pattern resulting from the prehistoric contractions were synchronically anomalous. This is manifest in the following survey:

The Accentual System

Sg					
Nom	βασίλεια	σφαῖρα	χώρα	συκῆ	θεά
Acc	βασίλειαν	σφαῖραν	χώραν	συκῆν	θεάν
Gen	βασιλείας	σφαίρας	χώρας	συκῆς	θεᾶς
Dat	βασιλείᾳ	σφαίρᾳ	χώρᾳ	συκῇ	θεᾷ

a) Thematic proparoxytones (βασίλεια) and properispomenons (σφαῖρα) show the *rightward* shift of accent in weak cases according to the general limiting rule. b) Paroxytones (χώρα) and perispomenons (συκῆ) keep the accent distributed *columnarly* in both strong and weak cases. However, c) oxytones (θεά) show the *leftward* shift of accent in weak cases:[11]

                                                   accent shift

a) Strong cases   3́ 22 1   2́2 1
   Weak cases   3 22́ 1   22́ 11   rightward
b) Strong cases   22́ 11 (22) 1́1
   Weak cases   22́ 11 (22) 1́1   ∅
c) Strong cases   (22) 11́
   Weak cases   (22) 1́1   leftward

How realistic is the assumption that the description in (b) and (c) corresponds to what was really heard in colloquial Attic? Did speakers really have the contrast between the acute in θεά and the circumflex in θεᾶς if they did not in the same environment in συκῆ/συκῆς?

We know from the living tone-accent languages that contour contrasts on the ultima are extremely rare. They do not exist in Serbo-Croatian i.e. Štokavian (see under 4.6); in Lithuanian, there are minimal pairs involving rare grammatical contrasts such as Dat vs. Instr Dual (e.g. *galvóm* vs. *galvõm*), which are limited to the literary language.

Obviously, the contrast between the acute and circumflex on the ultima is possible only in a phrase, since the realization of the rising tone requires a disyllabic sequence; for instance, in connection with enclitics we see the following:

θεάς	τινας	/tʰeás + tìnas/	'some goddesses' (Acc Pl) vs.
θεᾶς	τινος	/tʰeâs + tinos/	'of a goddess' (Gen Sg)
θεά	τις	/tʰeá + tìs/	'a goddess' (Nom Sg) vs.
θεᾷ	τινι	/tʰeâ + tini/	'to a goddess' (Dat Sg)

Similar examples indicate that speakers of Attic may have relied on the contrast between rising and falling pitch even on the ultima of polysyllabic words at phrase level. The tonal criteria could, of course, be easily overridden by segmental contrasts in other syntactic collocations, e.g. with the definite article:

ἡ θεά	/hē̜ + t^heā́/	'the goddess' vs.
τῇ θεᾷ	/tē̜̂ + t^heā̂î̯/	'to the goddess'
τὰς θεάς	/tās + t^heā́s/	'the goddesses' vs.
τῆς θεᾶς	/tē̂s + t^heā̂s/	'of the goddess'

It may be noted that in certain Doric dialects (e.g. Laconian, Heraclean), which simplified the cluster *-ns* in the Acc Pl and lengthened the preceding vowel (see under 2.5.2), the latter pair would be homophonous even with the article, e.g. Laconian τᾱ́ς θεᾱ́ς (Acc Pl = Gen Sg).

It is tempting to hypothesize that for many speakers of colloquial Attic similar forms could be homophonous. Of course, it is beyond the capacity of historical linguistics to say something more specific about local prosodic systems within other dialects and even more difficult to indicate when the contour contrasts on the ultima ceased to represent something psychologically real. (This problem has to be discussed in connection with the overall disintegration of the tone-accent typology of Ancient Greek, which could have taken place earlier than the end of the Graeco-Roman period, see Bubeník (1979)). The resulting homophony of certain grammatical forms was no problem (certainly not in 'strict' Doric dialects and Lesbian) since the grammatical contrasts were always indicated by syntactic collocations. Furthermore, such grammatical homophones actually occurred elsewhere in the Attic nominal system of contract nouns μνᾶς 'mina' Gen Sg = Acc Pl; ἁπλοῦς 'simple' Nom Sg = Acc Pl.

The issue centres around the problem of synchronic recoverability of underlying disyllabic forms, which could justify the circumflex. Whereas in the case of contract nouns (σῡκῆς < σῡκέας) or adjectives (χρῡσῆς < χρῡσέας) the disyllabic forms were synchronically recoverable (at least in the sense that here the contractions were recent, or that many dialects did not carry them out), the circumflex in the inflections of thematic feminines had to be learnt separately by each new generation as a new linguistic symbol - here the circumflex was 'underlying'. In any case, the contractions in the Gen and Dat Sg of the 1st Declension were older than 13/14th c. B.C. (Mycenaean evidence in Vilborg (1960:65)). What is of particular interest is the fact that we have to reckon with contemporary contractions in the Gen Pl of the same declension (ψυχάων < ψυχῶν). The Dat ψυχαῖς could have resulted from the early Attic *-ā̂si* → *-ais* by metathesis (see under 5.1).

Thus we may conclude that it was not impossible for contours to function contrastively on the ultima at the sentence level (oxytones pronounced in isolation would, of course, sound identical with perispomenons). Since typological parallels from living tone-accent languages indicate that this contrast is extremely rare, the question still remains: When Alexandrian grammarians introduced the acute in strong cases and the circumflex in weak cases did they really 'hear' the difference in the contour? And if they did, was the contrast fairly common or found only in the speech of grammarians who knew how to read Homeric poems correctly? There is still one more possibility: namely, that these marks could have been introduced on the basis of analogy of the masculine oxytones of the 2nd Declension, where the acute in strong cases was the only possible accent.

That it is perfectly possible for a feminine form to have the accent of its masculine counterpart by analogy is clearly shown by adjectives:

		Masculine	Feminine
Sg	Nom	δίκαιος	δικαία
	Gen	δικαίου	δικαίας
Pl	Nom	δίκαιοι ⟶	δίκαιαι
	Gen	δικαίων ⟶	δικαίων

While the masculine forms show a regular rightward shift of accent according to the general limiting rule, in the feminine instead of expected *δικαῖαι we find the analogical form δίκαιαι, and instead of expected *δικαιῶν we find δικαίων with the accent of the masculine counterparts.

The same analogical extension is found in adjectives which are accented on the long penult like δῆλος 'visible'. In the Gen Pl Fem the accent is not the expected *δηλῶν but rather δήλων, which again is the accent of the masculine. In other words, these forms show the very same leftward shift of accent as θεά. If the operation of analogy in the accentuation of θεά might seem hard to believe, there are very good reasons for analogical extensions in the accentuation of feminine adjectives:

	expected forms	cf.	actual forms
Nom Sg	δικαία	χώρα	δικαία
Nom Pl	*δικαῖαι	χῶραι	δίκαιαι
Gen Pl	*δικαιῶν	χωρῶν	δικαίων

Adjectival forms predicted on the basis of the nominal forms would include *δικαῖαι (Nom Pl) and *δικαιῶν (Gen Pl). Instead of this three-way distribution of high pitch we find the accent fixed on the penult with the exceptional shift leftwards in the Nom Pl. This is a typical accent pattern of the feminine adjectives, which is without parallel in the nominal inflection. This may be shown in the following survey of the distribution of the accent in feminine nouns and adjectives:

		Location of accent	Contour	
NOUN (FEMININE)	βασίλεια	antepenult	acute	Sg N,A; Pl N
		penult	acute	Sg G,D; Pl A,D
	σφαῖρα	penult	acute	Sg G,D; Pl A,D
		ultima	circumflex	Pl G
	χώρα	penult	circumflex	Pl N
		penult	acute	Sg N,A,G,D; Pl A,D
		ultima	circumflex	Pl G
	θεά }	ultima	circumflex	Sg G,D; Pl G,D
ADJECTIVE (FEMININE)	καλή }	ultima	acute	Sg N,A; Pl N,A
	δικαία	antepenult	acute	Pl N
		penult	acute	Sg N,A,G,D; Pl A,G,D
(MASCULINE) NOUN	δίκαιος }	antepenult	acute	Sg N,A; Pl N
	ἄνθρωπος }	penult	acute	Sg G,D; Pl A,G,D

As this survey shows, there are two possible sources of the analogical extension of the antepenult accentuation in the feminine plural forms: the masculine adjectival counterpart (δίκαιοι → δίκαιαι) or feminine nominal pattern (βασίλειαι → δίκαιαι). We may favour the first source since the Gen Pl Fem δικαίων is definitely adopted from the masculine paradigm.

Actually, it may be argued that the analogical extension took place only in the Gen Pl since historically the leftward shift of accent in both Masc and Fem Nom Pl may be described by Vendryes' Law (see under 4.2.1): Old Attic *δικαῖοι → Classical Attic δίκαιοι. The Doric form δικαίοι preserves the original location of accent.

Kuryłowicz's theory (1958 and 1968) regarding the origins of the circumflex in the final syllables of thematic nouns is based on the assumption that the regular accent on a long vowel or diphthong is an acute, while the circumflex appeared as a result of analogy with the circumflex that developed in other declensions. In his 1958 theory the analogical source is the contracted paradigm of s-stems, e.g. *dusmenḗs* 'evil-minded' – where the -s- was aspirated intervocalically, -h- was lost, and the preceding -e- underwent contraction with the vowel of the ending – the resulting circumflex was analogically transferred to the $\bar{a}$- and o-stems. The table demonstrates these analogical extensions:

The Accentual System

	s-stems		o-stems	ā-stems
	uncontracted	contracted (after s→h→∅/V-V)		
Sg Nom	dusmenḗs	dusmenḗs	agrós	tʰeā́
Acc	dusmenésa	dusmenē̃	agrón	tʰeā́n
Gen	dusmenésos	dusmenō̃s →	agrō̃	tʰeā̃s
Dat	dusmenési	dusmenei̯ →	agrō̃i	tʰeā̃i
Pl Nom	dusmenéses	dusmeneîs	agroí	tʰeaí
Acc	dusménesens	dusmeneîs	agrós	tʰeā́s
Gen	dusmenéson	dusmenō̃n →	agrō̃n	tʰeō̃n
Dat	dusménessi	dusmenési	agroîs	tʰeaîs
Dual N/A	dusmenése	dusmeneî	agrṓ	tʰeā́
G/D	dusmenésoin	dusmenoîn →	agroîn	tʰeaîn

As this table shows, only half of the forms (those connected with arrows) can be accounted for in a such way. Consequently, Kuryłowicz is forced to assume various constraints on analogical process, which are sometimes hard to believe. Thus Acc Sg Fem should be *tʰeā̃n* (cf. *dusmenē̃*) but the final nasal is supposed to block the analogy. This assumption is totally unnecessary, since the acute in *tʰeā́n* is actually analogical with the acute in Acc Sg Masc *agrón*, where the acute in the final syllable is the only possible accent. On the other hand, Acc Pl Fem cannot be explained in such a way; according to Kuryłowicz's analogy with s-stems, the Acc Pl of both genders should have circumflex in the final syllable (cf. *dusmeneîs*) - this time the operation of analogy is supposed to be blocked by the vowel differences. The Nom/Acc Dual did not develop an analogical circumflex because the dual is rather a derivational category.

Kiparsky's theory (1973:794 ff) regarding the origins of the circumflex accent in the final syllables of thematic nouns in Greek is based on the hypothesis that thematic and athematic nouns (belonging to the group of basically unaccented words) are accented by exactly the same rules, even if they receive superficially different accent patterns. These rules are:

1) Strong cases have presuffixal accent
2) Weak cases have post-stem accent

The derivations of πόδα (Acc Sg), ποδός (Gen Sg) 'foot' and φυγήν (Acc Sg), φυγῆς (Gen Sg) 'flight' according to Kiparsky are given below:

```
    pod + a      phug + ee + n    pod + os      phug + ee + s
1   pód + a      phug + eé + n
2                                 pod + ós      phug + ée + s
```

In athematic nouns, the alternation between presuffixal and post-stem accent produces a shift in the location of the accent from the stem to the ending, while in the thematic nouns the thematic vowel 'intercepts' both the presuffixal and the post-stem accent (i.e. the accent does not move but merely changes its contour from acute to circumflex).

Basically two objections can be raised against this proposal. First of all, the statement that theme-accented stems are related to movable athematic nouns is *true only for a part of the Greek dialectal world,* namely the Attic-Ionic dialect, whereas this statement is a misrepresentation in Aeolic and Doric dialects. There are no theme-accented stems (oxytones) in Aeolic and oxytones in Doric do not show the change in contour from acute to circumflex - consequently there can be no relationship between theme-accented stems and movable athematic stems in Aeolic or Doric dialects. In addition, there are in fact no movable athematic stems in Aeolic (admittedly, this is only a hypothesis based on what we know about the accentuation of the Lesbian dialect).[12] Compare the following data:

	Acc Sg	Gen Sg	Acc Sg	Gen Sg
Attic-Ionic	πόδα	ποδός	φυγήν	φυγῆς
Aeolic	πόδα	πόδος	φύγην	φύγης
Doric	πόδα	ποδός	φυγάν	φυγᾱ́ς
Attic-Ionic	CV́CV	CVCV́C	CVCV́VC	CVCV̂VC
Aeolic		CV́CV(V)(C)		
Doric	CV́CV		CVCV́C	

The second point is that only mora analysis can show that the change in contour from acute to circumflex (VV́ → V́V) is a movement of accent. However, as rightly pointed out by Martinet (1954:51), the syllable corresponds to a phonetic reality whereas the same is not true for the mora, which is a purely analytic descriptive device. In other words, if a shift in the location of the accent from the stem to the ending in πόδα-ποδός represents a psychologically real process, the change from acute to circumflex does not necessarily entail the breaking down of long vowels into psychologically real components: moras. Consequently, even in Attic-Ionic there is no relationship between theme-accented stems and movable thematic stems, at least in that sense, that these two phenomena are not comparable on the same level.

169   The Accentual System

The whole issue centres around the problem of how speakers of Attic interpreted synchronically the strong/weak accentual pattern πόδα ~ ποδός which represented an archaic survival from PIE. There could be two ways (at least):

i) According to Kiparsky they could realize that the accentual relationship between the mobile athematic nouns and thematic oxytones is reversed:

    strong case   πόδα   θεά
    weak case   ποδός   θεᾶς

ii) They could relate the rightward accent shift in the mobile athematic nouns to that of all other thematic nouns (with the exception of the contract nouns), as shown above:

    strong case   πόδα ——— βασίλεια, ἄνθρωπος
    weak case   ποδός — βασιλείας, ἀνθρώπου

The first hypothesis depends mainly on the psychological reality of tonal contrasts on the ultima; the latter hypothesis depends on the likelihood of the relatability of the penult-ultima allomorphy found in the athematic nouns and the antepenult-penult allomorphy of the thematic nouns. It may be noted, however, that the thematic nouns behave 'normally', i.e. they are accented according to the general limiting rule, whereas athematic monosyllables are highly marked in that the accent could still move one syllable leftwards in weak cases. Obviously, both hypotheses are highly speculative and aim ultimately at deriving accented forms from underlying unaccented ones. Let us emphasize again that only speakers with the contrast acute-circumflex on the ultima would be able to relate this pattern to that of either mobile athematic nouns or other thematic nouns. It also means that when the tonal system of Ancient Greek started changing its typology toward a stress-accent system the relatability was automatically out of question. We do not know when this happened in the Attic-based Hellenistic Koine, but the fact is that this problem was never faced by the speakers of Doric and Aeolic dialects. Finally, I think it is needless to say that even if we manage to derive πόδα ~ ποδός and φυγήν ~ φυγῆς by the same rule for a certain group of speakers we still do not explain the phenomenon of the shift of accent in athematic nouns.[13]

4.5   FUNCTION OF ACCENT IN ANCIENT GREEK DIALECTS

If the accent constantly occurs at a certain point in the word, it fulfills a demarcative function. It was especially in Aeolic (Lesbian) that this function was clearly pronounced, since the location of the accent in all full words was invariably fixed by the general limiting rule, i.e. the high pitch always receded to its full limit.[14] (Among living languages the Lesbian accent pattern is reminiscent of that found in certain Madeconian dialects which stress automatically the antepenult, e.g. *vodénica* 'mill' - *vodenícata* 'the mill').

This becomes more obvious if we compare the situation in Attic, where the accent also fulfilled a demarcative function by virtue of the same rule but only in the verbal system; nominal and quasi-nominal forms have to be described as underlyingly accented. Among quasi-nominal forms the most notable cases are the following: the Verbal Adjective in -*tós* (ἀγαπητός 'loveable'), the Perfect Participle Middle in -*ménos*, and the Participle and the Infinitive of the 2nd Aorist (λιπών, λιπεῖν 'leave'). It can be said that in these cases one of the functions of the accent was to indicate the morphological structure of these words. Attic dialect by using accent 'freely' could maximize its morphological contrasts whereas Aeolic had to rely only on segmental contrasts.

Attic nouns have to be classified as underlyingly accented on the ultima, penult or antepenult, e.g. σοφός 'wise', ποταμός 'river', φίλος 'friend', ἄνθρωπος 'man'. All these form belong to a set of nominatives of the 2nd Declension but they are accented differently. We may say that the accent is a lexical property of these nouns, which means that each generation of speakers had to learn the accent separately. A look at the words in Aeolic σόφος, πόταμος, φίλος, ἄνθρωπος reveals that here the accent is describable automatically by the general limiting rule. As expressed neatly by Garde (1968:148) 'in Lesbian the law of limitation becomes the law of fixation'. (Generativists would say that Lesbian accent is completely unmarked in the lexicon, whereas in Attic the accent has to be marked for nouns and quasi-nominals).

Consequently it may be said with Garde (1968:148) that the concept of 'mora' is irrelevant in Aeolic, since only syllables are essential to accentual description. From the viewpoint of the demarcative function of accent, cases such as 'accentable' monosyllabic suffixes or polysyllabic oxytones or paroxytones (with the short final syllable) are non-existent in Aeolic. In all polysyllabic words the location of the accent is simply predictable on the antepenult (if the last syllable is short) and on the penult (if the last syllable is long). Thus the alternation between acute and circumflex is predictable in all cases (in contrast with

Attic which has minimal pairs between the falling melodic pattern and the high pitch without fall on final syllables).

On the other hand, this fact eliminates the possibility of a distinctive function of the accent in Aeolic. This can be demonstrated easily if we examine the pairs assembled by Vendryes (see under 4.1). Only the left column (with both meanings) is possible in Aeolic:

πατρόκτονος   'killed by the father' or 'parricide'
θηρότροφος   'feeding on beasts' or 'feeding wild beasts'

Unfortunately, we know much less about the accent pattern of numerous West Greek dialects. Undoubtedly, the number of local prosodic systems in 'mild', 'middle' and 'strict' Doric dialects could be high. As seen above, the reconstructed Doric paradigms show the accent distributed columnarly as a result of the process of analogical accent levelling. The permutations of accent familiar from the inflectional paradigms of Attic were severely limited - at least in the 'strict' Doric dialects (Laconian). It is unfortunate that we do not know anything about the accent pattern of the 'mild' Doric dialects belonging to the Saronic group (Corinthian, Megarian and East Argolic), which were situated midway between Attic and Laconian. In the 'strict' Doric the resulting paradigmatic immobility of accent did not allow for the maximization of morphological contrasts as in Attic. ('Strict' Doric accent pattern is thus reminiscent of the 'logical' accent of the Germanic languages, which never shift the accent in the inflection as Romance or Slavic languages do).

We may compare some Laconian nominal and verbal forms with their Attic counterparts:

			Laconian		Attic
i)	Pl	1	ἐλέγομες	'we called'	ἐλέγομεν
		2	ἐλέγετε		ἐλέγετε
		3	ἐλέγον		ἔλεγον
ii)	Pl	Nom	ἄγγελοι	'messengers'	ἄγγελοι
		Gen	ἀγγέλων		ἀγγέλων
		Dat	ἀγγέλοις		ἀγγέλοις
		Acc	ἀγγέλως		ἀγγέλους
iii)	Positive		γεραιός	'older'	γεραιός
	Comparative		γεραιτέρος		γεραίτερος
iv)	Participle Middle:				
	Present, Aorist		-ύμενος		-ύμενος
	Perfect		-ύμενος		-ύμενος
v)	Participle Active Present:				
	Sg Gen		φερώhας		φερούσης
	Pl Nom		φερώhαι		φέρουσαι

172   Phonological Interpretation of Ancient Greek

4.6   TYPOLOGY OF ACCENT IN ANCIENT GREEK DIALECTS

According to Martinet (1954:22) there are three types of languages with respect to the utilization of frequency modulation:
1) Tone but no accent (Chinese)
2) Accent but no tone (English, Czech)
3) Accent and tone in the accented syllable (Serbo-Croatian, Attic-Ionic)

It is well-known that in languages which do not use the lexical accent, like Chinese, virtually all syllables are intoned, whereas in *tone-accent languages only accented syllables are intoned*.[15] As suggested by Garde (1968:142), the neutralization of tonal oppositions in unaccented syllables of these languages is similar to the neutralization of certain vocalic oppositions in unaccented position, e.g. degree of opening in Russian.

Also, it is generally known that it is possible to eliminate the tonal opposition from the description of the lexical accent in tone-accent languages if the moraic analysis is adopted. The long vowel or diphthong, which carries the opposition, in this approach will be analyzed as comprising two morae; there will be no opposition between two different pitch accents. With acute the high pitch will be located on the second mora /oó/ = /ő/, and with circumflex the high pitch will be located on the first mora /óo/ = /ô/.

Since Doric dialects do not show two different locations of the pitch accent in the same syllable (= there is no opposition between two different pitch contours), Doric can be classified as belonging to the stress-accent type. Since Attic is a tone-accent dialect, we find Ancient Greek dialects internally differentiated in the same way as Modern Slavic or Baltic languages:

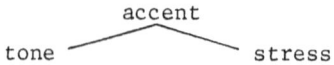

Attic	Doric	Ancient Greek Dialects
Serbo-Croatian	Macedonian	Modern Slavic Languages
Lithuanian	Latvian	Modern Baltic Languages

Aeolic (Lesbian dialect) occupies an intermediate position between Attic and Doric, since the alternations between pitch contours are completely automatic, i.e. the high pitch recedes always to its full limit. Aeolic may contrast two different pitch contours on the penult (minimal pairs like οἶκοι ~ οἴκοι are at least theoretically possible) but may not contrast two different pitch contours on the ultima (Attic minimal pairs of the type φῶς ~ φώς are impossible in Aeolic). In regard to the penult Aeolic looks like a tone-accent type, but in regard to the antepenult and ultima as stress-accent type. In other words, from the point of view of accentuation (disyllabic versus monosyllabic) Attic has disyllabic accentuation on both the penult and ultima, Aeolic only on the penult and Doric has only monosyllabic accentuation:

A T T I C   tone-accent (the accentable unit is mora)

accentuation	penult = long	penult = short	accentable unit		
1	ἄνθρωποι	ἄγγελοι	3́	(2)2	1
mono-2	ἀρχαῖος		3	2́2	1
di- 3	ἀνθρώπων	ἀγγέλων	3	(2)2́	11
mono-4	παῖδες	ἵππος		2́(2)	1
di- 5	παίδων	ἵππων		(2)2́	11
mono-6	φῶς				1̂1
di- 7	φώς				11́

A E O L I C   tone-accent (the accentable unit is sometimes mora and sometimes syllable)

	penult = long	penult = short			
1=2	ἄνθρωποι, ἀρχαιος	ἄγγελοι	3́	(2)2	1
3	ἀνθρώπων	ἀγγέλων	3	(2)2́	11
mono-4	παῖδες	ἵππος		2́(2)	1
di- 5	παίδων	ἵππων		(2)2́	11
6=7	φῶς				(1́)

D O R I C   stress-accent (the accentable unit is syllable)

	penult = long	penult = short			
mono- {1=2	ἀνθρώποι, ἀρχαῖος	ἀγγέλοι	3	(2́)	1
{3	ἀωθρώπων	ἀγγέλων	3	(2́)	1
mono- {4	παῖδες	ἵππος		(2́)	1
{5	(παιδῶν)	ἵππων		(2́)	1
6=7	φώς				(1́)

In the case of Aeolic polysyllabic words such as ἀνθρώπων the accentuation was phonetically disyllabic [ant^{h}roópþon]. However, there was no phonemic contrast of monosyllabic and disyllabic accentuation on the penult in polysyllabic words as in Attic: ἀρχαῖος /ark^{h}aîos/ versus ἀρχαίου /ark^{h}aiǫ̂/.

It might be of interest to compare the functional load of monosyllabic and disyllabic accentuation in Ancient Greek and Modern Serbo-Croatian dialects (Čakavian and Štokavian), since both show distributional interaction between tone and vowel length. In the Čakavian dialect of Serbo-Croatian (Belić (1909)), all syllables containing long vowels are intonable (i.e. the contours are contrastive in *any* long syllable not only initially as in Štokavian):

syllable	contour	moraic analysis	(traditional spelling)
long	rising /á/	aá	á
long	falling /ȁ/	áa	â
short		á	ȁ

In the Štokavian dialect of Serbo-Croatian even short vowels are intonable; consequently, the concept of mora is irrelevant for the description of this dialect. In terms of the traditional Vukovian system, restrictions on the distribution of the two contours are as follows:

a) the falling accent occurs only on the first syllable
b) monosyllabic words show only falling accent
c) internal syllables of polysyllabic words can have only rising accent (they can have falling accent in Čakavian)
d) final syllables of polysyllabic words cannot be accented (as in Čakavian)
e) length cannot occur before the accent (the length does occur before accent in Čakavian)

syllable	contour	traditional spelling	
long	rising /á/	grádu (Loc)	'city'
long	falling /ȁ/	grâdu (Dat)	'city'
short	rising /ó/	nòsak	'small nose'
short	falling /ȍ/	nȍsak	'easy to carry'

Notice that Serbo-Croation has 'better' tonal minimal pairs than Attic (discussed under 4.1) which are only of the *grammatical* type (οἶκοι 'houses' vs. οἴκοι 'in the house'). In addition to examples such as the difference between Dative and Locative found in a large number of words, Serbo-Croatian has examples of *lexical* tone, seen in pairs such as: mâjka 'mother' vs. májka 'grandmother' or examples whose grammaticality is not so obvious: pûstīm 'I empty' vs. pūstīm 'I become empty'.

In Štokavian (as shown by Ivić (1958), (1965:136)) the traditional phonetic analysis of four accents can be put in terms of simple phonological analysis, which reinterprets the surface contrast between rising and falling melodic pattern in the same syllable as a difference in the fundamental frequency of the posttonic syllable. The fundamental frequency of the posttonic syllable is higher in the words with rising accents than in words with falling accents.

175 The Accentual System

Thus, according to Ivić (1965:136), there are not four accents
but only one with two positional variants: the initial
(= falling) and the medial (= rising). The initial variant
appears within one syllable (and is therefore *monosyllabic*),
whereas the medial variant appears within two syllables (it
is *disyllabic*). In his phonemic analysis of Štokavian Ivić
marks only the *place* of accent and *quantity*. Thus the above
two pairs of words can be distinguished by means of a single
accent in its two positional variants:

	location of accent	accentuation
[grádù]	/grā'du/	disyllabic
[grâdu]	/'grādu/	monosyllabic
[nósàk]	/no'sak/	disyllabic
[nôsak]	/'nosak/	monosyllabic

Notice that the place of accent corresponds to the place
of the falling glide.

Similarly, in the following contrastive survey of Ancient
Greek and Serbo-Croatian we may mark the location of the
falling glide in terms of monosyllabic and disyllabic accentuation. Thus the interaction between tone and length in
Ancient Greek and Serbo-Croatian disyllabic and trisyllabic
words may be formally stated as below:

	Ancient Greek	Serbo-Croatian
Accentuation:	Disyllabic words	(high pitch on the ultima)
	2í 2í́	2í 2í́ (only Čakavian)
	2̄í 2̄í́ (only Attic)	2̄í 2̄í́
		(high pitch on the penult)
monosyllabic	2̂1 ∅	2̂1 2̄̂1
disyllabic	∅ 2̂1	2̂1 2̄̂1
	Trisyllabic words	(high pitch on the ultima)
	32í 3̄2í 32̄í 3̄2̄í (only Attic)	32í 3̄2í 32̄í 3̄2̄í (only Čakavian)
	32í 3̄2í 32̄í 3̄2̄í	32í 3̄2í 32̄í 3̄2̄í
		(high pitch on the penult)
monosyllabic	32̂1 3̄2̂1 ∅	∅ (only Attic) 32̂1 3̄2̂1 32̄̂1 3̄2̄̂1
disyllabic	∅ ∅ 32̂1 3̄2̂1	32̂1 3̄2̂1 32̄̂1 3̄2̄̂1 (only Čakavian)

176 Phonological Interpretation of Ancient Greek

                                      (high pitch on the antepenult)

monosyllabic ∅ ∅ ∅ ∅ $\hat{3}21$ $\hat{3}21$ $\hat{3}2\bar{1}$ $\hat{3}2\bar{1}$

disyllabic $\hat{3}21$ $\hat{3}21$ ∅ ∅ $3\hat{2}1$ $3\hat{2}1$ $3\hat{2}\bar{1}$ $3\hat{2}\bar{1}$

The following observations may be made on the basis of this survey:

i) The distribution of contrastive contours:

    Ancient Greek

Attic - long penult and ultima
Aeolic- long penult of disyllabic words (i.e. initially in
       disyllabic words)

    Serbo-Crotian

Čakavian - any long syllable
Štokavian - initially

ii) As mentioned above, in Štokavian final syllables of polysyllabic words cannot be accented (Štokavian retraction of accent took place in the 15th century). Similarly, in Aeolic polysyllabic words the accent has to move as far as permitted by the general limiting rule (see under 4.3.2, p. 154).

iii) Most typically in both 'mora-counting' dialects (Attic and Čakavian) the circumflex may occur on the penult of polysyllabic words while it may not in 'syllable-counting' Aeolic and Štokavian.

Finally, we may procede to typological classification of several groups of IE language families to show more clearly internal differentiation of the Hellenic branch on the basis of typological parallels. Kiparsky's insightful typology of IE accent (1973) is based on a relationship between accentual mobility and the existence of contour accents. In this connection, we might recall Trubetzkoy's restriction, that only languages with distinctive vowel-length represent a real tone-accent type; contrastive contours, as shown on examples from Ancient Greek and Serbo-Croatian, tend to appear only on syllables containing long vowels (Lehiste (1970:82)). The best known cases are among Slavic and Baltic languages, which are supposed to represent the older IE type (whereas tone-accent of modern Scandinavian and Indo-Aryan languages developed secondarily). What is of interest from the point of view of comparative accentology is the development of secondary fixed accent in all these groups. Thus Latvian, in the Baltic group, immobilized stress-accent on the initial syllable (there are only a

177 The Accentual System

few exceptions) and may be described (Garde (1968:100)) as having a 'quasi-fixed' accent. Similarly, in the West Slavic group Polish immobilized the accent, which is misleadingly described as pitch-accent (Lehiste (1970:133)), on the penultimate syllable; Macedonian in the South Slavic group immobilized its accent, which is a purely stress accent, on the antepenultimate syllable. Ancient Greek, which belongs to the Kentum languages, exhibits parallels reminiscent strongly of the accentual differentiation of Balto-Slavic languages belonging to the Satem subphylum of IE. Attic-Ionic developed contrastive contours by early contractions; Doric presumably fixed the contourless accent of Proto-Greek by analogical levelling of paradigms. On the other hand, Aeolic immobilized its accent purely phonologically by the limiting rule. We may summarize all these data in Table 4-1.

Table 4-1. Accent typology of Balto-Slavic languages and Ancient Greek dialects.

	tone-accent		stress-accent		
	free	quasi-fixed	free	quasi-fixed	fixed
Baltic	Lithuanian	Latvian			
Slavic			Russian	Polish	Czech
(Southern group)	Čakavian	Štokavian	Bulgarian	Macedonian	
Greek	Attic-Ionic	Aeolic			Doric

4.7 SITUATION IN MODERN GREEK DIALECTS

I will discuss the following Modern and Ancient Greek forms:

Modern Greek Dialects:

Katharevusa

Sg Nom	ánϑropos	Pl	ánϑropi
Acc	ánϑropon		anϑrópus
Gen	anϑrópu		anϑrópo(n)

Demotike

Sg Nom	ánϑropos	Pl	ánϑropi
			(or anϑrópi)
Acc	ánϑropo		anϑrópus
Gen	anϑrópu (or ánϑropu)		anϑrópo(n)

	Sg Nom	ðáskalos	'teacher'	Pl	ðaskáli
	Acc	ðáskalo			ðaskálus
	Gen	ðáskalu			ðaskálo(n)

Ancient Greek Dialects: Attic-Ionic

Sg Nom	ánt^{h}rǫ̆pos	Pl	ánt^{h}rǫ̆poi
Acc	ánt^{h}rǫ̆pon		ant^{h}rǫ́pǭs
Gen	ant^{h}rǫ́pǭ		ant^{h}rǫ́pǭn

Doric

Sg Nom	ánt^{h}rōpos	Pl	ant^{h}rópoi
Acc	ánt^{h}ropon		ant^{h}rópōs
Gen	ant^{h}rópō		ant^{h}rópōn

The preceding page shows the striking identity of the place of accent in Ancient and Modern Greek in the nominal paradigm of the 2nd Declension. The difference, however, is obvious. The vowels of Modern Greek are only of two types: accented and unaccented; whereas in Ancient Greek the distinctive vowel length makes for a fourfold division (long and short accented, long and short unaccented). As we know, the phonological distinction of length was lost sometime at the end of the Graeco-Roman period (about the 3rd c. A.D. according to Allen (1968:89)). Since those times vowel length became only an accentual feature and stopped functioning distinctively.

Thus, in Modern Greek the problem is how to explain synchronically the shift of stress in Gen Sg and Pl, and Acc Pl. The movement of stress in these forms cannot obviously be explained in phonological terms as in Ancient Greek, where the length of the ultima governed the movement (i.e., accent could not be placed on the antepenult if the ultima was long).

Nevertheless, some linguists (Warburton (1970:110), Newton (1972:12)) tried to account for the shift of stress in these forms phonologically by postulating short and long vowels in underlying representations. The strong appeal of this solution seems to be rooted in the striking identity of the place of accent in both Ancient and Modern Greek - in other words, the old limiting rule still 'limits' the accent of Modern Greek by not allowing it to occur more than three syllables from the end. Consequently, the Modern Greek version of the limiting rule has to differ from the old one in one important respect - the 'length' of the three vowels, i, o, u in certain suffixes in Modern Greek (the three above plus the 1st, 2nd, 3rd Sg and 3rd Pl of Act Ind or Perf Pass) is only 'abstract'. The length of

the suffixes is not a feature of the vowels but of the
respective morphemes which must be marked for this feature.
Thus the old limiting rule could be reworded for the purposes
of Modern Greek accentuation as follows:

an acute (high stress) is placed on the penult if the
vowel of the ultima belongs to a morpheme marked 'LONG',
otherwise on the antepenult (Warburton (1970:111)).

Subsequently, it is necessary to get rid of the feature
'LONG' by another rule of vowel shortening, operating under
the same conditions. Thus the derivation of the Gen Sg in
Modern Greek (Katharevusa) would be the same as in Ancient
Greek, the only difference being the vowel shortening rule,
which must be ordered after the antepenult rule in Modern
Greek:

	Modern Greek (Katharevusa)	Ancient Greek
	ánϑropū	ánthrōpū
Limiting rule	anϑrópū	anthrṓpū
Vowel Shortening	anϑrópu	–

However, new problems emerge. These concern the accentuation of certain forms in Demotike such as Gen Sg ðáskalu (or even ánϑropu). In terms of abstract phonology the first form could be derived from the same underlying representation as that of Katharevusa by blocking the limiting rule:

	Katharevusa	Demotike	
	ánϑropū	ánϑropū	ðáskalū
Limiting rule	anϑrópū	–	–
Vowel Shortening	anϑrópu	ánϑropu	ðáskalu

On the basis of these phenomena we may conclude that the old limiting rule does not govern the movement, in many instances, in the Gen Sg (especially of compound nouns, e.g. αντίλαλου 'of the echo' and proper names, e.g. Χριστόφορου 'of Christopher').[16] On the other hand, the accent may move against all expectations (based on the old limiting rule) in Nom Pl anϑrópi (versus Katharevusa ánϑropi, cf. Classical ἄνϑρωποι), ðaskáli etc. All these difficulties (unnatural underlying representations containing a feature, which never appears in any of Modern Greek dialects; vowel shortening rule, which is motivated only by this artificial underlying representation) seem to indicate that we should be looking for the real solution not in the framework of abstract phonology but rather in terms of concrete morphology. More recently, Warburton (1976:259) showed that a natural way to

account for the accentual changes of Modern Greek is not to
postulate abstract length in underlying representations but
to consider morphological criteria. The essence of her proposal is based on the accentual dichotomy of the verbal and
the nominal part of the lexicon. We may recall the well-
known phenomenon of the verb's 'recessive' accent in Ancient
Greek - the limiting rule simply 'predicts' the accent on all
verbal forms - which thus may be considered underlyingly
unaccented. On the other hand, nouns were underlyingly
accented in Attic-Ionic (but not in Aeolic, see p. 170).
Similarly for Modern Greek, Warbarton suggests that verbs are
to be considered underlyingly unaccented, whereas the nouns
have to be marked for accent. With the exception of the Gen
Sg, Gen Pl, and Acc Pl, the nouns of the 2nd Declension,
which are stressed underlyingly on the antepenult, keep
their accent.

Since these three suffixes do not form any natural morphological class they have to be learned as 'exceptions' by each
new generation of speakers of Modern Greek. It is easy to
imagine that various speakers will reinterpret these alternations differently.[17] In other words, the paradigm of *ánϑropos*
is exposed to analogical levelling of accent. A result of
this analogizing is an opposition *en bloc* of the singular
(antepenult accentuation) and the plural forms (penult
accentuation):

Sg	Nom	ánϑropos	Pl	anϑrópi
	Acc	ánϑropo		anϑrópus
	Gen	ánϑropu		anϑrópon

However, as commented by Warburton (1976:267),

> This reinterpretation has not become established in the
> language because it involves changes that are counter-
> acted by standardization and education and also because
> it goes against the tendency to columnal accentuation
> (retain stress as far as possible).

The best we can do in describing a similar situation is
to say that speakers of Demotike tend to minimize the mobility
of accent within a nominal paradigm, which is typical of
Katharevusa. This is not surprising since parallels of the
immobilization of accent within a nominal paradigm are available from other languages. In Russian about 90% of nouns
have fixed accent - however, the remaining 10% have mobile
accent. Among these 10% there are fairly common nouns such
as *golová* 'head' and *ruká* 'hand':

Sg	Nom	golová	ruká
	Acc	gólovu	rúku

181   The Accentual System

Pl	Nom	gólovy	rúki
	Gen	golóv	rúk
	Dat	golovám	rukám

A look at these forms in <u>Byelorussian</u> will reveal that a far-reaching reinterpretation of the nominal paradigms took place here. The accent does not shift leftwards in the Acc Sg (Acc was the only one among six cases showing this shift); the plural forms of *galavá* have the fixed accent on the second syllable of the stem (plural forms of *rúki* (Dat, Loc, Instr) with mobile accent are classifiable as 'semantic' cases in both Russian and Byelorussian):

Sg	Nom	galavá	ruká
	Acc	galavú	rukú
Pl	Nom	galóvy	rúki
	Gen	galóv	rúk
	Dat	galóvam	rukám

Returning to Greek we may notice that similar phenomena of accent immobilization exist in verb paradigms. In the Passive Imperfect the shift of accent characterizes 1st Person of both numbers only in Katharevusa, while Demotike shows stress distributed columnarly in all forms:

Katharevusa	Sg	1	ἐλειπόμην	Demotike	1	ἐλειπόμουν
		2	ἐλείπεσο		2	ἐλειπόσουν
		3	ἐλείπετο		3	ἐλειπόταν
	Pl	1	ἐλειπόμεθα		1	ἐλειπόμαστε
		2	ἐλείπεσθε		2	ἐλειπόαστε
		3	ἐλείποντο		3	ἐλειπόνταν

It is a pity that our Doric data do not allow us to make any conclusions about the accentuation of singular forms of the 2nd Declension, which were accented on the antepenult in Attic-Ionic. However, we know that Nom Pl forms were accented on the penult, not on the antepenult as in Attic (in the Laconian dialect of Alkman there are forms such as ἀγγέλοι, ἀνθρώποι (see Schwyzer (1939:384)). It could be that there has been a trend in Classical Doric dialects to immobilize the accent in nominal paradigms. As shown under 4.3.2, there has been a trend in Doric and Hellenistic Greek, to immobilize the accent in verb paradigms. In both cases, a shift of the accent, which is in perfect agreement with the *phonological* rule of limitation, causes 'irregularity' in *morphology* - the shift of accent introduces allomorphy the functionality of which is exposed to reinterpretation by learners of the language:

182 Phonological Interpretation of Ancient Greek

		Attic	analogy	Doric
Pl	Nom	ántʰrō̧poi	→	antʰrópoi
	Acc	antʰrṓ̧pōs		antʰrópōs
	Gen	antʰrṓ̧pōn		antʰrópōn
Pl	1	elábomen		elábomen
	2	elábete		elábete
	3	élabon	→	elábon
				elábosan (Hellenistic)

NOTES

1 There are quite numerous cases breaching the general
   limiting rule, arising as a result of the Attic-Ionic
   metathesis of vowel-length, which followed the date of
   fixation of the accent - so far the traditional explanation. These cases include:
   a) Genitives in -εω (= 1st Decl Masc), e.g. Ἀτρείδεω

	Atreídāo
Fronting	Atreídǣo
Raising	Atreídę̄o
Metathesis	Atreídeǭ

   b) so-called Attic declension ἵλεως 'gracious' (ἵλᾱος →
   ἵληος → ἵλεως)

Homeric	Fronting-Raising	Metathesis	Analogical stress levelling
ἵλᾱος	ἵληος	ἵλεως	
ἱλᾱου	ἱλήου	*ἱλέω	ἵλεω
ἱλᾱῳ	ἱλήῳ	*ἱλέῳ	ἵλεῳ
ἵλᾱον	ἵληον	ἵλεων	

   Notice that the metathesis of vowel-length still does not
   explain the retraction of accent in Gen and Dat Sg and
   the location of accent must be explained as due to the
   analogy with strong cases. It seems, however, that these
   two forms can be derived from /hílāo/ and /hílāoi/; see
   the derivation of all forms:

	Nom Sg	Gen Sg	Dat Sg	Acc Sg
	hílāos	hílāo	hílāoi	hílāon
Fronting	hílǣos	hílǣo	hílǣoi	hílǣon
Raising	hílę̄os	hílę̄o	hílę̄oi	hílę̄on
Metathesis	híleǭs	híleǭ	híleōi	híleǭn

   c) the Genitive of the 3rd Declension nouns with stems in
   -i and -u e.g. πόλεως and πήχεως. Again both forms are
   explainable by metathesis from *pólējos* and *pákʰewos*.

183 The Accentual System

However, there is no such explanation for the Gen Pl
πόλεων, and only the paradigmatic levelling, which limits
the permutation of accent within the paradigm, will work.
On the other hand, both forms ἄστεων and ἀστέων are documented, which indicates that the allomorphy within the
paradigm was minimized only optionally. Notice that
typologically the same situation exists in Modern Greek:
Gen Sg ἀνθρώπου 'man' and δάσκαλου 'teacher' (Demotike).
The general rule was formalized by Kiparsky (1967a):
$$V \rightarrow \acute{V} \; / \; — \; C_o V_o C_o V_o^1 \; C_o \#$$
This schema functions as shown below for ἄστυ 'city',
σῶμα 'body', σώματος (Gen Sg), σωμάτων (Gen Pl), φῶς
'light':

```
              a         st u
         s    o      o  m  a
        so    o   m  a  t  o  s
       soom   a   t  o        o  n
        ph    o              o  s
           -  C_c V_o C_o V_o^1 C_o#
```

2 Doric φερομένοι (Masc Pl) is postulated on the basis of
   documented Doric forms such as τυπτομένοι, καλουμένοι
   (versus Attic τυπτόμενοι, καλούμενοι). See Thumb-Kieckers
   (1932:76).
3 According to Kuryłowicz (1958:158) circumflex in pronominal Gen Pl Masc in Doric ἀλλῶν, τηνῶν, τουτῶν results
   from an analogical extension from the Gen Pl Fem (where
   circumflex results from the contraction $\bar{a} + \bar{o}n \rightarrow \bar{a}n$):

	Feminine	Masculine
Pl Nom	ἄλλαι	ἄλλοι
Gen	ἀλλᾶν ⟶	ἀλλῶν

An analogy in the opposite direction took place in Attic-
Ionic:

	Feminine	Masculine
(instead of *δίκαῖαι) Pl Nom	δίκαιαι	δίκαιοι
(instead of *δικαιῶν) Gen	δικαίων ⟶	δικαίων

However, an analogical extension cannot explain circumflex in nominal Gen Pl Masc παίδων, Τρώων.

	Proto-Greek	Attic	Doric
Sg Nom	páwis	παῖς	παῖς
Gen	páwidos	παιδός	παιδός(?)
Pl Nom	páwides	παῖδες, Τρῶες	παῖδες, Τρῶες
Gen	pawídōn	παίδων, Τρώων	παιδῶν, Τρωῶν

Taking into account the situation in reconstructed
Proto-Greek, Attic παίδων very likely shows the original
accent *pawídōn → paídōn. On the other hand, Doric
regularized the paradigm in that this noun is accented

like monosyllabic nouns inherited from PIE, which have desinential accent in weak cases (γῦψ 'vulture' versus γῡπός, γῦπες versus γῡπῶν). This represents an innovation of Doric, which could take place only after the disyllabic *páwis was no longer synchronically recoverable (= after the restructuring *disyllabic noun → monosyllabic noun* took place).

4 Kuryłowicz (1958:157) explains Doric paroxytons, corresponding to Attic properispomenons, as a result of the Doric innovative process labelled 'paroxytonèse':

il paraît que la paroxytonèse ≃ ⌣ > ⸗ ⌣ des formes γυναῖκες, παῖδες, ...est une innovation dorienne. C'est que nous font supposer les corollaires morphologiques du changement ⸗ > ≃ (πωλίον:πόδιον, ψυχοπομπός:πατροκτόνος) qui ne paraissent pas bornés à l'ionien-attique.

Furthermore, Kuryłowicz comments on the correspondence between Doric paroxytons and Attic proparoxytons (p.158):

le changement ≃ ⌣ > ⸗ ⌣ éclaircit l'accentuation inattendue ἀγγέλοι, ἀνθρώποι etc. L'assimilation de ≃ οι à ⸗ οι provoque nécessairement celle de x̂x - οι à xx̂ - οι parce que ≃ οι et x̂x - οι, ⸗ οι et xx̂ - οι représentent des couples dont les membres sont isofonctionnels au point de vue de l'accentuation. C'est à dire que la suppression de la différence entre οἴκοι et οἶκοι (> οἴκοι) entraîne le déplacement ἄποικοι > ἀποίκοι.

I certainly do not see how the suppression of the difference between οἴκοι and οἶκοι could entail a rightward shift of accent in Doric. The alleged suppression is a fact of simple neutralization (= synchronic process), while the rightward shift of accent in ἄποικοι represents a historical metatony (or better analogical stress levelling with other members of the paradigm); consequently I do not see any casual nexus between these two.

5 The uncontracted forms of the Gen and Dat Sg are postulated on the basis of documented forms such as Gen Pl εὐνόων (Thuc. 6.64), elsewhere εὔνοων.

6 Ancient writers variously ascribe the Hellenistic type ἐλάβοσαν to Boeotian, Doric, Chalcidian, Alexandrian, οἱ τῇ 'Ασιάνῃ φωνῇ and οἱ ἑλληνίζοντες ἐν Κιλικίᾳ See Hainsworth (1967:73).

7 Kuryłowicz's explanation (1958:159) of why in Doric the accent in the 3rd Pl Imperfect is located on the penult (e.g. ἔφερον, ἔλαβον) runs as follows:

Par opposition à -ον de la 1re p. sing. les désinences fondées -αν, -εν, -ον furent appréciées comme -ᾱν, -ην, -ων avec abrégement morphologique de la voyelle longue. Mais la longueur postule l'accentuation de la pénultième. Au point de vue structural une forme comme ἐλάβον serait donc d'abord, avant la limitation de l'accent, appréciée comme *ἔλαβων > ἔλαβον (abrégement morphologique), puis, après la limitation, *ἔλαβων > *ἐλάβων (déplacement de l'accent) > ἐλάβον (abrégement morphologique). Car au point de vue structurel le fait morphologique (l'abrègement) se superpose au fait phonologique (limitation).

8   This claim is based on the following observations:

	Lithuanian		Greek	
Strong case	gálvos 'heads'	(Nom Pl)	phugā́s	(Acc Pl)
Weak case	galvõs	(Gen Sg)	phugē̃s	(Gen Sg)
	galvomìs	(Instr Pl)		

While Greek is accented by IE rules
1) Strong cases have presuffixal accent
2) Weak cases have post-stem accent
these rules are replaced in Lithuanian by Baltic rules
1') Strong cases have word-initial accent
2') Weak cases have word-final accent

	Lithuanian		Greek		Cf.
Nom Pl	*galv+aá+s	Acc Pl	phug+aá+s		pód+a
Gen Sg	*galv+áa+s	Gen Sg	phug+ée+s		pod+ós
Instr Pl	*galv+áa+mis				

The IE ancestor of Lithuanian after application of Baltic rules 1' and 2' yields the correct accent and contour for Lithuanian, i.e. in Instr Pl the new marginal alternation puts the accent in prepausal environment and in Gen Sg, where the shift occurs in the same syllable, the high pitch shifts to the second mora. In Nom Pl the new marginal alternation puts the accent on the initial syllable:

Nom Pl	gálv-aa-s	gálvos
Gen Sg	galv-aá-s	galvõs
Instr Pl	galv-aa-mìs	galvomìs

9   Any analysis of Greek which fails to distinguish between prehistoric and late Greek contractions (even if the rules are the same!) is heading for serious confusions.

Prehistoric contractions
inside morpheme-boundaries   dówelos → δοῦλος
across morpheme-boundaries   tīmá+es → τῑμῆς
                              tīmá+ei → τῑμῆι
(thematic vowel + ending)

Historical contractions
across morpheme-boundaries   sūké+ā   → συκῆ
                              sūké+ās → συκῆς
(thematic vowel + ending)   sūké+ai → συκῆι
                              sūké+ān → συκῆν

10 It is tempting to 'explain' the split in contour accents between the strong and weak cases of thematic oxytones in Attic by drawing on dialect mixing. Western Attic was under the influence of Boeotian (= Aeolic dialect) since the sub-Mycenaean period and Ionic spoken in the Saronic gulf was overlaid by Doric dialects before the end of the 2nd Millenium. Thus, the Attic accent pattern in thematic oxytones may be said to represent a mixture of both Aeolic type (in weak cases) and Doric type (in strong cases):

Aeolic	Attic	Doric
θεᾶ	θεά	θεά
θεᾶν	θεάν	θεάν
θεᾶς	θεᾶς	θεάς
θεᾷ	θεᾷ	θεᾴ

11 Kiparsky (1973:800) wonders why the weak cases (= Gen, Dat) show a forward shift in athematic nouns, but a backward shift in the thematic nouns and consequently the accentual relationship between the two classes is just the reverse of what we might have expected. However, as shown above the backward shift in the thematic nouns takes place only in oxytones (feminine), whereas in proparoxytones and properispomenons of both genders the forward shift is as normal as in the athematic nouns:

```
           Acc Sg              Gen Sg
    pód - a                pod - ós    rightward shift
 basílei - a             basileí - aas
 spháir - a              spháir - aas
           but
    the - aán              the - áas    leftward shift
```

12 I base this assumption on data such as χθόνος (vs. Attic χθονός) in Alcaeus B10₁₀ (Lobel (1927:14)). This Aeolic accentual shift is quite remarkable since mobile athematic monosyllables survived until Modern Greek times (πᾶν, παντὸς 'everything'; φῶς, φωτὸς 'light'). On the other hand, immobile athematic monosyllables occurred even in Vedic, e.g. śvā́n, śúnas (Gen) 'dog' (cf. Aeolic κύνος vs. Attic κυνός).

13 As I see this problem *one* of the reasons for the mobility of accent in PIE monosyllabic athematic nouns was to avoid homonymic clashes. Thus, in Vedic Gen Sg (or Acc Pl) *padás* 'foot, step' (*pāt*) would be homophonous, if accented on the root, with Nom Sg *pádas* 'step, stride, foot'. There are quite a few examples like those listed below, where the only difference between the two different lexical items is the location of accent. On the other hand, notice that Acc Sg *pā́dam* 'foot, step' (*pāt*) is

homophonous with Acc Sg *pā́dam* 'foot, bottom, fourth part' (*pā́das*). See Macdonell (1916) for data.

Athematic Monosyllabic Nouns (movable stems)			Thematic Nouns (fixed stems)	
pāt 'foot, step',	(Gen Sg)	padás	(Nom Sg) pádas	'step, stride'
vāk 'speech, voice'	(Instr Sg)	vācā́	(Nom Sg) vā́cā	'speech, word'
	(Gen Pl)	vācā́m	(Acc Sg) vā́cām	
sāt 'victorious'	(Gen Sg)	sahás	(Nom Sg) sáhas	'powerful'
ap 'water'	(Gen Sg)	apás	(Nom Sg) ápas	'work'

14 Actually there are some underlyingly accentable morphemes even in Lesbian, e.g. prepositions and conjunctions are accented on the ultima as in other dialects: ἀνά, διά, κατά, ἀτάρ (Schwyzer (1938:383)).

15 This statement oversimplifies the issues. Tone-accent languages with a polysyllabic type of accentuation such as Latvian and some nonstandard Lithuanian dialects make tonal distinctions even in unstressed syllables. In the Zemaitish (Samogitian) dialect of Lithuanian the stress was retracted from a circumflex accented syllable to the initial syllable and the initial syllable received a new intonation (acute if the previously unstressed syllable was acute, and middle tone if the initial syllable was circumflex).

16 According to Householder et al. (1964:54), the Gen Sg and the Gen and Acc Pl of proparoxytone substantives are stressed on the penult, but the stress remains on the antepenult in the Gen Sg of some compound nouns, some (especially family) names - e.g. ἀντίλαλος 'echo', Gen Sg ἀντίλαλου; μανδρόσκυλον 'sheep dog', Gen Sg μανδρόσκυλου, Gen Pl μανδρόσκυλων. Furthermore, some substantives occur with or without stress alternation in the plural - e.g. συμπέθερος 'child's father-in-law', Gen Sg συμπέθερου, Gen Pl συμπέθερων ∿ συμπεθέρων, Nom Pl συμπέθεροι ∿ συμπεθέροι. The shift in the Nom Pl was formerly common on all proparoxytones and it is still common with some nouns - e.g. δασκάλοι 'teachers'.

17 At this point we may recall Kuryłowicz's statement (1945-1949:37):
   il résulte d'un système grammatical concret quelles transformations "analogiques" sont possibles...mais c'est le facteur social...qui décide si et dans quelle mesure ces possibilités se réalisent...les actions de l'"analogie" ne sont pas des nécessités.

5

Interplay between Sound Change and Analogy

5.1 PERSONAL ENDINGS OF THEMATIC AND ATHEMATIC VERBS

In my discussion of personal endings I will be frequently referring to PIE, Vedic and Avestan forms, which I list below:

			Indicative	Subjunctive	
PIE	Sg	2	bhéresi	bhérēs	
		3	bhéreti	bhérēt	
	Pl	3	bhéronti	*bhérōnt	
Vedic			bhárasi	bhárās(i)	
			bhárati	bhárāt(i)	
			bháranti	bhárān	
Avestan			barahi	barāhi	
			baraiti	barāit(i)	
			barainti	barān	
					Athematic Verb
Proto-Greek			phéresi	phérēs(i)	títhēsi
			phéreti	phérēt(i)	títhēti
			phéronti	phérōnt(i)	títhenti

Kiparsky (1967b:112) proposed a metathesis rule describing an early sound change which took place in the prehistory of Greek. This rule inverts word-final -*i* with preceding dental consonants, which were probably palatalized in this position. By this rule PIE 2nd Sg *légesi* becomes Greek λέγει, and 3rd Sg *légeti* becomes *légeit*, which then turns into λέγει by the Greek loss of word-final obstruent stops (cf. *sōmat*→ σῶμα). In the same way the corresponding PIE subjunctives (reconstructed by Brugmann, *Grundriss II. 3538*) *legēsi* and *legēti* develop into Greek λέγῃς /légēis/ and λέγῃ /légēi/. However, there are several dialectal variants of the 3rd Sg Subjunctive:

189   Interplay between Sound Change and Analogy

      λέγῃ   Attic
      λέγη   Arcadian, Cypriot, Boeotian, Elean
      λέγῃσι   Homeric

A common source of both λέγη and λέγῃ, according to Schwyzer (1938:661), is PIE $leg\bar{e}t$. This form after the loss of word-final -t gives Arcadian etc. λέγη. The Attic λέγῃ is explained by the analogy with indicative λέγει.

According to Kiparsky the form *$leg\bar{e}t$ is only a superficially plausible comparison with Vedic subjunctive $bhar\bar{a}t$, which furthermore seems to ignore the fact that subjunctives of the type λέγη are restricted in two ways. First, they occur only in the 3rd Pers Sg, whereas the secondary endings in the Vedic subjunctive are not restricted. Second, subjunctives of the type λέγη, apart from scattered examples elsewhere, occur only in two dialect areas: in the Aeolic group (Thessalian, Boeotian, isolated examples also in Lesbian) and in Arcado-Cypriot (no decisive examples in Cypriot).

Kiparsky modifies his metathesis rule to explain forms like λέγῃσι, which occur in the Homeric dialect. The final -i, which would be obliterated by the metathesis rule, must optionally be retained. This revision would then generate $leg\bar{e}ti \rightarrow leg\bar{e}iti$, which would yield Homeric λέγῃσι (after affrication and frication $t \rightarrow t^s \rightarrow s$ before front vowels). Kiparsky's two versions of the metathesis rule are as follows:

a) $\begin{bmatrix} -\text{cons} \end{bmatrix} \begin{bmatrix} +\text{cons} \\ -\text{grave} \end{bmatrix} \begin{bmatrix} -\text{cons} \\ -\text{grave} \\ +\text{diffuse} \end{bmatrix}$ #

        1   2   3   4

Structural change: 1 2 3 4 $\Longrightarrow$ 1 2 3 4
                        e.g. $\bar{e}ti \longrightarrow \bar{e}it$

b) structural change 1 2 3 4 $\Longrightarrow$ 1 3 2 3 4
                        e.g. $\bar{e}ti \longrightarrow \bar{e}iti$

It is worth mentioning that there is support for the metathesis rule outside of Greek in Avestan. Compare some Avestan and Aeolic forms:

		Indicative	Subjunctive	
Avestan				
	Sg 2	barahi	barāhi	
	3	baraiti	barāiti	or barāts̆
	Pl 3	barainti	baran	
Aeolic	Sg 2	φέρεις	φέρῃς	
	3	φέρει	φέρῃσι	(Homeric)
	Pl 3	φέροισι	φέρωισι	

As is obvious, the environment of metathesis (b) in Avestan is limited to dental stop and nasal; but metathesis did not take place before the dental fricative s, which later changed to h. In Greek, the environment of metathesis (b) includes the dental fricative s. However, even before the dental stop metathesis (b) was only optional in Avestan, as shown by the alternating form of the 3rd Sg *barāts*. The sequence of historical sound changes may be reconstructed in this fashion.

	Avestan			
	barāsi	barāti	barāti	baranti
Metathesis (b)	-	barāiti	-	barainti
Fricative Weakening	barāhi	-	-	-
Affrication	-	-	barāt^{s}i	-
i-Loss	-	-	-	barāts̪

	Aeolic			
	pʰérēsi	pʰéreti	pʰérēti	pʰéronti
Metathesis (a)	pʰérēis	pʰéreit	-	-
Metathesis (b)	-	-	pʰérēiti	pʰérointi
$t \rightarrow \emptyset\ /\ $-	-	pʰérei	-	-
Affrication	-	-	pʰérēit^{s}i	pʰéroint^{s}i
Frication	-	-	pʰerēisi	pʰéroinsi
$n \rightarrow \emptyset$	-	-	-	pʰéroisi

At this point we can demonstrate that the traditional assumption regarding the derivational history of φέρῃς (from *pherēsi) and Homeric φέρῃσι (from *pherēti) is wrong. Schwyzer (1938:661) suggests that fricative weakening ($s \rightarrow h \rightarrow \emptyset$) took place in the PIE personal endings-*esi* and -*ēsi* (apparently because it undoubtedly took place in Avestan) and derives these two forms as follows (the formalization is mine):

	pʰérēsi	pʰérēti
Fricative Weakening	pʰérēhi	-
h-Loss	pʰérēi	-
Affrication	-	pʰérēt^{s}i
Frication	-	pʰérēsi
Metathesis	-	pʰerēisi

-*s* in the 2nd Sg Subj is explained as analogical with other forms, such as the Optative. But this is completely unnecessary if we assume with Kiparsky that there were sound changes, which were formalized by him as two versions of the metathesis rule. But above all, the mistake of various traditional hypotheses consists of the assumption that fricative weakening and subsequent loss of -*h*- obliterated the crucial -*s*- of the ending -*esi* (as in *genesos → *genehos*

→ geneos→γένους). This assumption seems to be rooted in the
Neogrammarian belief that sound change is 'blind', and in
our concrete case it could be supported by the observation
that this change really took place im Avestan (compare *barahi*
with Vedic *bharasi*).[1] Finally, that this assumption is
totally mistaken can be demonstrated by its application to
the indicative endings, where it would necessitate the derivation of φέρει from *phéreti via phéresi (!), and the -s in
the 2nd Sg would again have to be explained as analogical,
although its source would remain unclear:

	phéresi	phéreti
Fricative Weakening	phérei	-
Affrication + Frication	-	phéresi
Fricative Weakening	-	phérei

Further complications emerge if we try to apply metathesis
rules on athematic verbs. The main problem here is that
postulated underlying forms of the Indicative of athematic
verbs, *tithēsi and *tithēti, correspond to the underlying
forms of the Subjunctive of thematic verbs, *legēsi and
*legēti. Homeric forms τίθεις, τίθει (versus Attic τίθης,
τίθησι) are derived from these underlying forms by Kiparsky
in the following fashion:

	títhēsi	títhēti
Metathesis (a)	títhēis	títhēit
Osthoff's Law	títheis	títheit
t→ ∅ / - #	-	títhei

The traditional solution (see Thumb-Scherer (1959:277) is
definitely much simpler: athematic verbs began being
inflected as thematic verbs (φέρεις, φέρει→ τίθεις, τίθει
instead of τίθης, τίθησι). In other words, the thematic
endings were extended from thematic verbs to the athematic
ones. Furthermore, Kiparsky's process analysis cannot
explain the fact that some originally athematic verbs began
being inflected as contract (thematic) verbs in West Ionic
dialects. Thumb-Scherer (1959:280), for example, provide
the forms τιθεῖν (Eretria and Oropos), καθιστᾶν (Eretria),
διδοῦν (Oropos) etc.; there are also literary forms like
τιθεῖ, διδοῖ, supported by inscriptional forms διδοῖ in
Miletos and Samos. However, my basic objection concerns the
use of Osthoff's Law, which is a diachronic rule of Greek (or
better, a synchronic rule of Mycenaean Greek, see Lejeune
(1972:220)) in a synchronic derivation.

Arcado-Cypriot and Aeolic Subjunctive forms like τίθη are
explained by Kiparsky by a monophthongization rule, applying
to word-final long diphthongs (which are preserved in Attic

λέγῃ). This seems to be a likely explanation in the framework of process analysis:

	títhēti
Metathesis (b)	títhēit
$t \rightarrow \emptyset \;/\;\_\#$	títhēi
Monophthongization	títhē

Yet even here the traditional solution - see Buck (1955:119) - surpasses the above solution in its simplicity. Buck assumes that the original endings of the Subjunctive were *-ēs and *-ē; later on, they were replaced by -ēis and -ēi by analogy to the indicative -εις and ει; but only in Arcado-Cypriot and Aeolic dialects was the original 3rd Sg -ē preserved. What this means is that Buck reconstructs the Proto-Greek Subjunctive forms *phérēs and *phérēt with secondary endings. (Kiparsky works with the forms *phérēsi and *phérēti showing primary endings). The only difficulty of Buck's hypothesis consists in the fact that there is no evidence for the 2nd Sg Subj *φέρης which seems to be peculiar in view of the preserved 3rd Sg Subj φέρῃ. However, this objection might be obviated by showing that such a form in the case of athematic verbs would be homonymous with the 2nd Sg Indic τίθης (but there is also τίθησθα). In terms of external comparative evidence it is hard to prefer either one of the two reconstructions, since Vedic shows both primary and secondary endings in the 2nd and 3rd Sg Subj *bháras(i)* and *bhárat(i)* (but only a secondary ending in the 3rd Pl Subj *bháran*).

Another difficulty appears in deriving Attic forms τίθης and τίθησι by means of the alternate form of the metathesis rule (b), which leaves the final vowel in place. Metathesis (a) is out of question for the sake of the 3rd Pers τίθησι. Now the problem is to eliminate long diphthongs in medial position by monophthongization (Osthoff's Law does not apply here):

	títhēsi	títhēti
Metathesis (b)	títhēisi	títhēiti
Monophthongization	títhēsi	títhēti
Frication	-	títhēsi
$i \rightarrow \emptyset$	títhēs	-

What happens in this case is that there appear intermediate forms which are identical with underlying forms. Consequently, we can assume that neither metathesis (b) nor (a) applied in Attic and we obtain the following scheme (a lower part of the above scheme):

	títʰēsi	títʰēti
Frication	-	titʰḗsi
$i \to \emptyset$	títʰēs	-

The loss of final -*i* in the primary ending of the 2nd Sg is to be understood as a simple resolution of a homonymic clash, which was a result of the East Greek palatalization and frication of /t/ before /i/.

Finally, let us compare the derivation of all the above forms according to Kiparsky with a formalized traditional solution. Notice that, according to Kiparsky, Osthoff's Law cannot apply in the Subjunctive of thematic verbs in the Homeric dialect (although it applies in athematic verbs). If it applied the forms of the 2nd and 3rd Sg Subjunctive would be identical with the corresponding Indicative forms. In my view, the invocation of Osthoff's Law in this case is spurious, since the long diphthong of the Subjunctive represents an exception to Osthoff's Law.

In summary, Attic forms of the Subjunctive φέρῃς and φέρῃ may be explained (a) as analogous to the Indicative φέρεις and φέρει (Buck) or (b) as a result of metathesis of Proto-Greek *pʰérēsi* and *pʰerēti* (Kiparsky).

I am inclined to favour the traditional solution since, in my view, Homeric forms τιθεῖς and τιθεῖ are definitely analogical formations with thematic verbs. In addition certain Doric forms are undoubtedly to be analyzed as analogical formations. The ending of the 2nd Sg Ind in Cypriot ἔρπες = ἔρπεις 'creep' (Hesychius), συρίσδες = συρίζεις 'pipe' (Theocritus), is obviously a secondary ending extended analogically in the Present from the Imperfect. It is unlikely that these forms are a result of the loss of -*i* in the primary ending *-esi* (*pʰéresi* → *pʰéres* → *titʰēsi* → *titʰēs*) in view of all we know about the history of primary and secondary endings.

5.2 ATHEMATIC INFLECTION OF CONTRACT VERBS

The athematic inflection of contract verbs (s.c. 'Aeolic' inflection) is characteristic of some Aeolic dialects (Lesbian and Thessalian of Pelasgiotis) and Arcado-Cypriot. For Boeotian, the ancient grammarians teach the athematic inflection (Sg 1 φίλειμι, Pl 3 φίλεντι); this however is not supported by the evidence of inscriptions (Impf ἐπολέμιον = ἐπολέμεον, Participle ποιιόμενος = ποιεόμενος, both with height dissimilation).

In Lesbian, according to one grammatical papyrus (see Thumb-Scherer (1959:102)), contract verbs are inflected in certain forms as athematic verbs:

	THEMATIC VERBS				ATHEMATIC VERBS			
Kiparsky (1967b)	Indicative		Subjunctive		Indicative		Subjunctive	
AEOLIC								
Metathesis (a)	*phéresi	*phéreti	*phérēsi	*phérēti	*títhēsi	*títhēti	-	-
t → ∅ / — #	phéreis	phéreit	-	phérēit	-	tithēit	-	-
Monophthongization	-	phérei	-	phérēi	-	tithēi	-	-
i → ∅	-	-	?	phérē	tithēs	tithē	-	-
HOMERIC								
Metathesis (a)	phéreis	phéreit	phérēis	phérēiti	tithēis	tithēit	-	-
Metathesis (b)	-	-	-	phérēiti	-	-	-	-
Osthoff's Law	-	-	-	-	tithēis	tithei	-	-
t → ∅ / — #	-	phérei	-	-	tithēis	tithei	-	-
Frication	-	-	-	phérēisi	-	-	-	-
ATTIC								
Metathesis (a)	phéreis	phéreit	phérēis	phérēit	tithēisi	tithēiti	-	-
Metathesis (b)	-	-	-	-	tithēsi	tithēti	-	-
Monophthongization	-	phérei	-	phérēi	-	tithēi	-	-
t → ∅ / — #	-	-	-	-	-	-	-	-
Frication	-	-	-	-	tithēs	tithei	-	-
i → ∅	-	-	-	-	tithēs	-	-	-

	THEMATIC VERBS				ATHEMATIC VERBS	
	Indicative		Subjunctive			
Traditional solution	*phéresi	*phéreti	*phérēsi	*phérēti	*títhēsi	*títhēti
AEOLIC						
Metathesis (a)	phéreis	phéreit	-	-	-	-
t → ∅ / -#	-	phérei	-	-	-	-
Frication	-	-	-	phérēsi	-	títhēsi
(homonymic clash)	-	-	-	phérēs	-	títhēs
-i → ∅	-	-	phérēs(undoc)	-	títhēs	-
(homonymic clash)	-	-	-	phérē	-	títhē
HOMERIC						
Metathesis (a)	-	phéreit	phérēis	phérēiti	-	-
Metathesis (b)	-	-	-	-	-	-
t → ∅ / -#	-	phérei	-	-	-	-
(analogical extension of thematic endings)	-	-	-	phérēisi	títheis	títhei
ATTIC						
Metathesis (a)	phéreis	phéreit	phérēis	phérēit	-	-
t → ∅ / -#	-	phérei	-	phérēi	-	-
Frication	-	-	-	-	-	títhēsi
(homonymic clash)	-	-	-	-	títhēs	-

Sg 1 πόημι
 2 πόεις and πόησθα (with the ending of the Perfect, cf. οἶσθα < *woid-t^{h}a).
 3 πόει

This is supported by evidence from literary and inscriptional Lesbian.[2]

Aeolic athematic forms are quite divergent from thematic forms of West Greek and Attic-Ionic dialects. Compare Lesbian and Attic:

Present of Contract Verbs

	3rd Sg	3rd Pl
Ionic (Attic)	φιλεῖ	φιλοῦσι
	τιμᾷ	τιμῶσι
	στεφανοῖ	στεφανοῦσι
Aeolic (Lesbian)	φίλει	φίλεισι
	τίμαι	τίμαισι
	στεφάνοι	στεφάνοισι

The main difference between Ionic and Aeolic forms consists in the location of accent. In Attic, the circumflex on the ultimate or penultimate is a result of contraction of the stem-vowel and the thematic vowel (p^{h}ilé+ei → p^{h}ilêi, p^{h}ilé+onti → p^{h}ilôsi). In Aeolic, the thematic vowel is syncopated and the accent is located on the syllable which precedes the syllable containing the stem-vowel (p^{h}íle+(o)nti).

There are basically two ways to reduce Ionic and Aeolic forms to a common proto-form:

a) if *p^{h}iléonti, with the accent on the antepenultimate, is chosen, then there must be a metatony (leftward shift of accent) accompanied by the syncopation of the thematic vowel in Aeolic:

	Ionic	Aeolic
	p^{h}iléonti	p^{h}iléonti
Metatony + Syncope	-	p^{h}ílenti

b) if *p^{h}íleonti is chosen, then there must be a different type of metatony (rightward shift of accent) in Ionic and the syncopation of the thematic vowel in Aeolic. The accent in this case belongs to the PIE ancestor of Greek and the metatony is nothing other than the Greek general limiting rule.

Note that in Aeolic the diphthongs *ei, oi, ai* result not only from metathesis in the environment before a cluster -*ns*- followed by -*i*, but also before a word final -*ns* (*nts),

where metathesis is out of question (e.g. Pres Participle
φίλεις < *phílents).³

3rd Sg PRESENT OF CONTRACT VERBS
φιλέει τῑμάει στεφανόει

	Ionic Attic	Aeolic (Lesbian)
	phíleei	phíleei
Metatony	philéei	-
Syncope	-	phílei
Contraction	philêi	-
Monophthongization	philẽ	-
	tímaei	tímaei
Metatony	tīmáei	-
Syncope	-	tímai
Contraction	tīmâi	-
	stephánoei	stephánoei
Metatony	stephanóei	-
Syncope	-	stephánoi
Contraction	stephanôi	-

3rd Pl PRESENT OF CONTRACT VERBS
φιλέντι διψάοντι στεφανόοντι

	Ionic (Attic)		Aeolic (Lesbian)	
	phíleonti		phíleonti	
Metatony	philéonti	*Syncope*	phílenti	
Affrication	philéontsi		phílentsi	
t → ∅ / C - C	philéonsi		phílensi	Arcadian
		Metathesis	phíleinsi	
n → ∅	philéọsi	n → ∅	phíleisi	
+ Compensating Lengthening				
Raising	philéʊsi			
Contraction	philôsi			
	dípsaonti		dípsaonti	
Metatony	dipsáonti	*Syncope*	dípsanti	
Affrication	dipsáontsi		dípsantsi	
t → ∅ / C - C	dipsáonsi		dípsansi	
		Metathesis	dípsainsi	
n → ∅	dipsáọsi	n → ∅	dípsaisi	
+ Compensatory Lengthening				
Raising	dipsáʊsi			
Contraction	dipsǫ́si			

Metatony	stepʰánoonti		stepʰánoonti
Affrication	stepʰanóonti	Syncope	stepʰánonti
$t \rightarrow \emptyset / C - C$	stepʰanóont^{s}i		stepʰánont^{s}i
	stepʰanóonsi		stepʰánonsi Arcadian
		Metathesis	stepʰánoinsi
$n \rightarrow \emptyset$	stepʰanóǫsi	$n \rightarrow \emptyset$	stepʰánoisi
+ Compensatory Lengthening			
Raising	stepʰanóǭsi		
Contraction	stepʰanǫ̂si		

The Subjunctive of contract verbs in Attic is largely identical with the Indicative ($tīmáēi \rightarrow tīmâi$, $stepʰanóēi \rightarrow stepʰanôi$, yet $pʰiléēi \rightarrow pʰilêi$ versus indicative $pʰiléei$ $pʰilê$). It is most unfortunate that we do not know anything about the subjunctive of contract verbs in the Aeolic dialects (or in Arcado-Cypriot), but we may hypothesize that the syncope of the first component of the diphthong /ēi/ could take place as well:

$$\breve{\bar{e}} \rightarrow \emptyset / \begin{Bmatrix} e \\ a \\ o \end{Bmatrix} - i$$

Further complications emerge in the analysis of the Present Participle of contract verbs since there are at least six different forms in dialects:

φίλεντι	Lesbian
φιλέντι	Arcadian, Thessalian (Pelasgiotis)
φιλεῦντι	Ionic, Doric (East Aegean, Megara)
φιλοῦντι	Attic
φιλίοντι	Boeotian, Cypriot, 'Strict' Doric (Cretan, Laconian, Heraclean)
φιλέοντι	Thessalian (Thessaliotis)[4]

Deriving all these forms from *$pʰíleonti$, we can say that Lesbian kept the pre-Greek accent but syncopated the thematic vowel; Arcadian and Thessalian (Pelasgiotis) shifted the accent rightward and syncopated the thematic vowel; Attic shifted the accent rightward and contracted the stem-vowel and thematic vowel; finally, the sequence /e+o/ could remain unchanged as in Thessaliotic, or undergo progressive or regressive height dissimilation:

/eo/ → /eu/ (Progressive) in Ionic, Doric (East Aegean, Megara)
/eo/ → /io/ (Regressive) in Boeotian, Cypriot, 'Strict' Doric

All these forms could have developed as shown below:

199 Interplay between Sound Change and Analogy

PRESENT PARTICIPLE OF CONTRACT VERBS
φιλέων   (Dat Sg φιλέοντι)

	Arcadian		
	Thessalian (Pelasgiotis)		Lesbian
Metatony	pʰíleonti		pʰíleonti
Syncopation	pʰiléonti		—
	pʰilénti		pʰílenti
	Ionic		Boeotian
	Doric (East Aegean, Megara)		Cypriot
			'Strict' Doric (Cretan, Laconian, Heraclean)
Metatony	pʰíleonti		pʰíleonti
Progressive	pʰiléonti		pʰiléonti
Height	pʰiléonti	Regressive	pʰilíonti
Dissimilation		Height Dissimilation	
	Attic		
Metatony	pʰíleonti		
Contraction	pʰiléonti		
Raising	pʰilỗnti		
	pʰilǒ̃nti		

We may tabulate all these forms (and also plural forms of the Participle) in Figure 5-1 to show their dialectal distribution.

The location of the accent is uncertain in the case of athematic verb in Doric and particularly in the case of athematic and contract verbs in Arcadian. In Arcadian the accent could be situated on the antepenultimate as in Aeolic, or on the penultimate as in Ionic:

Lesbian	Arcadian		Ionic
φίλεντι	φίλεντι or φιλέντι		φιλέοντι
*φίλενσι (→ φιλέντεσσι)	φίλενσι	φιλένσι	φιλέουσι
φίλεισι (<* φίλενσι)	φίλενσι	φιλένσι	φιλέουσι

In terms of process analysis, both sets of Arcadian forms can be derived in the same way; however, the forms with accent located on the antepenultimate do not undergo metatony as in Aeolic (cf. the derivation of contract verbs in Ionic with metatony and in Aeolic without metatony):

Figure 5-1. The dialect geography of thematic, athematic and contract verbs

	Part Pres (Dat Sg)	Part Pres (Dat Pl)	Pres Indic (3rd Pl)
Aeolic (Lesbian)	φέροντι	φερόντεσσι	φέρουσι
	τύθεντι	τυθέντεσσι	τύθεισι
	φίλεντι	φιλέντεσσι	φίλεισι
Attic	φέροντι	φέρουσι	φέρουσι
	τιθέντι	τιθεῖσι	τιθέασι
	φιλοῦντι	φιλοῦσι	φιλοῦσι
Ionic	φιλεῦντι (also East Aegean Doric)		τιθεῖσι
Doric ('Strict')	φέροντι	φέρονσι	φέροντι
	τιθέντι	τιθένσι	τίθεντι
	φιλίοντι	φιλίονσι	φιλίοντι
		(φερόντοις in North-West)	
		(φιλεόντοις in North-West)	
Arcadian	φέροντι	φέρονσι	φέρονσι
	τιθέντι	τιθένσι	τιθένσι
	φιλέντι	φιλένσι	φιλένσι

Arcadian

	Part Pres (Dat Sg)	Part Pres (Dat Pl)	Pres Indc (3rd Pl)
	pʰíleonti	pʰíleontsi	pʰíleonti
Metatony	pʰiléonti	pʰiléontsi	pʰiléonti
Syncope	pʰilénti	pʰiléntsi	pʰilénti
Affrication	-	-	pʰiléntsi
$t \to \emptyset\ /\ C-C$	-	pʰilénsi	pʰilénsi
	pʰíleonti	pʰíleontsi	pʰíleonti
Metatony	-	-	-
Syncope	pʰílenti	pʰílentsi	pʰílenti
Affrication	-	-	pʰílentsi
$t \to \emptyset\ /\ C-C$	-	pʰílensi	pʰílensi

5.3 ATHEMATIC VERBS 'BE', 'GO' AND 'SAY'

There are several different forms of εἶναι 'to be' in the Present:

	Attic	Homeric	Aeolic	Doric
Sg 1	εἰμί		ἔμμι (Lesbian)	ἠμί
			ἐμμί (Thessalian)	
2	εἶ	εἶς, ἔσσι		
				West Greek
Pl 3	εἰσίν	ἔασι	εἰσί (Lesbian)	ἐντί
			ἐνθί (Thessalian)	

The 1st Sg is easy to explain. The Aeolic group underwent a regressive dissimilation of sibilant /s/, whereas elsewhere the sibilant was subjected to fricative weakening. If the accent of Thessalian ἐμμί is genuine, then we can imagine the sequence of sound changes as follows:

			Lesbian	Thessalian
Fricative Weakening	esmí		ésmi	esmí
Compensatory Lengthening	ehmí	*Voicing*	ézmi	ezmí
Raising	ēmí Doric	*Assimilation*	émmi	emmí
	ēmí Attic-Ionic			

The 2nd Sg εἶ 'you are' is from Proto-Greek *éssi (↦ ési → éhi → éi), but a problem is presented by Homeric εἶς. According to Schwyzer (1938:659), this form consists of εἶ+s, with -s extended analogically from the other forms of the 2nd Sg. Schwyzer explains εἶς 'you will go' (in Hesiod WD 208) in exactly the same way. Yet this assumption is unnecessary, since the first form can be derived by metathesis (a) and, in

the second case, the loss of final -*i* from the primary ending
*-*si* seems to be more likely:

	éssi	éssi		
Degemination	ési	ési	éisi	éisi
Metathesis (a)	-	éis	-	-
Fricative Weakening	éhi	-	éihi	-
$h \rightarrow \emptyset\ /\ V - V$	éi	-	éii	-
$-i \rightarrow \emptyset$			éi	éis
	εἶ	εἶς	εἶ	εἶς

The expected form of the 3rd Pl is *εἶσί in Attic-Ionic,
*ἐντί in West Greek (and *εἶσι could be predicted for Aeolic
after 'psilosis'), all these going back to Proto-Greek *senti.
On the other hand, the Mycenaean form /e(h)ensi/, spelled
e-e-si, suggests Proto-Greek *esenti, with the full grade
*es generalized throughout the whole paradigm:

	esénti	sénti		
Fricative	ehénti	hénti		
Weakening			or	
Affrication	ehént^{s}i	hént^{s}i		
$t \rightarrow \emptyset$	ehénsi	hénsi		hénsi
$h \rightarrow \emptyset\ /\ V-V$	eénsi *Metathesis (b)* héinsi	*Comp.Length.*	hêsi
	$n \rightarrow \emptyset$	héisi	*Raising*	hẽsi

The expected form would be quite inconvenient since it
would be almost homonymous (only the accent is different)
with the expected form of 'they will go' (from *jénti).
Furthermore, there is another form εἶσι, belonging to the
Aorist Participle (Dat Pl) of ἵημι 'send'. Since languages
usually do not tolerate homonymy involving the most frequent
verbs 'be' and 'go', both forms were replaced by more distinctive formations:

ἵημι	ἰέναι	εἶναι
*jént+si	j+énti	*s+entí
⋮	⋮	⋮
εἶσι	εἶσι	εἰσί
	replaced by	replaced by
	ἴασι	εἰσί
'having sent' (Dat Pl)	'they will go'	'they are'

The inflection of the verb ἰέναι 'to go' in the Present
Indicative is remarkably close to the corresponding inflection in PIE (some forms are identical). The desinential
accent in the 1st and 2nd Pl is preserved only in Vedic, and
Greek regularized the initial accent in all forms:

	Vedic	PIE	Greek
Sg 1	émi	*éimi	εῖμι
2	éṣi	*éisi	εῖ, εῖς (Hesiod), εῖσθα (Homeric)
3	éti	*éiti	εῖσι, εἰτι (Cyrenaean)
Pl 1	imás	*imés/n	ἴμεν
2	ithá	*ité	ἴτε
3	yánti	*jénti	ἴᾱσι

The situation in the 2nd Sg is an interesting one. Here we may assume that -s- of the ending *-si underwent a fricative weakening in Attic; on the other hand, -s- was not obliterated in the forms preserved in Hesiod and Homer:

Fricative Weakening		éisi	éisi
$h \rightarrow \emptyset / V - V$		éihi	-
$-i \rightarrow \emptyset$		éii	-
		éi	éis (+ tʰa)
		εῖ (Attic)	εῖς (Hesiod)
			εῖσθα (Homeric)

The form of the 3rd Pl ἴᾱσι 'they will go', occurring in Homeric and Attic, is a new formation for the expected ἴεισι or εῖσι. The ending -asi is borrowed from the Perfect (λελοίπ +ασι). The same phenomenon occurred in athematic verbs: τιθέασι (instead of τίθεισι, which occurs in Aeolic; this form is from *titʰenti, which is preserved by Doric τίθεντι). The PIE ending of the 3rd Pl *-enti has been replaced everywhere in Attic-Ionic, with the exception of the verb 'to be', εἰσί 'they are' (cf. Doric ἐντί). In the case of 'they will go', the sequence of changes could have been the form *jénti ⟶ hénti ⟶ héntˢi ⟶ hénsi ⟶ hêsi or héinsi ⟶ héisi, the reason for the innovation being the indistinctiveness of *hêsi.

We may hypothesize that in Aeolic εῖσι could be not only singular 'he will go' but also plural 'they will go':

	éiti	jénti
$j \rightarrow h$	-	hénti
Psilosis	-	énti
Affrication	éitˢi	éntˢi
$t \rightarrow \emptyset$	éisi	énsi
Metathesis (b)	-	éinsi
$n \rightarrow \emptyset$	-	éisi

In exactly the same way we may derive Aeolic φαῖσι 'he says' < *pʰaiti and homophonous φαῖσι 'they say' < *pʰanti. Another piece of indirect evidence for this reconstruction is supplied by Lesbian (Sappho) ἴεισι 'they send', from Proto-Greek *jíenti, versus Attic ἱᾶσι:

	Proto-Greek	Attic	Aeolic
'they send'	*jíenti	ἱᾶσι	ἵεισι
'they will go'	*jénti	ἴᾶσι	x = εἶσι

Of course, even x = ἵεισι is possible (with -ι analogically with ἵμεν, ἵτε). A result of various sound-changes from Proto-Greek to classical dialects was the undesirable indistinctiveness of certain forms in both Ionic and Aeolic. As pointed out above, this can be considered a main reason why some of these forms were replaced by new, more distinctive formations:

	Proto-Greek	Attic	Aeolic
'they are'	*sentí	εἰσί	εἰσί
'he will go'	*éiti	εἶσι	εἶσι
'they will go'	*jénti	(ἴᾶσι)	new form εἶσι
'they send'	*jíenti	(ἱᾶσι)	new form ἵεισι

We may hypothesize that the accent in Aeolic εἰσί 'they are' was located on the last syllable, even if this breaches the Aeolic rule of recession of accent, since otherwise εἶσι would be semantically overloaded.

A large variety of forms exists in the Imperfect of εἶναι 'to be':

	Lesbian	Homeric	Attic	West Greek Aeolic Arcado-Cypriot
Sg 1	ἔον	ἦα	ἦ (Old Attic), ἦν	
2	ἦσθα	ἦσθα	ἦσθα	
3	ἦς	ἦεν, ἤην	ἦν	ἦς
Pl 1		ἦμεν	ἦμεν	
2		ἦτε	ἦστε, ἦτε	West Greek
3	ἔον ἦσαν ἔσαν		ἦσαν	ἦν

Historically, this variety is explainable by the assumption that Proto-Greek could form the Present, Imperfect and Perfect from the same PIE root *es as did Vedic (1 Sg Impf ásam - 1 Sg Perf ása, 2 Sg Impf ásīs - 2 Sg Perf ásitha etc.). Later on, however, the Perfect Paradigm was given up and there are only a few forms surviving in the Homeric dialect. The dissolution of the Proto-Greek system can be imagined as shown below:

Homeric	Proto-Greek		Attic-Ionic	West Greek
	Perfect	Imperfect		
ἦα	*és-a	*és-ņ ⟶	ἦ	
ἦσθα	*és-tha	*és-s		
	*és-a	*és-t ⟶		ἦς

205 Interplay between Sound Change and Analogy

            *és-men   ἦμεν
            *és-te   ἦστε
            *ēs-ent

As is well-known, PIE knew another *verbum existentiae* formed from the root *bhū. Vedic shows nicely that all forms from the root *es could be paralleled by forms from the root *bhū. In the development of various IE languages this situation presented a choice in the formation of paradigms - thus Latin used the root *bhū in the Perfect, whereas Old Church Slavonic used the same root in both Imperfect and Aorist. In Greek, the suppletive form replacing the old Perfect is taken from γίγνομαι 'be born, be produced, take place' (with a basic meaning 'to come into being').

	Present	Imperfect	Perfect	
Vedic	ásmi	ā́sam	ā́sa	
	bhávāmi	ábhavam	babhū́va	
			ábhuvam	(Aorist)
Proto-Greek	*ésmi	*ḗsṇ	*ḗsa	
Attic	εἰμί	ἦ(ν)	γέγονα	
			ἐγενόμην	(Aorist)
Latin	sum	eram	fuī	
Old Church Slavonic	jesmь	bjēaxъ	bjexъ	(Aorist)
			byxъ	(Aorist)

The 3rd Sg Impf ἦς in West Greek, Aeolic and Arcado-Cypriot goes back to Proto-Greek Imperfect *ēs-t (with loss of word-final -t). On the other hand, Homeric ἦεν (and Attic-Ionic ἦν) is an odd form. Schwyzer (1938:677) suggests that this form represents the PIE plural form *es-ent (cf. Vedic ā́san); this assumption seems to be unwarranted since it is based on a rather superficial resemblance. It could be that this form goes back to *ē-se(n) plus an Aorist ending, which was introduced in the plural ἦ+σαν:

ἦεν   ē-se(n)   cf.   ἔλυ -σε(ν)
ἦσαν   ē-san   ἔλυ -σαν

The trouble with this hypothesis is that ἦσαν is a recent (?) formation, whereas ἦεν might be old. The problem is connected with the change s ⟶ h (fricative weakening) with subsequent loss of intervocalic /h/. It can be argued that Greek lost /s/ in the Imperfect formed from the root *es. As shown by the 2nd Pl forms ἦστε ∿ ἦτε two synchronic analyses presented themselves to speakers of Greek - with or without /s/. The second 'etymological' analysis would of course be supported by the Present forms:

	Imperfect			Present
Sg 2	ê̓ - stʰa	or	ê̓s-tʰa	
Pl 1	ê̓ - men			es - mén
2	ê̓ - te		ê̓s - te	es - té
3	ê̓ - san		ê̓s - an	

The first analysis with /s/ synchronically irrecoverable comes into play also for some Homeric Present forms (Pl 1 εἰμέν versus Attic ἐσμέν):

	Present		
Sg 1	ei - mí	or	
2	ei - s		es - sí
3			es - tí
Pl 1	ei - mén		
3	ei - sín		

The situation for the Imperfect of ἰέναι 'go' parallels that for εἶναι 'be', in collapsing Proto-Greek Imperfect and Perfect forms:

	Ionic	Homeric	Attic
Sg 1	ἤιον	ἤια	ᾖα
2			ᾔεις, ᾔεισθα
3	ἤιε, ᾔιε		ᾔει
Pl 1	ᾔιομεν		ᾖμεν
2			ᾖτε
3	ἤιον	ἤισαν, ᾖσαν	ᾖσαν

The reconstruction of these forms for Proto-Greek is difficult, but we can imagine a state of affairs similar to that of Vedic, which still shows a distinct morphology of Imperfect and Perfect formed from the same root *ei (Impf áyam, áis ... versus Perf iyáya, iyátha). Homeric ἤια (and Attic ᾖα) continue the Proto-Greek Perfect *ēi+a (but even the Proto-Greek Imperfect *ēi+m would give the same result). The Proto-Greek 2nd Sg Perfect could be reconstructed as *ēi+tʰa; the forms actually documented show that the original ending *-tʰa was replaced by -eis, which superficially looks as if it were taken from the thematic Present, but is probably the same -eis (and -ei in the 3rd Sg) which is typical of the Pluperfect: ἐλελοίπ+εις (and ἐλελοίπ+ει). Another form of the 2nd Sg occurring in Attic has the ending *-tʰa suffixed to ēi+eis in the same way as in the Present:

207 Interplay between Sound Change and Analogy

```
'you will go'              'you went'
ei
ei + s                     ēi + eis
ei + s + tʰa               ēi + eis + tʰa
```

As shown by Ionic, the Imperfect of ἰέναι could also be inflected in a completely 'regular' way as a thematic Imperfect.

Equally diversified are the Present forms of the verb φάναι 'to say':

	Attic	Homeric	Lesbian	Doric
Sg 1	φημί		φαῖμι	
2	φῄς	φῆις, φῆισθα	φαι, φαῖσθα	
3	φησί		φαῖσι	
Pl 1	φαμέν			
2	φατέ			
3	φᾱσί		φαῖσι	φαντί

The difference between Ionic (Attic) and Aeolic (Lesbian) is due to the fact that metathesis (b) took place in Lesbian, while Attic underwent the usual loss of nasal and compensatory lengthening in the 3rd Pl, and fronting and raising in the 3rd Sg:

	Lesbian	
	3rd Sg	3rd Pl
	pʰáti	pʰánti
Affrication	pʰátsi	pʰántsi
$t \rightarrow \emptyset$	pʰási	pʰánsi
Metathesis (b)	pʰáisi	pʰáinsi
$n \rightarrow \emptyset$	-	pʰáisi

	Attic	
	3rd Sg	3rd Pl
	pʰāti	pʰantí
Affrication	pʰatsi	pʰantsí
$t \rightarrow \emptyset$	pʰasí	pʰansí
Fronting	pʰæsí	-
Raising	pʰẹsí	-
$n \rightarrow \emptyset$ + *Compensatory Lengthening*		pʰāsí

The 2nd Sg is more complicated. We must postulate

metathesis (a) to explain Homeric φῇς, φῇσθα, Lesbian (Sappho) φαῖσθα, and metathesis (b) to explain Lesbian (Alcaeus) φαι; furthermore, in the case of φαι, we must assume that fricative weakening obliterated the -s- of the ending *-si.

	Attic		Homeric
	pʰási		pʰási
-i ⟶ ∅	pʰás	Metathesis (a)	pʰáis
Fronting	pʰǽs		pʰǽis
Raising	pʰę́s		pʰę́is (+tʰa)

	Lesbian		
	pʰási		pʰási
Metathesis (b)	pʰáisi	Metathesis (a)	pʰáis
Osthoff's Law	pʰáisi		pʰáis (+tʰa)
Fricative Weakening	pʰáihi		
h ⟶ ∅ / V - V	pʰáii		
-i ⟶ ∅	pʰái		

5.4 PERFECT WITH ASPIRATE

Perfect with aspirate appears in the 5th c. in Attic and Ionic dialects. Only stems in a labial or velar obstruent display this formation: stems in /p/, /b/ and /pʰ/ have Perfect in /pʰ/, and stems in /k/, /g/ and /kʰ/ have Perfect in /kʰ/, e.g. κρύπτω 'hide', κέκρυφα, φυλάττω 'guard', πεφύλαχα.[5] In the Homeric dialect there are forms of the 3rd Pers Pl Middle Voice Perfect where we find the aspirates /pʰ/ and /kʰ/ in exactly the same environment, e.g. τετράφαται (from τρέπω 'turn'), τετάχαται (from τάττω 'arrange'). Various hypotheses have been elaborated to explain these facts. Thus according to Meillet (in Schwyzer (1938:772)), the aspiration in all these forms is a result of an analogical extension from the roots where it was etymological. In ἔσκαφα (from σκάπτω 'dig') the aspiration is etymological (cf. σκάφη 'the hull of a ship', σκάπτω < *skapʰjō), whereas in βέβλαφα (from βλάπτω 'disable') the aspiration is unetymological (cf. βλάβη 'harm', βλάπτω < *blabjō). According to Schwyzer (1938:771), the aspiration in the 3rd Pl Middle τετράφαται originated in forms with clusters φθ and χθ (e.g. 3rd Sg Imper τετράφθω, Infinitive τετράφθαι with the accent located on the same syllable), and the aspiration was extended from such cases to all persons of the active Perfect, starting with the 3rd Pl.

Interplay between Sound Change and Analogy

Both hypotheses apparently lack any deeper and more cogent reasons. Schwyzer's explanation, in particular, seems to be unsatisfactory.

A more plausible explanation has been elaborated by Christol (1972:69), according to whom φ and χ are to be analyzed as archiphonemes /p/ and /k/ plus a suffix /h/, which functioned as a marker of the active Perfect. Thus the similarity between the structure of the Perfect and Aorist becomes obvious in the case of the verb σκάπτω, where reduplication is impossible and the only difference between the Perfect and Aorist is the difference between markers:

	Perfect	Aorist
Sg 1	éskap+h+a	éskap+s+a
Pl 1	eskáp+h+amen	eskáp+s+amen

A Perfect marker $-h-$, whatever its origin, was undoubtedly quite inconvenient for a language with aspirate phonemes /p^h/, /t^h/ and /k^h/, since the sequence of two phonemes /p+h/ could be reanalyzed as a single phoneme /p^h/. Consequently, we may hypothesize that the historical stage of Greek with the Perfect marker $-h-$ was rather short and unstable. After the introduction of the new Perfect marker $-k-$, the old marker $-h-$, if it was ever used elsewhere than after the stems in labial and velar stops, was given up. The reason was that Greek also knew Perfects in which reduplication functioned as the external marker, and which showed ablaut in the stem, e.g. λείπω - λέλοιπα (not always, however, e.g. φεύγω - πέφευγα). Consequently, two synchronic analyses of ἔσκαφα were available:

lélu + k + a   pépheug + a
éskap + h + a   éskap^h + a

These prehistoric stages can be reconstructed in the following sequence:

Stage 1 (a) Inherited PIE Aorist marker $-s-$
        (b) Perfect marker $-h-$ (origin?)
            Aorist   élū + s + a   éskap + s + a
            Perfect   lélu + h + a   éskap + h + a

Stage 2 (a) Greek *fricative weakening*: $s \rightarrow h\ /\ V - V$
        (b) Greek Perfect Marker $-k-$
            Aorist   élū + h + a   éskap + s + a
            Perfect   lélu + k + a   éskap + h + a

Stage 3 (a) Aorist marker $-s-$ used even intervocalically
            (analogy with postconsonantal s)
            Aorist   élū + s + a   éskap + s + a
            Perfect   lélu + k + a   éskap + h + a

During Stage 2, there arose a certain ambiguity when $-h-$ could be used as a marker of both Aorist (where intervocalical $-h-$ represented underlying $-s-$) and Perfect (where $-h-$ stood for underlying $-h-$). This situation might have provided an incentive for the Greek introduction of the new Perfect marker $-k-$. Of course, Greek relied on the reduplication in contrasting Perfect and Aorist, e.g. βέβλαφα vs. ἔβλαψα; consequently, the danger of homonymic clash would be limited only to cases where reduplication was not possible (in verbs like σκάπτω, ῥίπτω, ἄρχω, ἀνοίγνυμι, etc.). All this discussion, however, remains purely speculative since we simply do not possess any direct evidence that the Aorist marker $-s-$ (the same is true for Future) ever underwent fricative weakening. In other words, analogy with the postconsonantal Aorist marker $-C-s$ could prevent the sound change $s \longrightarrow h\ /\ V - V$ from happening. As far as our data reach, there never was a stage in the history of Greek, when the Aorist marker $-s-$ was obliterated by sound change as it was in Avestan or Old Church Slavonic.[6]

All this still does not explain the form of the 3rd Pl Middle Perfect in the Homeric and Ionic dialects τετράφαται. This rather inconvenient form (contrast stems in a vowel, such as λέλυνται, showing the characteristic 3rd Pl cluster $-nt-$, and stems in a consonant, such as *tetrápntai $\longrightarrow$ *tetrápatai $\longrightarrow$ τετράφαται without $-nt-$) was replaced in Attic by the analytic form τετραμμένοι εἰσίν. Christol hypothesizes that Homeric τετράφαται is a result of an extension of h from active forms (compared with Schwyzer's hypothesis this extension works in the opposite direction):

Christol (1972)

Perfect Active	Perfect Active	Perfect Middle
éskap + h + a	tétrop + h + a	tetráp + h + atai

Schwyzer (1938)

| éskap^h + a | tétrop^h + a | tetrap^h + t^{h}ai |
| | | tetrap^h + atai |

A question to be asked is why Perfect with aspirate occurs only with stems in a labial or velar obstruent. If formed with stems in a dental obstruent, πείθω 'persuade' *pepeit^{h}ntai, we would predict forms like *pepeit^{h}atai (with etymological aspirate). On the other hand, the extension of /h/ is impossible in the case of stems in the voiced dental obstruent /d/, κομίζω 'provide for' *kekomídṇtai, where the form *kekomídatai is predictable, but *kekomid^{h}atai impossible; the reason is that Greek does not have voiced aspirates. Our documented forms, however, are invariably analytical ones: πεπεισμένοι εἰσίν, κεκομισμένοι εἰσίν.

The only relics of the prehistoric aspect marker -h- in Attic are preserved in the Perfect of stems in a labial or velar obstruent (the preservation of -h- was here conditioned by a certain inconvenience in pronouncing medial clusters $-p^{(h)} + k-$ and $-k^{(h)} + k-$). It could be that there are other relics elsewhere in dialects, such as the forms of the 2nd Aorist athematic verbs (3rd Pl Active) found in various dialects:

Boeotian ἀνεθεαν   versus Attic ἀνέθεσαν   other dialects
                                              ἀνεθεν

Locrian ἀνεθεαν
Arcadian συνεθεαν
Cypriot κατεθυjαν

In the singular there is a marker -k- which appears to have been borrowed from the Perfect ἔθη + κ + α. Plural forms have a short vowel in the stem with endings attached directly, e.g. ἔθετμεν and ἔθετε. The 3rd Pl form in -αν might be a descendent of prehistoric $*\acute{e}t^h e+h+an$, where -h- was the old aspect marker used intervocalically. A further supporting reason for this hypothesis could be sought in the fact that the only difference between singular Aorist and Perfect forms of certain athematic verbs is reduplication:

Aorist ἔθη + κ + α
Perfect τέθη + κ + α

This parallels the situation in the prehistoric stages 1 and 2 before the introduction of the new Perfect marker -k-, where the only difference between Perfect and Aorist forms of all persons consisted of reduplication:

(Stage 2) Aorist   *élū + h + a   levelled analogically into
                                              élū + s + a
(Stage 1) Perfect *lélū + h + a   later replaced by
                                              lélū + k + a

However, all this might be purely speculative, since the most likely origin of such forms as ἀνεθεαν was apparently the 3rd Pl of certain common verbs like εἶπαν 'they said' (also εἶπον) or ἤνεγκαν 'they carried' (also ἤνεγκον). The reason for the analogical extension could simply be the fact that the old form ἀνεθεν was not distinct enough, since it looked rather like a singular form - i.e., the motive was a maximization of morphological contrasts.

5.5 PERFECT PARTICIPLE

As stated traditionally, Aeolic dialects (Lesbian, Thessalian and Boeotian) show thematic inflection of the Perfect Participle, Buck (1955:118). It is more appropriate to say

that Aeolic dialects have the marker -ont- in the Perfect
Participle (whereas non-Aeolic dialects have the original
marker -ót-) by analogy with the Present Participle.

Attic-Ionic

		Present Participle			Perfect Participle		
Masc Sg	N	λείπ	ων		γεγον	ώς	
	G		οντ	ος		ότ	ος
	D		οντ	ι		ότ	ι
	A		οντ	α		ότ	α
Fem Sg	N		ουσ	α		υῖ	α

Aeolic

Masc Sg	N	λείπ	ων		γεγόν	ων	
	G		οντ	ος		οντ	ος
	D		οντ	ι		οντ	ι
	A		οντ	α		οντ	α
Fem Sg	N		οισ	α		οισ	α

Attic-Ionic shows two distinct patterns in the morphology
of the Present and Perfect Participle:

Present Participle =   ROOT ont CASE (root is
                                      accented)
Perfect Participle = reduplication ROOT ót CASE (accent is
                                      located on the marker -ót-)

Speakers of Aeolic dialects no doubt found these patterns
too complicated and simplified the whole matter by the analogical extension of the marker -ont- from the Present Participle
to the Perfect Participle. The immediate incentive for this
analogy was that Aeolic does not allow for the accent on the
penultimate if the antepenultimate is accentable, i.e. Aeolic
does not display the accentable morpheme -ót- functioning as
the Perfect Participle marker elsewhere:

Present Participle =   ROOT ont CASE
Perfect Participle = reduplication ROOT ont CASE

The grammatical simplification lies in the fact that while
the Perfect Participle is double-marked in Attic-Ionic (by
reduplication and distinctive accent), it is marked only by
reduplication in the Aeolic dialects. We may assume that the
situation in Aeolic is secondary by hypothesizing that in this
case the Attic-Ionic accent corresponds to the Proto-Greek
accent. External evidence for this hypothesis is offered by
Vedic, where the Perfect Participle is accented on the marker,
e.g. *dad+ús+as* 'having given' (Gen Sg), but the Present
Participle either on the root or on the inflection, e.g.
dád+at+as 'giving' (Gen Sg) and *ad+at+ás* 'eating' (Gen Sg).

213 Interplay between Sound Change and Analogy

Consequently, we may reconstruct historical changes in Aeolic in terms of metatony and analogical extension as shown below:

```
Proto-Greek        Aeolic
leíp+ont+os        leíp+ont+os
gegon+wót+os  ──▶  *gegón+wot+os  | (metatony)
                   gegón+ont+os   | (analogical extension
                                     of -ont-)
```

The feminine form γεγονυῖα, especially, was exposed to various analogical extensions for quite obvious reasons. Its morphology was a sort of historical relic (notice the rare diphthong /ui/ limited to the environment before non-high vowels) and there are basically two types of analogical leveling of this cumbersome form in various dialects:
i) In Aeolic and North-West dialects (evidence from the late Delphian) the ending -οισα or -ουσα was extended from the Present Participle:

	Present Participle	Perfect Participle
Attic-Ionic	λείπουσα	γεγονυῖα
Aeolic (Lesbian)	λείποισα	τετόκοισα
North-West (late Delphian)	λειπουσα	δεδωκουσα

ii) In some Doric dialects (Theran, Heraclean), and also late Attic, the ending -εια was extended from the nominal u-stems (γλυκύς, Fem γλυκεῖα - the alteration us : eia goes back to the old ablaut pattern *us : *ewja i.e. zero : full grade):

| Theran | ἑστακεια | Attic | ἑστηκυῖα | (rare) |
| Heraclean | ἐρρηγεια | | ἐρρωγυῖα | (theoretical) |

In trying to avoid the analogical extension of -ont- into the Perfect Participle in terms of more abstract phonology, it would be a mistake to postulate a single underlying representation -wont- for both Present Participle -ont- and Perfect Participle *-wot-, which would generate both Attic-Ionic γεγονότος (*gegon+wót+os) and Aeolic γεγόνοντος. The same reasoning could be pursued in the case of the feminine form, and a single underlying -wontja- could be reconstructed, which would generate both Attic-Ionic γεγονυῖα (gegon+ús+ja *gegon-wót-ja) and Aeolic γεγόνοισα. Compare these two sets of underlying representations:

	Abstract Phonology		Concrete Phonology	
	Present	Perfect	Present	Perfect
Masc	ont	wónt	ont	wót
Fem	ontja	wóntja	ontja	wótja

One of the reasons why underlying representations like *wónt* and *wóntja* are to be rejected is that the evidence for them comes from two different dialects – Attic-Ionic γεγονυῖα enables us to postulate /w/ in underlying representations of the Perfect Participle, and Aeolic γεγόνοντος seems to indicate that a cluster /nt/ should figure in underlying representations of the same participle. In other words, a 'discovery procedure' applied in this case is nothing other than a cumulative method (used in Neogrammarian historical reconstructions or in generative phonology). This of course is not to deny that it is possible to derive even Aeolic γεγόνουσα from underlying *wontja*. Another point against the assumption of such forms is that such an assumption necessitates a morphological rule whereby a cluster /nt/ is simplified to /t/ in the non-phonological environment of the Perfect Participle; notice that after this step one reaches the representations *wot*, *wotja* (p. 215).

It could be that some supporting evidence for the more abstract underlying representations -*wont*-, -*wontja*- could come from the analysis of forms belonging to ἑστάναι 'stand';

Attic	ἑστώς (Masc)	Ionic	ἑστεώς (Masc)
	ἑστῶσα (Fem)		ἑστεῶσα (Fem)

These forms are traditionally analyzed as syncopated forms of ἕστηκα. Besides the participle forms there are only dual and plural forms of the Perfect and Pluperfect. They occur in Homer and Herodotos and in Attic Literature they are already archaisms.

ἑστ(ήκ)αμεν   ἕσταμεν
ἑστ(ηκ)ώς   ἑστώς

However, there is no *ἑστυῖα which would be syncopated from ἑστηκυῖα. Similarly, it is unnecessary to analyze Attic τεθνεώς and Homeric τεθνηώς as syncopated forms of τεθνηκώς (both come from *teth nāwōs) or Homeric τεθνηυῖα (Od. 4.734) as syncopated form of τεθνηκυῖα (this form may be traced back to *teth nawsja = zero-grade of *teth nāwosja*). Thus the best we can do is to assume that the analogical extension of -*ont*- from the Present Participle could have already taken place very early in the pre-history of Greek. That analogical extension is still the most reasonable explanation may be supported by similar phenomena in the Perfect Participle of Vedic.

Vedic Present (and Future and Aorist) Participles have two stems: the strong in -*ant*, and the weak in -*at*, e.g. *adánt*- 'eating'. If the suffix is accented, the accent shifts in weak cases to the endings that begin with vowels. The participles of verbs with a reduplicating Present do not

Attic-Ionic

	leípontos	leípontja	gegonwóntos	gegonwóntja
nt → t / - Perfect Participle	–	–	–	gegonwóntja
∅ - Grade Formation	–	–	gegonwótos	gegonwótja
w → ∅ / C -	–	–	gegonótos	gegonútja
Affrication	–	leípont^{s}ja	–	gegonút^{s}ja
t - Loss	–	leíponsja	–	gegonúsja
Depalatalization	–	leíponsa	–	gegonúhja
Compensatory Lengthening	–	leípǭsa	–	gegonújja
Raising	–	leípōsa	–	–
Fricative Weakening h → j / -j				

Aeolic

	leípontos	leípontja	gegónwontos	gegónwontja
w → ∅ / C -	–	leípontja	gegónontos	gegónontja
Affrication	–	leípont^{s}ja	–	gegónont^{s}ja
t - Loss	–	leíponsja	–	gegónonsja
Metathesis	–	leípoinsa	–	gegónoinsa
n - Loss	–	leípoisa	–	gegónoisa

distinguish a strong and weak stem, and keep -*at* (= weak stem) throughout, e.g. *dádat-* 'giving'.

PRESENT PARTICIPLE
(non-reduplicating stem)

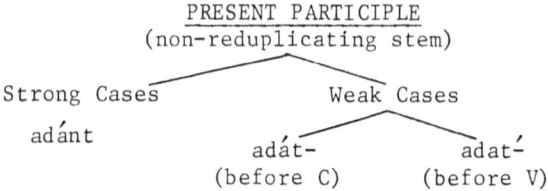

The Perfect Participle, e.g. dadvā́s 'having given', shows three stems: the strong in -vā́s occurring in strong cases (Nom, Acc of Sg, Dual and Nom Pl) and two weak stems in -vát and úṣ. The first occurs before consonants, the second before vowels. The suffix of uncompounded forms is always accented. The stem in -vát represents an analogical extension of the stem -át from the Present Participle. The reason for this extension is quite simple. Proper phonological forms *dadvóbhis (Instr Pl) and *dadvóbhyas (Dat Pl), according to the rule *as* ⟶ *o* / - *bh*, would destroy paradigmatic unity in the sense that the characteristic marker of the Perfect Participle *vas* ∿ *ús* would be obliterated. Thus instead of variants vā́s ∿ úṣ ∿ *vó we find vā́s ∿ úṣ ∿ vát. Unfortunately, we do not have any documents for the Locative; we can reconstruct *dadvátsu* (cf. *patsú* 'feet' Loc.).

PERFECT PARTICIPLE

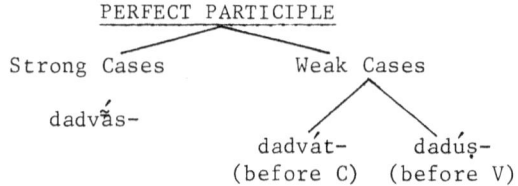

See the following chart (p. 217) for a more detailed description of the distribution of morphemic variants of both participles.

The same derivation in terms of more concrete phonology with two underlying representations *dadváns-* (generating *dadvā́s* and *dadúṣ-as*) and *dadvót-*, which is extended analogically from *dádat-* (Present Participle) are presented below:

Solution (1)

	dadvánsam	dadvánsas
Nasalization	dadvā́sam	dadvā́sas
Ø-Grade Formation	-	dadúsas

Figure 5.2 Distribution of morphemic variants of Present and Perfect Patriciple in Vedic

	PRESENT PARTICIPLE		PERFECT PARTICIPLE	
	(No reduplication)	(reduplication)		
Sg N	ad án	dád at		dad vā́n
A	ánt am	at am		vā́s am
N Pl	ánt as	at as		vā́s as
Sg I	ad at ā́	at ā́		dad úṣ ā
D	at é	at e		úṣ e
Ab, G	at ás	at as		úṣ as
L	at í	at i		úṣ i
Pl A	at ás	at as		úṣ as
I	ád bhis	ad bhis	ANALOGY →	dad vád bhis
D, Ab	ád bhyas	ad bhyas	→	vád bhyas
G	at ā́m	at ām		úṣ ām
L	át su	at su	→	vát su (undocumented)
STEM	strong	weak	weak	weak strong

Retroflexion — dadúṣas

Solution (2)

	dadvánsam	dadvánsas
Ø-Grade Formation	–	dadúnsas
Cluster Simplification	–	dadúsas
Nasalization	dadvā́sam	–
Retroflexion	–	dadúṣas

However, even this derivation is probably beside the point since the matter may be further simplified if we assume that the nasal in *vā́s* (<*váns*) is *analogically* extended from the Present Participle in *-ant*. As shown above on the chart, forms with nasal have the same distribution in both Present and Perfect Participle (Nom, Acc of Sg, Dual and Nom Pl), which could facilitate analogical extension. In other words, there is no point in deriving *uṣ* from VANS; *uṣ* should be derived from VAS and *vā́s* from VANS as shown below:

	dadvánsam	dadvásas
Ø-Grade Formation	–	dadúsas
Nasalization	dadvā́sam	–
Retroflexion	–	dadúṣas

Summarizing, we may say that some forms of Perfect Participle in both Vedic and Greek are best explained as analogical extensions from the Present Participle:

Present Participle		Perfect Participle				
	analogy					
ant	⟶	vant	∾	vat	∾ us	Vedic
ont	⟶	(w)ont	∾	(w)ot	∾ us	Greek

NOTES

1 However, to do justice to the old hypothesis, it seems that even in Greek in some instances the personal ending *-(e)si* was really obliterated by fricative weakening and subsequent loss of intervocalic /h/. In this way, Attic εἶ 'you will go' (from **eisi*) and εἶ 'you are' (from **esi*) can be best explained:

219 Interplay between Sound Change and Analogy

	eisi	esi
Fricative Weakening	eihi	ehi
h ⟶ ∅ / V - V	ei i	e i
i ⟶ ∅	ei	

2 See Thumb-Scherer (1959:102) for data:
Pres Sg 1 φίλημμι
       2 λύπης   and   φίλησθα
       3 ποίη   and   φίλει, τίμαι, στεφάνοι
    Pl 1 φορήμμεθα
       2
       3 ἐπιρρόμβεισι, δίψαισι, στεφάνοισιν, διασάφηνται

3 Compare the following forms:
Aeolic (Lesbian)

3rd Pl Pres	φίλεισι	δίψαισι	στεφάνοισι
Participle Pres	φίλεις	γέλαις	διδούς

Attic-Ionic

3rd Pl Pres	εἰσί	φᾶσί	φέρουσι
Participle Pres	τιθείς	ἱστᾶς	διδούς
Proto Greek	*-enti	*-anti	*-onti
	*-ents	*-ants	*-onts

Aeolic

	enti		anti		onti		
Affrication	ent^si	ents	ant^ssi	ants	ont^si	onts	
t ⟶ ∅ / C - C	ensi	ens	ansi	ans	onsi	ons	
Metathesis (b)	einsi		ainsi		oinsi		
n ⟶ ∅	eisi	eis(!)	aisi	ais(!)	oisi	ois(!)	

Attic-Ionic

	enti		anti		onti		
Affrication	ent^si	ents	ant^si	ants	ont^si	onts	
t ⟶ ∅ / C - C	ensi	ens	ansi	ans	onsi	ons	
n ⟶ ∅	ẹ̄si	ẹ̄s	āsi	ās	ǭsi	ǭs	
+ *Compensatory Lengthening*							
Raising	ẹsi	ẹs			ǫsi	ǫs	

This difficulty would be removed if we assumed that Greek dialects went through a stage with nasalized vowels. The nasalized vowels could be diphthongized and later on denasalized yielding historical -*oisi* (Aeolic) or -*ousi* (Attic-Ionic):

	Aeolic	Attic-Ionic
	-onti	-onti
Nasalization	õti	õti
Postnasal n ⟶ ∅	õti	õti
Diphthongization	õĩti	õũti
Denasalization	oiti	outi

	Aeolic	Attic-Ionic
Affrication	oit^{s}i	out^{s}i
t ⟶ ∅	oisi	ousi
	φέροισι	φέρουσι
	-ants	-ants
t ⟶ ∅	ans	ans
Nasalization	āns	āns
Postnasal n ⟶ ∅	ās	ās
Diphthongization	āis	–
Denasalization	ais	ās
	παίς	πᾶς

4 See Thumb-Scherer (1959) and Thumb-Kieckers (1932) for the actually documented forms:
<u>Arcadian</u>   ἐπιορκέντι 'swearing falsely' (Dat)
<u>Cypriote</u>   ἰό(ν)τα 'being' (Acc)
<u>Thessalian</u> (Pelasgiotis) στρατα]γέντος 'being general'
                                                              (Gen)
               (Thessaliotis) στραταγ] έο‹ι›ντος
                                       'being general' (Gen)
<u>Boeotian</u>   ῥύοντος 'running' (Gen)
<u>Lesbian</u>   [ὁ]μονόεντες 'agreeing together' (Gen)
<u>Cretan</u>   καλίων 'calling'
<u>Laconian</u>   ἀνιοχίων (= ἡνιοχέων) 'holding the reins'
<u>Heraclean</u> ἀναγγελίοντι 'reporting' (Dat)
<u>Ionic</u>   φιλεῦντας (Homeric) 'loving' (Acc Pl)

5 Some verbs had two Perfect forms - one in a stop, the other in an aspirate - and there usually was a difference in meaning. Forms in a stop were used intransitively, whereas later formations in an aspirate had transitive meaning:
ἀνέῳγα 'I am open'   vs. ἀνέῳχα 'I have opened'
πέπρᾱγα 'I am in a state...'   πέπρᾱχα 'I have done'
ἔρρωγα 'I am broken'   ἔρρηχα 'I have broken'
πέπηγα 'I am stuck'   πέπηχα 'I have fixed'

6 The situation is quite complicated in Old Church Slavonic. Basically, the PIE Aorist marker is unchanged in the cluster -s-te (2nd Pl) and in underlying sequences of consonant + s. Elswhere, s occurred subject to so-called Pedersen's Law (= 'ruki' rule), according to which PIE *s becomes a dorsovelar fricative x after i, u, r, and k. The resulting x is palatalized before front vowels. See the plural forms of the old sigmatic Aorist of *rešti* (*rek-ti*) 'say':

          Pl 1   rěxomъ   <   *rēk-s-omu
             2   rěste   <   *rēk-s-te
             3   rěšě   <   *rēk-s-int

These forms can be derived in the following way:

221 Interplay between Sound Change and Analogy

	rēksomu	rēksint
Pedersen's Law	rēkxomu	rēkxint
Cluster Simplification	rēxomu	rēxint
Palatalization	–	rēšint
Nasalization	–	rēšẽ

However, x was extended analogically in many environments where it cannot be predicted as a result of Pedersen's Law, i.e. we may talk about the morphologization of the phonological process. See the Aorist forms of *pẽti* (< *pen-ti):

				analogical formations
Pl 1	pẽsomъ	<	*pen-s-omu	pẽxomъ
2	pẽste	<	*pen-s-te	pẽste
3	pẽsẽ	<	*pen-s-int	pẽšẽ

See Leskien (1969:49, 145) for data.

SELECT BIBLIOGRAPHY

Allen, W.S. (1953) *Phonetics in Ancient India:* London.
- (1958) 'Some problems of palatalization in Greek': *Lingua* 7, pp. 113-33.
- (1962) *Sandhi:* The Hague.
- (1967) 'Correlations of tone and stress in ancient Greek': *To honor Roman Jakobson: essays on the occasion of his seventieth birthday*, 1.46-62: The Hague.
- (1968) *Vox Graeca.* (A guide to the pronunciation of Classical Greek): Cambridge, University Press.
- (1973a) *Accent and Rhythm:* Cambridge, University Press.
- (1973b) 'Χθών, 'Ruki,' and related matters: a reappraisal': *Transactions of the Philological Society*, 1973, pp. 99-126.
- (1974) *Vox Graeca^2* (A guide to the pronunciation of Classical Greek): Cambridge, University Press.

Antilla, R. (1972) *An Introduction to Historical and Comparative Linguistics*, The MacMillan Company, New York.

Bartoněk, A. (1966) 'Development of the long-vowel system in ancient Greek dialects': Opera Universitatis Purkynianae Brunensis (Facultas Philosophica) 106, Praha.
- (1972) *Classification of the West Greek Dialects at the time about 350 B.C.:* Prague.

Bechtel, F. (1921-4) *Griechische Dialekte:* Berlin.

Beekes, R.S.P. (1973) 'The Greek i- and u- Stems and πόλις, -ηος': *Glotta* 51, pp. 228-245.

Belić, A. (1909) 'Zametki po čakavskim govoram': *Izvestija otdelenija russkogo jazyka i slovesnosti imperatorskoj akademii nauk*, XIV, 2, pp. 181-266.

Benveniste, E. (1968) 'Le système phonologique de l'iranien ancien': *Bulletin de la Société de Linguistique de Paris*, Tome 63, Fasc. 1, pp. 53-64.

Blass, F. (1888) *Über die Aussprache des Altgriechischen:* Berlin.

Select Bibliography

Blass, F., A. Debrunner (1961) *A Greek Grammar of the New Testament and other Early Christian Literature*: Chicago.
Bloomfield, M. (1888) 'The Origin of the Recessive Accent in Greek': *American Journal of Philology* 9, pp. 1-41.
Bourget, E. (1927) *Le dialecte laconien*: Paris.
Brause, J. (1909) *Lautlehre der kretischen Dialekte*: Halle.
Browning, R. (1969) *Medieval and Modern Greek*: London, Hutchinson.
Bubeník, V. (1975) Review of A. H. Sommerstein, The Sound Pattern of Ancient Greek, Oxford 1973: *Lingua* 33, pp. 170-8.
- (1976) 'Consonant Length in Ancient Greek Phonology': *Current Progress in Historical Linguistics* (W.M. Christie, Jr., ed.) North-Holland Publishing Company, pp. 157-165.
- (1979) 'Historical Development of the Ancient Greek Accent System': *Indogermanische Forschungen* 84, pp. 90-106.
Buck, C.D. (1955) *The Greek Dialects*: Chicago.
Chadwick, J. (1963) 'The prehistory of the Greek language': *Cambridge Ancient History*, rev. edn., Vol. II, Ch. XXXIX. C.U.P.
- (1969) 'Greek and Pre-Greek': *Transactions of the Philological Society*, pp. 80-98.
- (1973) *Documents in Mycenaean Greek*^{2}: Cambridge, University Press.
Christol, A. (1972) 'Phonologie des aspirées grecques et parfait à aspirée: *Bulletin de la Société de Linguistique de Paris*. Tome LXVII, Fasc. 1, pp. 69-83.
Coleman, R. (1963) 'The Dialect Geography of Ancient Greece': *Transactions of the Philological Society*, pp. 58-126.
Debrunner, A., O. Hoffman (1954) *Geschichte der griechischen Sprache II: Grundfragen und Grundzüge des nachklassischen Griechisch*: Berlin, Sammlung Göschen.
Diver, W. (1958) 'On the prehistory of Greek consonantism': *Word*, 14. 1-25.
Dow, S. (1967) 'Ekphantos': *Glotta* 45, pp. 202-21.
Garde, P. (1968) *L'accent*: Paris.
Goodwin, W.W. (1894) *A Greek Grammar*: London.
Grammont, M. (1948) *Phonétique du grec ancien*: Lyon
Guarducci, M. (1939, 1942) *Inscriptions Creticae II, III*. Roma.
Hainsworth, J.B. (1967) 'Greek Views of Greek Dialectology': *Transactions of the Philological Society*, pp. 62-76.
Hamp, E.P. (1960) 'Notes on Early Greek Phonology': *Glotta* 38, pp. 187-190.
Householder, F.W. (1959) '*Pa-ro* and Mycenaean cases': *Glotta* 38, pp. 1-10.
- (1960) 'Early Greek -*j*-': *Glotta* 39, pp. 179-190.
Householder, F.W., K. Kazazis, A. Koutsoudas (1964) *Reference Grammar of Literary Dhimotiki*: The Hague.

Householder, F.W., G. Nagy (1972) *Greek, A Survey of Recent Work*: The Hague.
Ivić, P. (1958) *Die serbokroatischen Dialekte ihre Struktur und Entwicklung*: The Hague.
Ivić, P. (1965) 'Prozodijski sistem savremenog srpskohrvatskog standardnog jezika': *Symbolae linguisticae in honorem Georgii Kuryłowicz*: Warsaw: Polska Akademia Nauk, pp. 135-144.
Jakobson, R. (1937/1962) 'Über die Beschaffenheit der prosodischen Gegensätze': *Selected Writings. I. Phonological Studies*. The Hague.
Jakobson, R., C.G.M. Fant, M. Halle (1952) *Preliminaries to Speech Analysis*. MIT Acoustics Lab., Tech. Rep. No. 13: Cambridge, Mass.
Jakobson, R., M. Halle (1956) *Fundamentals of Language*: The Hague.
Jannaris, A.N. (1897/1968) *An Historical Greek Grammar Chiefly of the Attic Dialect*: Hildesheim.
Kiparsky, P. (1967a) 'A propos de l'histoire de l'accentuation grecque': *La phonologie générative*, ed. by Sanford A. Schane, pp. 73-93. Paris, Didier and Larousse (Languages 8).
- (1967b) 'A Phonological Rule of Greek': *Glotta* 44, pp. 109-134.
- (1973a) 'On comparative linguistics: the case of Grassmann's Law': *Current Trends in Linguistics* 11, pp. 115-134.
- (1973b) 'The Inflectional accent in Indo-European': *Language* 49, pp. 794-849.
Kuryłowicz, J. (1945-9) 'La nature des procés dits 'analogiques'': *Acta Linguistica* 5, 15-37.
- (1958) *L'accentuation des languages indo-européennes*. Polska Akademia Nauk, Prace Językoznawcze 17. Wrocław and Kraków.
- (1968) *Indogermanische Grammatik II*: Heidelberg, Winter.
Ladefoged, P. (1971) *Preliminaries to Linguistic Phonetics*: Chicago and London.
Lehiste, I. (1970) *Suprasegmentals*: Cambridge, Mass.
Lejeune, M. (1972) *Phonétique historique du mycénien et du grec ancien*: Paris.
Leskien, A. (1969) *Handbuch der altbulgarischen Sprache*: Heidelberg.
Lobel, E. (1927) ΑΛΚΑΙΟΥ ΜΕΛΗ: Oxford, Clarendon Press.
Lupaş, L. (1972) *Phonologie du grec attique*: The Hague.
Macdonnel, A.A. (1916) *A Vedic Grammar for Students*: London, Oxford University Press.
Martinet, A. (1954) 'Accents et tons': *Misc. Phon. II*: London, 13.
Meillet, A. (1965) *Aperçu d'une histoire de la langue grecque^7*: Paris.

Meisterhans, K., E. Schwyzer (1900) *Grammatik der attischen Inschriften³*: Berlin.
Miller, D.G. (1974) 'Some problems in formulating aspiration and deaspiration rules in Ancient Greek': *Glossa* 8:2, pp. 211-24.
Nagy, G. (1970) *Greek Dialects and the Transformation of an Indo-European Process*: Cambridge, Mass.
Newton, B. (1972) *The generative interpretation of dialect*: Cambridge.
Palmer, L.R. (1963) *The Interpretation of Mycenaean Greek Texts*: Oxford.
Risch, E. (1955) 'Die Gliederung der griechrischen Dialekte in neuer Sicht': *Museum Helveticum* 12, pp. 61-76.
Ruijgh, C.J. (1967) *Etudes sur la grammaire et le vocabulaire du grec mycénien*. Amsterdam, Hakkert.
Ruipérez, M.S. (1956) 'Esquisse d'une histoire du vocalisme grec': *Word* 12, pp. 67-81.
Sag, I.A. (1974) 'The Grassmann's Law Ordering Pseudoparadox': *Linguistic Inquiry* V, pp. 591-607.
Saussure, F. de (1916/1960) *Course in General Linguistics*: London. (Translated by W. Baskin from *Cours de Linguistique générale*: Lausanne/Paris).
Schwyzer, E., P. Cauer (1923) *Dialectorum Graecarum exampla epigraphica potiora*: Leipzig, Hirzel.
Schwyzer, E. (1939) *Griechische Grammatik. Vol. I: Lautlehre, Wortbildung, Flexion*: München, Beck.
Sommerstein, A.H. (1973) 'The Sound Pattern of Ancient Greek': *Publications of the Philological Society* XXIII.
Sturtevant, E.H. (1940) *The Pronunciation of Greek and Latin²*: Philadelphia.
Szemerényi, O. (1968) 'The Attic 'Rückverwandlung' or atomism and structuralism in action': Studien zur Sprachwissenschaft und Kulturkunde, *Gedenkschrift für Wilhelm Brandenstein (1898-1967)*, ed. by Manfred Mayrhofer, 139-57. IBK 14.
Thumb, A. (1909) *Handbuch der griechischen Dialekte*: Heidelberg.
Thumb, A., E. Kieckers (1932) *Handbuch der griechischen Dialekte I²*: Heidelberg.
Thumb, A., A. Scherer (1959) *Handbuch der griechischen Dialekte II²*: Heidelberg.
Vendryes, J. (1938) *Traité d'accentuation grecque*: Paris.
Vilborg, E. (1960) *A Tentative Grammar of Mycenaena Greek*: Göteborg.
Warburton, I.P. (1970) 'Rules of accentuation in Classical and Modern Greek': *Glotta* 48, pp. 107-121.
- (1976) 'On the boundaries of morphology and phonology: a case study from Modern Greek': *Journal of Linguistics*, pp. 259-278.

Whitney, W.D. (1889) *Sanskrit Grammar*: Cambridge, Mass.
Williams Jackson, A.V. (1892) *An Avestan Grammar*: Stuttgart.
Wyatt, W.F. (1968a) 'Greek Names in σσος -ττος': *Glotta* 46, pp. 6-14.
- (1968b) 'Early Greek /y/': *Glotta* 46, pp. 229-237.

INDEX OF NAMES

Allen 5, 14, 17, 44, 46, 74, 75, 79, 80, 85, 98, 115, 118, 134, 144, 178.
Anttila 14, 155.

Bartoněk 16, 17, 28, 45, 47, 58, 60, 63, 71, 75, 141.
Belić 174.
Bechtel 14.
Bubeník 85, 164.
Buck 14, 67, 68, 105, 151, 192, 211.

Chadwick 27, 28, 111, 131.
Christol 209, 210
Coleman 15

Dow 129
Debrunner 30

Garde 135, 170, 172, 177.
Goodwin 133.
Grammont 5.
Guarducci 76.

Hainsworth 184.
Householder 187.
Householder - Nagy 4.

Ivić 174, 175.

Jakobson 133.

Jakobson et al. 87.
Jakobson - Halle 16, 84.

Kiparsky 19, 101, 104, 138, 149, 161, 167, 176, 183, 186, 188, 194.
Kuryłowicz 155, 161, 166, 183, 184, 187.

Ladefoged 80, 87.
Lehiste 176, 177.
Lejeune 8, 18, 19, 51, 58, 70, 75, 79, 80, 99, 105, 108, 115, 117, 119, 127, 131, 141, 191.
Leskien 221.
Lobel 186.
Lupaş 16, 32, 34, 47, 74, 77, 79, 84, 85, 86, 98, 127, 128.

Macdonnel 187.
Martinet 62, 137, 168, 172.
Meisterhans - Schwyzer 45, 100.
Miller 103.

Newton 178.

Risch 28, 58.
Ruipérez 17.

Schwyzer 45, 47, 53, 58, 75, 106, 129, 145, 146, 160, 181, 187, 189, 190, 202, 205, 208.
Sommerstein 10, 19, 74, 141.
Sturtevant 5, 79, 80.
Szemerényi 17, 50.

Thumb 14.

Thumb - Kieckers 15, 76, 183, 220.
Thumb - Scherer 15, 191, 193, 219, 220.

Vendryes 135.
Vilborg 116, 164.

Warburton 178, 179, 180.

INDEX OF GREEK WORDS
AND WORD FORMS

ἀγαπητός 170.
ἀγασώς (ἀγαθούς) 105.
ἄγγελοι 171 (paradigm), 173.
ἀγγέλοι 171 (paradigm), 173, 181.
 ἀγγέλων 173.
ἀγκύλος 140.
ἄγκυλος (ἀγκύλος) 140.
ἄγριος 146, 152.
 ἀγρύοιο 152.
ἀγρός 167 (paradigm).
ἄγω
 ἦγον 10, 11.
αδευπιος (ἀδελφεός) 79.
αδικιων (ἀδικῶν) 67.
αζαθος (ἀγαθός) 110.
Ἀθήνηθεν 138.
Ἀθήνησι 138.
αἰδώ 70.
αιλος (ἄλλος) 126.
αιλοτρια (ἀλλότρια) 126.
αιμισεων (ἡμισέων) 115.
αἰχμή 80.
ἄχαντος (ἄκανθος) 97.
ἄλιος (ἥλιος) 71.
Ἀλκμήνη 93.
ἄλλοθεν 137-8.
ἄλλοθι 137-8.
ἄλλος 33, 39, 126-7.
ἅλς
 ἅλασι (ἁλσί) 123.
 ἅλεσσι (ἁλσί) 123.

ἅλσις 123.
ἁμές (ἡμεῖς) 25.
 ἁμέ (ἡμᾶς) 25.
ἅμμες (ἡμεῖς) 25.
 ἅμμε (ἡμᾶς) 25.
ἀμνός 120.
ἄνασσα 84.
ἀνδρεῖος 141.
ανεθεαν (ἀνέθεσαν) 211.
ανεθεν (ἀνέθεσαν) 211.
ανεθιαν (ἀνέθεσαν) 66.
ἀνεπίθετος 146.
ανεσηκε (ἀνέθηκε) 105.
ἄνθρωπος 166 (paradigm), 169, 170, 178.
 ἀνθρώπου 179.
 ἄνθρωποι 173.
 ἀνθρώποι (ἄνθρωποι) 173, 181.
 ἀνθρώπων 173.
αντροπος (ἄνθρωπος) 97.
ἄνυδρος 146.
ανφοτερος (ἀμφότερος) 79.
ἄξιος 155 (paradigm).
Απειλων (Ἀπόλλων) 126-7.
Ἀπέλλων (Ἀπόλλων) 126-7.
ἁπλοῦς 164.
 ἁπλᾶ 70.
απολογιττετθω (ἀπολογιζέσθω) 107.
αποδοσσαι (ἀποδόσθαι) 106.
αποϝειπαθθω (ἀπειπάσθω) 107.

ἀποκλείω 47.
ἀποκλῄω 47.
ἀπόλλυμι 126.
ἀπόφανσις 123.
ἀπόφασις 123.
ἀπυ (ἀπό) 25.
ἀπφῦς 17, 98.
ἀργυρός
  ἀργυροῖ 43.
  ἀργυρῷ 43.
ἁρπαγή 135.
ἁρπάγη 135.
ἄρρην 123.
ἄρσην 123.
ἀρχαῖος 173.
ἄρχαιος (ἀρχαῖος) 173.
ἀρχαίος (ἀρχαῖος) 173.
  ἀρχαίου 173.
ἆσθμα 95.
ατροπος (ἄνθρωπος) 97.

βαίνω 126.
Βάκχος 17.
βανα (γυνή) 120.
βάπτω
  ἐβάφη 103.
βασίλεια 163 (paradigm), 166, 169.
βδάλλω 93.
βδελλίζω 93.
βδελύττομαι 93.
βειλομαι (βούλομαι) 26, 118.
βελλομαι (βούλομαι) 26, 116-9.
βλάπτω
  ἔβλαψα 210.
  βέβλαφα 208, 210.
βοικιαρ (οἰκίας) 109.
βολή
  βολῶν 135.
βολλᾱ (βουλή) 26, 125.
βόλλομαι (βούλομαι) 26, 118.
βόλος
  βόλων 135.
βουλή 48, 126.
  βουλῆς 48.
  βουλῇ 48.

βούλομαι 116-9.
  βουλεῖ 46.
βροχυς (βραχύς) 26.
βωλᾱ (βουλή) 26, 48, 126.
βωλομαι (βούλομαι) 118.
Βωρθεα (Ὀρθία) 109.
Βωρσεα (Ὀρθία) 109.

γενεά 49, 51.
γενεή 49, 52.
γένος
  γένους 191.
  γένη 70.
γεραιός 171.
  γεραίτερος 171.
  γεραίτερος (γεραίτερος) 171.
γίγνομαι 205.
  γενοιτυ (γένοιτο) 25.
  ἐγενόμην 205.
  γέγονα 205.
  γεγονώς 212 (paradigm).
  γεγονότος 213, 215.
  γεγονυῖα 213, 215.
  γεγόνων (γεγονώς) 212 (paradigm).
  γεγόνοτος (γεγονότος) 213, 215.
  γεγόνοισα (γεγονυῖα) 213, 215.
γλυκύς 213.
  γλυκεῖα 213.
γνάμπτω 95.
γράφω
  γράψω 96.
γυνή
  γυναῖκες 4, 140.
  γυναίκες (γυναῖκες) 4, 140.

δαμάζω
  δμηθείς 95.
Δᾱρεῖος 58.
δάφνη 106.
δείκνυμι
  δειξαίμην 150.
  ἐδειξάμην 150.

Index of Greek Words and Word Forms

δειλομαι (βούλομαι) 26, 116-119.
δεύρη (δέρη) 60.
δεκεσθαι (δέχεσθαι) 107.
δερFᾱ (δέρη) 60.
δέρη 50, 60.
δέρκομαι
  ἐδέρχθην 98.
Δευς (Ζεύς) 111.
δηλομαι (βούλομαι) 116-9.
δῆλος 165.
  δήλων 165.
Δηνα (Δία) 111-3.
διαβειπαμενος (διαειπάμενος) 109.
διδάσκω 82.
δίδωμι 149 (paradigm).
  δίδωσι 23, 149.
  δίδωτι (δίδωσι) 23, 149.
  διδοῖ (δίδωσι) 191.
  διδοῦν (διδόναι) 191.
  δεδωκουσα (δεδωκυῖα) 213.
δικαδδω (δικάζω) 111-3.
  δικακσει (δικάσει) 23, 113.
δίκαιος 165-6 (paradigm).
διψῶ
  διψῶσι 197.
  δίψαισι (διψῶσι) 197.
δμώς 82.
δνοπαλίζω 82, 95.
δνόφος 82.
δōος (ζῶος) 111-3.
δōριαν (δωρεάν) 66.
δοῦλος 154.
  δούλου 154.
δραχμα (δραχμή) 37.
  δραχμαω (δραχμά) 37.
δυς- 95.
δυσγενής 81.
δυσμενής 81, 146, 167 (paradigm).
δῶλος (δοῦλος) 154.
  δώλω (δούλου) 154.
δῶρον 136-7.
  δώρων 136-7.
δωω (ζώω) 111.

ἕβδομος 146.

ἐγαμαντυ (ἐγήμαντο) 25.
ἔγερσις 123.
ἐγώ
  ἐμεο (ἐμοῦ) 24.
  ἐμιν (ἐμοί) 24.
ἔγωγε 141, 144.
  ἔμοιγε 141.
εἷμα 49.
εἱμάτιον (ἱμάτιον) 49.
εἰμί 6, 33, 46, 64-5, 122, 124, 201, 205-6.
  ἐμι (εἰμί) 26.
  ἔμμι (εἰμί) 6, 26, 122, 124, 201.
  ἐμμί (εἰμί) 201.
  εἶ 201-2.
  εἶς (εἶ) 201-2, 206.
  ἔσσι (εἶ) 201.
  ἐστί 82.
  εἰμέν (ἐσμέν) 206.
  εἰσίν 202-4, 206.
  ἔασι (εἰσίν) 201.
  ἐνθί (εἰσίν) 201.
  ἐντί (εἰσίν) 201.
  ἦ(ν) 204-5 (paradigm).
  ἦα (ἦ(ν)) 204-5 (paradigm).
  ἦεν (ἦν) 205.
  ἦς (ἦν) 25, 204.
  ἦσαν 159-60, 205-6.
  ἔον (ἦν, ἦσαν) 204.
  ἔσαν (ἦσαν) 159, 204.
  ἤν (ἦσαν) 159-60, 204.
  εμεν (εἶναι) 36.
εἶμι 203 (paradigm).
  εἶς (εἶ) 203, 207.
  εἶσθα (εἶ) 203, 207.
  εἶσι 203-4.
  ἴᾱσι 203-4.
  ᾖα 206 (paradigm).
  ᾔια (ᾖα) 206.
  ᾔιον (ᾖα) 206 (paradigm).
  ᾔεις 206-7.
εἵνυμι (ἕννυμι) 124.
εἰρήνη 50.
εἰς 93, 95.
εἷς 134.
εἰσδέχομαι 81.
εἰσρέω 81.

232 Index of Greek Words and Word Forms

ἐκ 93, 95, 99-100.
ἔκγονος 85, 100.
ἐκθλίβω 93, 97.
ἐκθνήσκω 93, 97.
ἐκκινέω 85.
εκομιττα (ἐκόμισα) 115.
ἐκτείνω 100.
ἔκφανσις 123.
ἔκφασις 123.
ἐκφέρω 99.
ἐκχέω 85, 99.
hελεσται (ἑλέσθαι) 107.
ἐλπίζω 19.
hεμισσον (ἥμισυ) 115.
hεμισυ (ἥμισυ) 115.
ἔμφασις 123.
ἐν 93, 95.
ενγυς (ἐγγύς) 79.
ἐνδεᾶ 51-5.
ἐνζεύγνυμι 81.
ἐνθαῦθα (ἐνταῦθα) 97.
ἐνθαῦτα (ἐνταῦθα) 97.
ἔννεκα (ἕνεκα) 61.
ἐνσβέννυμι 95.
ἐνστέλλω 81.
ἐξ 25.
εξαγοδι (ἐξάγουσι) 23.
ἐξημελγμένος 93.
ἐξκαίδεκα (ἑκκαίδεκα) 95.
ἐξμέδιμνος 95.
ἐξπηχυστί 95.
εοντος (ὄντος) 65.
επιδει (ἐπειδή) 48.
επιθιιανε (ἐπιθιγγάνη) 110.
ἐπίφασις 123.
επολεμιον (ἐπολέμουν) 193.
ἐρῆμος 141-2.
ἔρημος 141-2.
ἔρπες (ἕρπεις) 193.
ἔρσην (ἄρρην) 123.
εσκεθην (ἐσχέθην) 106.
ἑσπέρα 82.
ἔτος
  ἔτεα 66.
  ἔτη 66.
εὐέθωκεν (εἴωθε) 125.
εὐκλ(ε)ῆς
  εὐκλ(ε)έα 55.

εὐκλεῖα 55.
εὐκλεεῖς 55.
εὐκλεᾶ 55.
εὔνους 155-6 (paradigm).
εὔνων 42.
εὔνοος 155-6 (paradigm).
εὐνῶ 156.
ηὔνων 42.
εὐνῶν 156.
εὑρίσκω
  εὗρε 42-3.
  ηὗρε 42-3.
εὔφορος 146.
ευχαριστωμες (εὐχαριστοῦμεν) 66.
εὔχομαι
  εὔχου 42-3.
  ηὔχου 42-3.
  εὔξασθε 42-5.
  ηὔξασθε 42-5.
εχ (ἐκ) 99-100.
ἔχθρα 135, 146.
ἐχθρός 93, 97-9.
  ἐχθρά 135, 146.
Ἔχφαντος 99.
ἐχφέρειν 99.
ἐχφορήσαντι 99.
ἔχω 102.
  εχι (ἔχει) 48.
  ἔχει 85.
  ἔξω 102.
  ἔσχον 102.
εφαφιξατο (ἐφηφίσατο) 115.
ἔωθα (εἴωθα) 125.

Ϝευμενος (Ϝελμενος) 79.
Ϝεπιjα (ἔπη) 66.
Ϝετεα (ἔτη) 66.
Ϝετιια (ἔτη) 66.
Ϝημα 48.
Ϝρατρα (ῥήτρα) 36.
Ϝωρθεα (Ὀρθία) 109.

ζα (γῆ) 110.
ζειρά 82.
Ζενι (Διί) 111-3.
ζέω 82.
ζδος (ζῷος) 111-3.

233 Index of Greek Words and Word Forms

ζτεραιον 82.
ζώννυμι 124.

Ϻις (τίς) 82, 116-8.
ἥ 134.
ἥλιος 71.
ἡμέρα 50-4.
ἡμέρη 50-4.
ημι (εἰμί) 35, 64, 122, 124, 201.
ημισσον (ἥμισυ) 115.
ημιτυ (ἥμισυ) 115.

θάλασσα 84.
θάλαττα 84.
θάλπω
  ἐθάλφθη 100.
θάπτω
  ἐτάφη 103-4.
θαρρέω 124.
θάρρος 123.
θαρρύνω 124.
θαρσέω 124.
θάρσος 123.
θαρσύνω 123.
θαρσύς 123.
θεά 163-9 (paradigm).
  θεᾶς 135.
  θεάς 135.
θειβηω (Θηβαίου) 46.
θέλγω
  ἐθέλχθη 100.
θεός 66, 106.
θέρμανσις 123.
θεσμός 81.
Θετταλός 97.
θηρότροφος 136, 171.
θηροτρόφος 136.
θιθεμενος (τιθέμενος) 98.
θιος (θεός) 66.
θνῄσκω 97.
  τεθνηκώς (τεθνεώς) 214.
  τεθνηώς (τεθνεώς) 214.
θνητός 80.
θράσος 124.
θρασύνω 124.
θρασύς 124.

θρίξ 103.
  τριχός 103.
θρόνος 80.
θυκα (τύχη) 98.
θυμός 9, 33, 38, 48, 135.
θῦμος (θυμός) 135.
θύραζε 81.
θυφλος (τυφλός) 98.

ἰν (ἐν) 25.
ἰναλινω (ἐναλίνω) 25.
ἰνδικος (ἔνδικος) 25.
hιέρεα 46.
hιέρεια 46.
hιερομναμονσι (ἱερομνήμοσι) 123.
ἵημι
  ἱᾶσι 203-4.
  ἵεισι (ἱᾶσι) 203-4.
  ἥ 134.
  εἵς 134.
  εἵσι 202.
Ἰλιόθι 138.
ιοντα (ὄντα) 65.
ἵππος 173.
  ἵππου 7, 12.
  ἵππω 7, 12.
  ἵππων 173.
  ιππω (ἵππου) 7, 12.
  ιππω (ἵππου) 7, 12.
ἱπποφορβός 140.
ἱρᾱνᾱ (εἰρήνη) 50.
Ἰσθμοῖ 138.
ἵστημι
  ἔσταν (ἔστησαν) 159.
  ἐστάσαν (ἔστησαν) 159.
  στάν 160.
  ἑστώς 214.
  ἑστῶσα 214.
  ἑστεώς (ἑστώς) 214.
  ἑστεῶσα (ἑστῶσα) 214.
  ἑστηκώς 214.
  ἑστακεια (ἑστηκῖα) 213-4.
ἰών (ἐγώ) 65, 67, 110.

κάββαλε (κατέβαλε) 85.
καδδῦσαι (καταδῦσαι) 85.

καθαίρω
  εκαθᾶρα (ἐκάθαρα) 120.
  ἐκάθηρα (ἐκάθαρα) 122.
καθιστᾶν (καθιστάναι) 191.
καιρός 48.
κακχάζω 17, 98.
καλιων (καλῶν) 67.
καλός
  καλή 166 (paradigm).
καλχός (χαλκός) 79.
κάππεσον (κατέπεσον) 85.
καπφάλαρα (κατὰ φάλαρα) 85.
καρδία 52.
καρύσσω 26, 110-12.
καρύττω 26, 110-12.
κας (καί) 25.
κατά 85.
κατεθιjαν (κατέθεσαν) 66, 211.
κατεληλύθοντος (κατεληλυθότος) 26.
κάτθανον (κατέθανον) 85.
καττάνυσαν (κατετάνυσαν) 85.
καυχος (χαλκός) 79, 97.
κεῖμαι 64-5.
κείρω
  ἔκερσεν 123.
κέλλω
  κέλσαι 123.
κῆμαι (κεῖμαι) 46.
κεράννυμι 124.
κηρύσσω 110-12.
κηρύττω 110-12.
κιμενας (κειμένας) 48.
κίς (τίς) 14, 116.
κλεῖθρον 47.
κλείς 47.
κλῆθρον 47.
κλής 47.
κλίσις 123.
κνάω 95.
κομιδδω (κομίζω) 115.
κόρᾱ (κόρη) 60.
κορϜᾱ (κόρη) 60.
κόρη 50-6, 60-1.
Κορινθόθι 139.
κόρρη 51-2.

κοσμιοντες (κοσμοῦντες) 66.
κοσμοντες (κοσμοῦντες) 66.
κότερος (πότερος) 120.
κούρη 60-1.
κραδίη (καρδία) 52.
κρᾶνᾱ (κρήνη) 50.
κρατύς
  κρείττων 111.
  κράτιστος 111.
κρίων
  ἔκριννα 120, 122.
κρίσις 123.
κρύπτω 103.
  ἐκρύφη 103.
  κέκρυφα 208.
κτείνω 122, 126-7.
κτέννω (κτείνω) 122, 126.
κυεοσα (κυοῦσα) 68.
κυευσα (κυοῦσα) 68.
κωρᾱ (κόρη) 60.
κῶς (πῶς) 120.

λαμβάνω
  ἔλαβον 4, 153, 157.
  (paradigm) 157.
  ἐλάβομεν 153-5.
  ἔλαβον 4, 153-5, 158-9.
  ἐλάβοσαν 4, 158-60.
λασφη (λάσθη) 106.
λέγω
  λέγεις 139, 188.
  λέγει 139, 188.
  ἐλέγομεν 171 (paradigm).
  ἐλέγομες 171 (paradigm).
  λέγης 188-9.
  λέγη 188-9.
  λέγη (λέγη) 189.
  λέγησι (λέγη) 189.
  εἶπαν 211.
  λέλεγμαι 79.
λείπω 48.
  λείπων 212 (paradigm), 213, 215.
  λείπουσα 213, 215.
  λείποισα (λείπουσα) 213, 215.
λιπεῖν 170.

Index of Greek Words and Word Forms

λιπών 170.
λέλοιπα 209.
λελοίπασι 203.
ἐλείφθη 98, 101-2.
λειτουργῶ 47.
λεύκη 135.
λευκή 135.
λητουργῶ 47.
λεύσσω 84.
λύθεος (λύθινος) 65.
λύθιος (λύθινος) 65.
λυπηρός 38.
  λυπηρᾶς 135.
  λυπηράς 135.
λύω
  ἔλυον 155 (paradigm) 157.
  ἔλυσα 209-11.
  ἐλύσαν (ἔλυσαν) 159.
  λῦσαι 136-7.
  λῦσαι 136-7.
  λυσαστο (λυσάσθω) 106.
  λέλυκα 209-11.
  λέλυνται 210.
  ἐλύθεν (ἐλύθησαν) 159.
  ἐλύθην (ἐλύθησαν) 25, 159.

Μεγαροῖ 139.
μεδδων (μείζων) 88, 111.
μέδων 88.
μέζων (μείζων) 113.
μhεγαλαν (μεγάλην) 110.
μείζων 113.
μέλισσα 110.
μέλιττα 19, 110-12.
μένος 146.
μέσος 110-12.
μέσσος (μέσος) 16, 110-12.
μετά 85.
μεττος (μέσος) 26, 88, 110-12.
μευ (μου) 68.
μηλύχιος (μειλίχιος) 48.
μῦλύχιος (μειλίχιος) 48.
μισθῶ
  μισθοῦμεν 73.
  μισθοῦτε 73.
  μισθῶμες (μισθοῦμεν) 73.
  μισθῶτε (μισθοῦτε) 73.

μισθοῦντες 74.
μισθωντες (μισθοῦντες) 74.
μισθωοντες (μισθοῦντες) 74.
μιστος (μισθός) 107.
μνᾶ 162 (paradigm).
  μνᾶς 164.
μνάομαι 120.
μνέα (μνᾶ) 162.
μοῖρα 126.

νεᾶ 50-4.
νεή 50-4.
νέμω
  ἔνειμα 122.
  ἔνεμμα (ἔνειμα) 122.
νίκη 33.
  νίκης 36.
  νίκᾱς 36.
  νικαις (νίκᾱς) 36.
  νικανς (νίκᾱς) 36.

ξεῖνος (ξένος) 60-1.
ξέννος (ξένος) 61.
ξένος 60-1, 99.
ξηνος (ξένος) 60-1.
ξύλον 22.

οhεοι (ὅτεῳ) 82.
οζις (ὅτις) 82.
οἵ 134.
οἶδα
  οἶσθα 196.
οἰκία 49.
οἰκίη (οἰκία) 49.
οἰκοδόμος 141.
οἴκοθεν 138-40.
οἴκοθι 138-40.
οἴκοι 136-40, 173-4.
οἴκοι 136-8, 173-4.
οἰκονόμος 141.
οἰκτρός 93.
ὀλίος (ὀλίγος) 110.
ὀλοφύρομαι 127.
ὀλοφύρρω (ὀλοφύρομαι) 127.
ὀπυ (ὑπό) 25.
ὄρνυμι
  ὦρσε 123.

ὅς
  οἵ 134.
  ᾖ 134.
ὀστᾶ 70.
οὐρανόθι 138.
οὔτε 39.
ὀφέλλω (ὀφείλω) 125.
ὀφήλω (ὀφείλω) 126.
ὀφθαλμός 98, 106.

παῖς
  παῖδες 136, 140, 154, 173.
  παύδες (παῖδες) 136, 140, 154, 173.
  παίδων 136, 154, 173.
  παιδῶν 154, 173.
παυσα (πᾶσα) 19, 59, 61.
πανσα (πᾶσα) 19, 59, 123.
πᾶς 58-9.
  παντός 58-9.
  πᾶσι 18.
  πᾶσα 18, 58-60, 123.
πατήρ 145 (paradigm), 64-5.
πατρόκτονος 136, 140, 171.
πατροκτόνος 136, 140.
παχύς 103-4.
  πάσσων 103-4.
πεινῶ
  πεινῶμεν 71-3.
  πεινῆτε 71-3.
  πεινᾶμες (πεινῶμεν) 71-3.
  πεινᾶτε (πεινῆτε) 71-3.
Πελεᾶται 46.
Πελειᾶται 46.
περίπολος 146.
πέσσυρες (τέτταρες) 11, 120-1.
Πετθαλος (Θεσσαλός) 97.
πέτταρες (τέτταρες) 11, 120-1.
πηλόθεν (τηλόθεν) 14, 116-9.
πίσυρες (τέτταρες), 11, 120.
πλάττω 111.
πλήρη 51-55.
πόθεν 138.
πόθι 138.
ποῖ 138.
ποικίλος 140.

ποίκιλος (ποικίλος) 140.
ποιμήν
  ποιμέσι 123.
πόημι (ποιῶ) 196 (paradigm).
ποιηασσαι (ποιήσασθαι) 106.
ποιιομενος (ποιούμενος) 65, 193.
πολεμίξομεν (πολεμίσομεν) 113.
πόλις
  πόλεως 143.
  πόλεσιν 143.
πος (πρός) 25.
ποταμός 135.
  ποταμοῦ 43.
  ποταμῷ 43.
πόταμος (ποταμός) 135, 170.
πότερος 146.
πούς 145 (paradigm).
  ποδός 167-9.
  πόδα 167-9.
πραξιομεν (πράξομεν) 24.
πράσσω 84.
πράττω 21, 33, 84.
πράϋνσις 123.
πρεσβεύω 81-2.
πρήσσω (πράσσω) 21.
πρήττω (πράττω) 21.
πρό 42.
προβειπαhας (προειπα(σα)ς) 109.
προθθα (πρόσθεν) 107.
πρός 93, 95.
προσβολή 81.
προσλαμβάνω 81.
προσνέμω 81.
προστα (πρόσθεν) 107.
πρόσφθεγμα 100.
πρωϋδᾶν 42.
Πυθοῖ 138.
πυρρός 80.

ῥᾴδιος
  ῥαίων 41, 44.
  ῥᾶων 41, 44.
ρεοντα (ῥέοντα) 67.
ῥήγνυμι
  ἐρρηγεια (ἐρρωγυῖα) 213.
ῥήτωρ
  ῥήτορσι 123.

237 Index of Greek Words and Word Forms

ῥήτρα 36.
phoFαισι (ῥοαῖς) 80.
ῥύμη 80.

σβέννυμι 82, 124.
σελᾱνᾱ (σελήνη) 57, 63, 122, 124.
σελάννᾱ (σελήνη) 122, 124.
σελήνη 63, 122, 124.
σεμνός 120.
σιός (θεός) 105.
σκάπτω 103.
   ἔσκαφα 208-10.
   ἐσκάφη 103.
σκῆπτρον 93.
σκληρότηρ (σκληρότης) 22.
σκότος 82.
σοφός 135, 170.
σόφος (σοφός) 135, 170.
σπείρω 82.
   ἔσπερσαι 123.
σταθμός 80.
στᾱλᾱ (στήλη) 11, 57, 122, 126.
στάλλᾱ (στήλη) 122, 125.
στέλλω 122, 126.
   ἔστελλα (ἔστειλα) 122.
   εστηλα (ἔστειλα) 122.
   ἔσταλσαι 123.
στεφανῶ
   στεφανοῖ 196-7.
   στεφάνοι (στεφανοῖ) 196-7.
   στεφανοῦσι 196-8.
   στεφάνοισι (στεφανοῦσι) 196-8.
στήλη 11, 122, 126.
στόμα 82.
στορέννυμι 124-5.
στόρνυμι 124-5.
στρατηγός 140.
στρέφω 103-4.
   στρέψω 103-4.
στρότος (στρατός) 26.
σύ 115 (paradigm).
συζεύγνυμι 81.
συκέα 162 (paradigm).
συκέη 162.

συκῆ 162-3 (paradigm).
συκία 162.
σύν 95.
συνεθεαν (συνέθεσαν) 66, 211.
συρίσδες (συρίζεις) 193.
συστέλλω 81.
σφαῖρα 163 (paradigm), 166.
σχεθέειν 106.

Ταναγρηω (Ταναγραίου) 46.
τάττω
   τετάχαται 208.
ταχύς 103-4.
   θάσσων 103.
   θάττων 103-4.
τεᾱ 162 (paradigm).
τεή 162 (paradigm).
τεκνα (τέχνη) 97.
τελεως (τέλειος) 125.
τεληος (τέλειος) 125.
τέσσαρες 120-1.
τέσσερες (τέσσαρες) 11, 84, 120-1.
τέτορες (τέτταρες) 11, 120-1.
τέτταρες 11, 84, 120-1.
τζετρακατιαι (τετρακόσιαι) 82.
τηλόθεν 14, 116-9.
τίθημι 101.
   τίθη 191-2.
   τίθης 85, 191-3.
   τίθεις 191-3.
   τίθησθα (τίθης) 192.
   τίθησι 23, 191-3.
   τίθντι (τίθησι) 23.
   τίθει (τίθησι) 191-3.
   τιθεῖ (τίθησι) 191.
   τίθεισι (τιθέασι) 200, 203.
   τίθενσι (τιθέασι) 200.
   τίθεντι (τιθέασι) 200, 203.
   τιθεῖν (τιθέναι) 191.
   τίθεντι (τιθέντι) 200.
   τιθένσι (τιθεῖσι) 200.
   τίθενσι (τιθεῖσι) 200.
   τιθέντεσσι (τιθεῖσι) 200.
   ἔθηκα 211.

ἔθεν (ἔθεσαν) 25.
τέθηκα 211.
τίκτω
   τετόκοισα 213.
τιμά (τιμή) 49.
τιμή 49, 161-2 (paradigm).
τιμῶ
   τιμᾷ 196-7.
   τιμῶμεν 72-3, 140, 142.
   τιμᾶτε 51, 58-9, 72-3.
   τιμῶσι 196.
   τιμᾶν 58.
   τιμάετε 51, 58-9, 72-3.
   τιμάητε 58.
   τιμάειν 58.
   τύμαι (τιμᾷ) 196-7.
   τύμαισι (τιμῶσι) 196.
   τιμῶμες (τιμῶμεν) 72-3, 140, 142.
   τιμῆτε (τιμᾶτε) 72.
   τιμεονσα (τιμῶσα) 68-9.
   τιμιουσα (τιμῶσα) 68-9.
   τιμιωσα (τιμῶσα) 68-9.
   τιμουσα (τιμῶσα) 68-9.
   τιμεοντες (τιμῶντες) 68-9.
   τιμηοντες (τιμῶντες) 74.
   τιμιοντες (τιμῶντες) 68-9, 74.
   τιμουντες (τιμῶντες) 68-9.
τίς 14, 82, 116-18.
τίτθη 17, 98.
τλάω 95.
τνατος (θνητός) 97.
τόμος 135, 146.
τομός 135, 146.
τόσος 111.
τότον (τούτων) 46.
τούσδε 144.
τράπεζα 81-2.
τρέπω
   ἐτρέφθη 102.
τρέφω 101-3.
   θρέψω 101-3.
   τέτροφα 102, 210.
   τετράφαται 208-10.
   τετραμμένοι εἰσίν 210.
   τετράφθω 208.
   τετράφθαι 208.

   ἐθρέφθην 102-4.
τρέχω 96, 103.
   θρέξω 96, 103.
τρίβω
   τέτριμμαι 79.
τρόπαιον 141.
τροπαῖον 141.
τρόχος 135, 146.
τροχός 135, 146.
τρύχω
   τρύξω 103.
(Τ)τηνα (Δία) 111-13.
τυ (σύ) 115 (paradigm).
   τεο (σοῦ) 24.
   τιν (σοῦ) 24.
τυτθός 17.
τως (τούς) 59.
τωὐτό (ταὐτό(ν)) 42.

ὑγιής
   ὑγιᾶ 54-5.
   ὑγιῆ 54-5.
υἱεος (υἱοῦ) 67.
ὑμες (ὑμεῖς) 25.
ὑμε (ὑμᾶς) 25.
ὔμμες (ὑμεῖς) 25.
ὔμμε (ὑμᾶς) 25.
ὑμοιος (ὁμοῖος) 25.
ὑπέρ 93, 95.
υποσκεθην (ὑποσχέθην) 106.
ὕστερος 152.
   ὑστέρoιο 152.

φαεσφόρος (φωσφόρος) 135.
φαιδρός 106, 135.
φαῖδρος 135.
φαῖμι (φημί) 207 (paradigm).
   φαι (φής) 207-8.
   φαῖσι (φασί) 207.
φαίνω
   ἔφηνα 10, 122.
   εφανα (ἔφηνα) 10-11, 57-9, 62, 122.
   πέφανσαι 123.
φαμί (φημί) 49.
φάος (φῶς) 135.
φαρθενος (παρθένος) 98.
φάσγανον 81-2.

Index of Greek Words and Word Forms

φέρω 149 (paradigm).
  φέρεις 153, 188-193.
  φέρει 153, 188-193.
  φέρομες (φέρομεν) 23, 147.
  φέρετε 147.
  φέρουσι 23, 37, 59-60, 200.
  φέροισι (φέρουσι) 23, 37, 41, 59, 189-90, 200.
  φέρονσι (φέρουσι) 23, 37, 59-60, 200.
  φέροντι (φέρουσι) 23, 37, 59-60, 147, 200.
  φέρωσι (φέρουσι) 60.
  ἔφερον 147.
  ἐφερέτον 151.
  ἐφερέτην 150-1.
  ἐφέρομεν 147.
  φέρῃς 188-93.
  φέρῃ 188-93.
  φέρησι (φέρῃ) 189-90.
  φέρωσι 37.
  φέρωισι (φέρωσι) 37, 41, 189.
  φέρωνσι (φέρωσι) 37.
  φέρωντι (φέρωσι) 37.
  φέρετον 151.
  φερέτω 147, 150-1.
  φερόντω (φερόντων) 150-1.
  φέροντον (φερόντων) 150-1.
  φερέτωσαν (φερόντων) 151.
  φερόντωσαν (φερόντων) 151.
  φέροντι (Part.) 200.
  φέρουσα 7-10, 13-14, 60.
  φερούσης 171.
  φέρουσαι 171.
  φέροισα (φέρουσα) 7-10, 12, 13, 59.
  φέρονσα (φέρουσα) 7-10, 11, 12, 59-60.
  φερωha (φέρουσα) 7-10.
  φερωhας (φερούσης) 171.
  φερώhαι (φέρουσαι) 171.
  φερωσα (φέρουσα) 7-10, 60.
  φέρονσι (φέρουσι Part.) 123, 200.
  φερόντεσσι (φέρουσι) 200.
  φερόντοις (φέρουσι) 200.
  φέρεται 147 (paradigm).
  ἐφερόμην 150.
  ἐφερέσθην 150.
  ἐφερόμεθα 148.
  ἐφέροντο 148.
  φερέσθω 150.
  φερέσθων 150-1.
  φερέσθον (φερέσθων) 151.
  φερέσθωσαν 151.
  φερόμενος 146, 152-3.
  φερομένοιο (φερομένου) 152-3.
  φερομένῳ 153.
  φερόμενοι 153-5 (paradigm).
  φερομένᾱ (φερομένη) 154-5.
  ἤνεγκαν 211.
Φέτταλος (Θεσσαλός) 97.
φεύγω
  πέφευγα 209.
φημί 47, 207 (paradigm).
  φησί 207-8.
  φασί 18, 207-8.
  ἔφασαν 159.
  ἐφάσαν (ἔφασαν) 159.
φθέγγομαι
  ἔφθεγμαι 80 (paradigm).
φθέγμα 80.
φθέρρω (φθείρω) 122, 126.
φθήρω (φθείρω) 122, 126-7.
φθόνος 99.
φίλος 156-7, 170.
  φίλου 156-7.
φιλῶ
  φιλεῖ 196-7.
  φίλει (φιλεῖ) 196-7.
  φιλοῦμεν 73, 141-2.
  φιλεῖτε 73, 141.
  φιλοῦσι 196-201.
  φιλέομεν 141-2.
  φιλέετε 141.
  φίλειμι (φιλῶ) 193.
  φίλεισι (φιλοῦσι) 197, 200-1.
  φίλενσι (φιλοῦσι) 197, 200-1.
  φιλένσι (φιλοῦσι) 201.

φίλεντι (φιλοῦσι) 193, 196, 200.
φιλέομες (φιλοῦμεν) 142.
φιλέοντι (φιλοῦσι) 196.
φιλίομεν (φιλοῦμεν) 142.
φιλίομες (φιλοῦμεν) 73.
φιλίετε (φιλεῖτε) 73.
φιλίοντι (φιλοῦσι) 200.
ἐφίλουν 155 (paradigm), 157.
ἐφίλεον (ἐφίλουν) 155 (paradigm).
ἐφίλιον (ἐφίλουν) 155 (paradigm).
φίλεις (φιλῶν) 197.
φίλεντι (φιλοῦντι Part.) 198-201.
φιλέντι (φιλοῦντι) 198-201.
φιλέοντι (φιλοῦντι) 198-201.
φιλεῦντι (φιλοῦντι) 198-201.
φιλίοντι (φιλοῦντι) 198-201.
φιλnοντες (φιλοῦντες) 74.
φιλιοντες (φιλοῦντες) 74.
φιλέντεσσι (φιλοῦσι) 199.
φιλέουσι (φιλοῦσι) 199.
φιλέοντας (φιλοῦντας) 68.
φιλεῦντας (φιλοῦντας) 68.
φιλειμενος (φιλοῦμενος) 73.
ἐφιλάθεν (ἐφιλήθησαν) 159.
ἐφιλήθην (ἐφιλήθησαν) 159.
φιλεῖσθαι 73.
φίλτρον 93.
Φλαβιος (Flauius) 108.
Φλαυιος (Flauius) 108.
φλέγω 80.
φρήν 80.
φυγή
  φυγῆς 167-9.
  φυγήν 167-9.
  φυγάς (φυγῆς) 168.
  φυγάν (φυγήν) 168.
φυλάττω 19.
  πεφύλαχα 208.
  πεφύλαχθε 98.
φῶς 134, 143, 173.

φώς 134, 143, 173.
χαμᾶθεν 137.
χαμαί 137.
χεύλιοι (χίλιοι) 48, 122, 124.
χέλλιοι (χίλιοι) 122, 124.
χέρρας (χεῖρας) 122, 124.
χηλιοι (χίλιοι) 48, 57, 122, 124.
χηρ (χείρ) 122, 124.
χθόνιος 93.
χναύω 95, 97.
χνοάζω 97.
χνόη 97.
χρεεσται (χρῆσθαι) 106.
χρησται (χρῆσθαι) 107.
χρητθαι (χρῆσθαι) 107.
χρόνος 80.
χρύσεος (χρυσοῦς) 65.
χρύσιος (χρυσοῦς) 65.
χρυσιππος (Crhysippus) 80.
χρυσομες (χρυσοῦμεν, χρυσῶμεν) 37.
χρυσοῦς
  χρυσῆ 71.
  χρυσῆς 164.
  χρυσέας 164.
χρυσωμες (χρυσοῦμεν, χρυσῶμεν) 37.
χώρᾱ 6, 49, 163 (paradigm), 165-6.
  χώρη 6, 49.

ψαφιδδω (ψηφίζω) 111-15.
ψευδῆ 56.
ψήφιζμα (ψήφισμα) 81.
ψῆφος 99.
ψυχή
  ψυχάων (ψυχῶν) 164.
  ψυχαῖς 164.
  ψυχᾶσι 164.

Index of Greek Words and Word Forms

MYCENAEAN WORDS

a-to-ro-qo (ἄνθρωπος) 64, 116.
a-pi-ko-ro (ἀμφίπολος) 119.
a-ro₂-e (cf. ἄριστος) 127.

e-ne-ka (ἕνεκα) 61.

ke-se-nu-wo (cf. ξένος) 61.

me-no (μηνός) 64.

qe-re- (τηλ-) 116.
qi (τίς) 116.
qo-u-ko-ro (βουκόλος) 64, 119.
qo-u-qo-ta (βουβότης) 116.

re-qo-me-no (λειπόμενος) 64.

tu-ro₂ (cf. τυρός) 127.

PHOENIX SUPPLEMENTARY VOLUMES SERIES

1 *Studies in Honour of Gilbert Norwood* edited by Mary E. White
2 *Arbiter of Elegance: A Study of the Life and Works of C. Petronius* Gilbert Bagnani
3 *Sophocles the Playwright* S.M. Adams
4 *A Greek Critic: Demetrius on Style* G.M.A. Grube
5 *The Coastal Demes of Attika: A Study of the Policy of Kleisthenes* C.W.J. Eliot
6 *Eros and Psyche: Studies in Plato, Plotinus, and Origen* John M. Rist
7 *Pythagoras and Early Pythagoreanism* J.A. Philip
8 *Plato's Psychology* T.M. Robinson
9 *Greek Fortifications* F.E. Winter
10 *Comparative Studies in Republican Latin Imagery* Elaine Fantham
11 *Orators in Cicero's Brutus: Prosopography and Chronology* G.V. Sumner
12 *Caput and Colonate: Towards a History of Late Roman Taxation* Walter Goffart
13 *A Concordance to the Works of Ammianus Marcellinus* Geoffrey Archbold
14 *Fallax opus: Poet and Reader in the Elegies of Propertius* John Warden
15 *Pindar's 'Olympian One': A Commentary* Douglas E. Gerber
16 *Greek and Roman Mechanical Water Lifting Devices: The History of a Technology* John P. Oleson
17 *The Manuscript Tradition of Propertius* James L. Butrica
18 *Parmenides of Elea Fragments: A Text and Translation with Introduction* David Gallop
19 *The Phonological Interpretation of Ancient Greek: A Pandialectal Analysis* Vít Bubeník

www.ingramcontent.com/pod-product-compliance
Lightning Source LLC
Chambersburg PA
CBHW051402070526
44584CB00023B/3263